Victorian Poetry

'THE CITY OF DREADFUL NIGHT' AND OTHER POEMS

Edited
with an introduction by
N. P. Messenger
ST PAUL'S COLLEGE OF EDUCATION,
NEWBOLD REVEL
and
J. R. Watson
DEPARTMENT OF ENGLISH,
UNIVERSITY OF LEICESTER

DENT, LONDON

ROWMAN AND LITTLEFIELD, TOTOWA, N.J.

© Introduction and notes, J. M. Dent & Sons Ltd, 1974

All rights reserved
Made in Great Britain
at the
Aldine Press · Letchworth · Herts
for
J. M. DENT & SONS LTD
Aldine House · Albemarle Street · London
First published in 1974
First published in the United States 1974
by ROWMAN AND LITTLEFIELD, Totowa, New Jersey

This book if bound as a paperback is
subject to the condition that it may not
be issued on loan or otherwise except in
its original binding

This book is set in 8 on 9 point Times New Roman 327

Dent edition
Hardback ISBN 0 460 10871 9
Paperback ISBN 0 460 11871 4

Rowman and Littlefield edition
Library of Congress Cataloging in Publication Data
Messenger Nigel P., comp.
Victorian poetry 'the city of dreadful night'
and other poems
(Rowman and Littlefield university library series)
Includes bibliographies.
1. English poetry—19th century. I. Watson,
John Richard, joint comp. II. Title.
PR1223.M44 821'.8'08 74-1125
ISBN 0-87471-518-0 (HARDBACK)
ISBN 0-87471-535-0 (PAPERBACK)

Contents

Introduction   ix

WILLIAM BARNES (1801–86)

Evenen in the Village   1
Woodley   1
Eclogue: The Common a-Took In   2
Grammer's Shoes   5
A Father Out, an' Mother Hwome   6
Day's Work a-Done   7
Hallowed Pleaces   8
Milken Time   9
The Water Crowvoot   10
Lydlinch Bells   11
The Wife a-Lost   12
Naighbour Playmeates   13
Woak Hill   14

R. S. HAWKER (1803–75)

Featherstone's Doom   16
The Silent Tower of Bottreau   17
The Poor Man and his Parish Church   18
The Burial Hour   21
A Legend of the Hive   22
The Fatal Ship   24

ELIZABETH BARRETT BROWNING (1806–61)

The Cry of the Children   25
from Sonnets from the Portuguese
    I, XVIII, XLIII, and XLIV   29
A Musical Instrument   31

CHARLES TENNYSON-TURNER (1808–79)

Wind on the Corn   33
Mary—a Reminiscence   33
Eustace and Edith   34
The Steam Threshing-Machine   34
The Drunkard's Last Market   35

On the Eclipse of the Moon of October 1865   35
The Seaside   35
Old Ruralities   36
To a Red-Wheat Field   36
To a Scarecrow, or Malkin, Left Long after Harvest 37
An Evening in Harvest Time   37
After the School-Feast   37
To a 'Tenting' Boy   38
Old Stephen   38
The Quiet Tide near Ardrossan   39
A Country Dance   39

ARTHUR HUGH CLOUGH (1819–61)

Duty   40
'Is it true, ye gods'   41
Qui Laborat, Orat   42
Qua Cursum Ventus   43
Epi-Strauss-Ium   44
Natura Naturans   44
Easter Day, Naples, 1849   46
Easter Day II   50
Say Not the Struggle Nought Availeth   51
from Amours De Voyage, Cantos I and II   51
from Dipsychus:
    'There is no God'   67
    'As I sat at the Café'   68
The Latest Decalogue   70
In the Great Metropolis   70

COVENTRY PATMORE (1823–96)

from The Angel in the House:
    The Cathedral Close   72
    Love at Large   74
    The County Ball   74
from The Unknown Eros:
    The Toys   76
    Magna est Veritas   77
1867   77
Night and Sleep   79
A London Fête   80

GEORGE MEREDITH (1828–1909)

The Old Chartist   82
from Modern Love
    I, XII, XIII, XXX, XXXVI, XLIII, XLIX, L   86
Lucifer in Starlight   89
Love in the Valley   89

DANTE GABRIEL ROSSETTI (1828–82)

The Blessed Damozel	95
Jenny	99
The Paris Railway-Station	108
Sudden Light	109
Alas, So Long!	109
The Woodspurge	110
An Old Song Ended	110
from The House of Life:	
The Dark Glass	111
Severed Selves	112
Barren Spring	112
A Superscription	113

CHRISTINA ROSSETTI (1830–94)

Goblin Market	114
Remember	127
A Birthday	127
Maude Clare	127
Echo	129
A Dirge	129
A Frog's Fate	130
Up-Hill	131

ALEXANDER SMITH (1830–67)

Glasgow	132

JAMES THOMSON, 'B.V.' (1834–82)

The City of Dreadful Night	136

WILLIAM MORRIS (1834–96)

The Defence of Guenevere	166
from The Earthly Paradise:	
An Apology	175
The Wanderers (Extract)	176
The Outlanders	176
August	178
October	179
February	179
L'Envoi	180

ALGERNON CHARLES SWINBURNE (1837–1909)

from Atalanta in Calydon:	
Chorus	183
The Triumph of Time	185

Hymn to Proserpine 194
The Lake of Gaube 198

W. E. HENLEY (1849–1903)

In Hospital 201

Notes, and select bibliographies 217
Index of First Lines 239

Introduction

On July 9th, 1864, a particularly unpleasant murder occurred on the North London Railway, when a man called Franz Müller killed Thomas Briggs in a compartment of a non-corridor coach between Bow and Hackney Wick. A commuter on the nearby Great Eastern line, Matthew Arnold, portrayed himself (in the Preface to *Essays in Criticism*, First Series, 1865) as teasing a fellow traveller about the possibility of being caught in another railway compartment with a homicidal maniac:

> 'Suppose the worst to happen,' I said, addressing a portly jeweller from Cheapside; 'suppose even yourself to be the victim; *il n'y a pas d'homme nécessaire*. We should miss you for a day or two upon the Woodford Branch; but the great mundane movement would still go on, the gravel walks of your villa would still be rolled, dividends would still be paid at the Bank, omnibuses would still run, there would still be the old crush at the corner of Fenchurch Street.' All was of no avail. Nothing could moderate, in the bosom of the great English middle class, their passionate, absorbing, almost bloodthirsty clinging to life.

Here we can discover Arnold's portrait of two faces of the Victorian period. The first is successful Victorian man, serious, comfortable, prosperous, the shopkeeper with his villa riding a wave of commercial prosperity. The other is the Victorian intellectual, here amused and sceptical, but elsewhere disturbed and directionless

> Wandering between two worlds, one dead,
> The other powerless to be born
> (Arnold, 'Stanzas from the Grande Chartreuse')

The antithesis, like many of Arnold's own contrasts, is over-simplified but convenient. On the one hand there are the undeniable signs of stability: the Great Exhibition of 1851, the middle-class crowds in the churches, the growth of speedy and convenient railway travel, the prosperity of the great industrial towns with their magnificent town halls, the great landowners on their estates. On the other hand there is the much more disturbing picture: an urbanized working class living in squalor and dying of disease, agricultural labourers starving and crippled with rheumatism, domestic servants exploited as a slave class, and mass emigration in search of work, food, and opportunity. Engels described it in 1845: 'Everywhere barbarous indifference, hard egotism on one hand, and nameless misery on the other, everywhere social warfare, every man's house in a state of siege . . .' And as Engels pointed out with some force, the victims of this 'social warfare' were the poor.[1]

Arnold's portly jeweller had a shop in Cheapside, but lived in a villa in the suburbs; he was a typical representative, as Arnold intended, of the prosperous middle class who moved out of the cities at this time and left them to the poor. The railway brought the middle class quickly and conveniently to their work, and out again at the end of the day to breathe the fresh country air over the cornfields of Leyton or the gardens of Denmark Hill. Behind them they left the worst problems of the age: overcrowding, poor air, bad sanitation, disease and crime; and while the administrators struggled, the populations of the great cities continued to grow at a rate which outstripped the best intentions of the commissioners and reformers. 'The colossal growth of London,' writes Francis Sheppard, 'is the central fact in the history of the capital in the nineteenth century,'[2] and the same could be said for the other great industrial cities, which acted as magnets for people from the surrounding countryside. Between 1841 and 1891 the population of London increased from 1,873,676 to 4,232,118; 'Our age is pre-eminently the age of great cities,' wrote Robert Vaughan.[3]

It might have been expected that Victorian poetry, like the novel, would become more comprehensively urban in order to deal more directly with contemporary life; but this was a challenge which many Victorian poets, major and minor, chose to ignore. Frequently they interpreted the present through the past by their use of myth, legend, and history. The reasons for this rejection of the city by poets were complex, involving not only their inheritance from the romantic movement, but also their conceptions of the poet and his art. From Wordsworth and Keats they derived ideas of what was good and beautiful, and of city-dwellers

> Living amid the same perpetual whirl
> Of trivial objects, melted and reduced
> To one identity, by differences
> That have no law, no meaning, and no end.
>
> (Wordsworth, *The Prelude*, vii, 725–8)

but the reasons for rejection were also related to the importance of traditional poetic language, the audience that the poet wrote for, and the shifting relationship between the poet and his audience.

One of the legacies of the romantic movement was the conception of the poet as *vates* or seer (re-affirmed by Carlyle in his lecture 'The Hero as Poet'[4]) and the Victorian public expected a poetry which was elevated above the level of ordinary speech, rich in sensuous imagery, well marked in rhythm and full in rhyme, that enshrined memorable insights or some moral truth. *In Memoriam*, published in 1850, exactly fitted this demand,

[1] *The Conditions of the Working Class in England*, ed. Eric Hobsbawm (London, 1969), p. 58.

[2] *London 1808–1870: the Infernal Wen* (1971), p. 1.

[3] Figures and quotation from Asa Briggs, *Victorian Cities* (new edition, 1968), p. 59.

[4] In *On Heroes, Hero-Worship, and the Heroic in History* (1841).

and although 'the long unlovely street' makes a brief appearance in section VII, the sustaining tradition behind the poem as a whole is the pastoral elegy. In the same way, Matthew Arnold can diagnose the 'strange disease of modern life,/With its sick hurry, its divided aims' in 'The Scholar Gipsy', but he finds himself unable to demonstrate this in an urban idiom. Instead he provides a Keatsian rhapsody on the Oxfordshire countryside which concludes in a splendid but irrelevant image of flight and rejection.

Apparently to the Victorians, poet and public alike, the democratic flux and utilitarian ugliness of the modern city were inimical to traditional poetic subjects and language, both of which were based on rapidly depreciating concepts of agrarian worth and aristocratic excellence. The scarcity of good satire in Victorian poetry is an indication of this. Pope could castigate the follies of the town with an authority that stretched back through Jacobean Drama to the classics; in comparison Patmore's attack on Disraeli in '1867' is shrill, peevish invective, and Clough's 'Duty' (perhaps in intentional contrast to Wordsworth's noble ode) splutters into near incoherence, baffled by what it sees as the debased meaning of the word itself:

> Moral blank, and moral void,
> Life at very birth destroyed.
> Atrophy, exinanition!

The Victorian city found its true poet in Dickens. In his hands the novel form, with its potential for chaotic and inclusive movement, effectively captures the urban vitality which it celebrates; it is the dominant art form of the age. While Dickens's novels exude a protean and eccentric life, the prevailing tone of much of the contemporary poetry is lassitude and weariness. For the poet, the industrial community thwarts and destroys; rather than being the centre for a new kind of growth, the city crudely contains the potential of its members and subdues their highest aspirations into a 'buried life'. For Arnold, the representative poet of this mood, the city is a 'brazen prison', and its inhabitants

> languidly
> Their lives to some unmeaning taskwork give,
> Dreaming of nought beyond their prison walls.
> ('A Summer Night')

while for poets wishing to make grand affirmations there was nothing heroic in Lancashire mill towns or London sweat-shops where pitiable wretches were subdued to a mere semblance of life by the machines they operated. Should they wish to expose these and other iniquities, such as child labour, the poets found themselves in difficulties. Elizabeth Barrett's 'The Cry of the Children', for instance, has its arresting urban images of the 'droning, turning' iron wheels and 'the black flies that crawl along the ceiling', but the poem's alternatives of pastoral innocence and sentimental religion are unconvincing in comparison.

Against the background of this uneasy confrontation between the poet and his age we must place and estimate the achievement of Clough. Arnold's portrait of him in 'Thyrsis' as 'Too quick despairer' prematurely silenced by religious doubt, though not without its truth, has concealed Clough's determination as an unfashionable experimenter in poetry. His poetry and his poetic theories form an instructive contrast to those of Arnold, with their insistence on great subjects and permanent thoughts. To read Clough's 1853 review 'Recent English Poetry' alongside Arnold's Preface to his *Poems* of the same year is to obtain a valuable insight into the difficulties facing poets who were reared in a classical tradition and who found themselves in an age of change and progress. 'We ask action', Clough's hero Dipsychus sadly exclaims,

> And dreams of arms and conflict; and string up
> All self-devotion's muscles; and are set
> To fold up papers. To what end? We know not.

Arnold's search for great actions led him to 'Sohrab and Rustum' and 'Balder Dead', as it later led William Morris to Icelandic literature and *Sigurd the Volsung*; but Clough rejected these subjects, and the ancient bardic role that went with them. Instead, he queries if the poetic gift is more than an accident of biology,

> a peculiar conformation,
> Constitution, and condition
> Of the brain and of the belly?
>   ('Is it true, ye gods')

He brought back into poetry a flexibility of tone and comprehensiveness of subject-matter, 'those positive matters of fact, which people, who are not verse-writers, are obliged to have to do with.'[1] In this he was influenced by Dryden, whom Arnold, in common with many Victorians (Hopkins, who thought Victorian English 'a bad business', was the great exception) did not consider a poet at all. Subjects of Clough's poetry included an Oxford reading-party, tourists caught up in a revolution, and mutual attraction in a railway carriage—attempts, like Meredith's *Modern Love*, to regain ground lost to the novel. His metre in his long poems, too, is a response to the age. In *Amours de Voyage* he descends into the swirling, reductive chaos of the streets and immerses himself in its 'destructive element':

> So, I have seen a man killed! An experience that, among others! ...
>   I was returning home from St Peter's; Murray, as usual,
> Under my arm, I remember; had crossed the St Angelo bridge; and
> Moving towards the Condotti, had got to the first barricade, when
> Gradually, thinking still of St Peter's, I became conscious
> Of a sensation of movement opposing me,—tendency this way
> (Such as one fancies may be in a stream when the wave of the tide is
> Coming and not yet come,—a sort of poise and retention);
>   (Canto II, vii)

[1] *Prose Remains of Arthur Hugh Clough* (London, 1888), p. 357.

A sort of poise and retention; the phrase, indeed the whole poem, shows Clough using the hexameter to represent the untidy ebb and flow of city life. Other poets, like Patmore in 'A London Fête' and Rossetti in 'Jenny', exposed the brutality of the mob and the sadness of prostitution; Clough writes in a way which is more inclusive, and extends the boundaries and possibilities of poetry. Meanwhile other poets, seeking to find some moment of significant thought or action, attempted to arrest the moment in art, and succeeded only in achieving a kind of frozen effect; this is particularly true of Pre-Raphaelite poetry and painting. Others sought some kind of certainty by concentrating on minute details of the natural world, as Rossetti does in 'The Woodspurge', or Tennyson in those minutiae which so delighted Mr Holbrook in *Cranford*. Closer to the city experience was the image which both Clough and Alexander Smith took from marine biology:

> But I must slave, a meagre coral-worm,
> To build beneath the tide with excrement
> What one day will be island, or be reef,
> And will feed men, or wreck them.
>
> ('Dipsychus')

> Slowly the city grew,
> Like coral reef on which the builders die
> Until it stand complete in pain and death.
>
> ('A Boy's Poem')

Clough declared that the 'lawful haunts of the poetic powers' were 'if anywhere, in the blank and desolate streets, and upon the solitary bridges of the midnight city'; but it is, perhaps, significant that the most daring and successful attempts to create poetry from such unpromising material were made by self-educated poets less hindered by cultural preconceptions. Besides, for Alexander Smith and James Thomson, representatives of the under-privileged, the city was a real prison; they had little else to write about. Alexander Smith mythopoeticizes the 'tragic heart of towns' in the manner of an inverse Wordsworth whose 'seed-time' has been fostered by a very different beauty and fear from that described in *The Prelude*:

> When sunset bathes thee in his gold
> In wreaths of bronze thy sides are rolled,
>   Thy smoke is dusty fire;
> And, from the glory round thee poured,
> A sunbeam like an angel's sword
>   Shivers upon a spire.
> Thus have I watched thee, Terror! Dream!
> While the blue Night crept up the stream.
>
> ('Glasgow')

Lit by the glare of its own foundry fires, the landscape of Smith's Glasgow is subject to its own laws and seasons. Instead of the movements of the tide, we have the migrations of labour; bridges are mountain ridges and the docks, with their masts and cranes, are its forests. All things mechanical flourish and prosper, but normal growth within this vast machine is stunted and pale. Cut off by miles of suburb, only the occasional glimpse of a flower or butterfly serves to remind its human prisoners of the seasonal change outside. Worse still, as Engels observed, was the effect upon them as human beings in a society: 'these Londoners have been forced to sacrifice the best qualities of their human nature, ... they crowd by one another as though they had nothing in common, nothing to do with one another, ... it occurs to no man to honour another with so much as a glance.'[1]

In Thomson's city the vision is intensified: 'The City is of Night; perchance of Death'. There is the same interest in labyrinthine streets and dark courts, with black rivers overhung by brilliantly lit bridges; but natural imagery is less frequent and more extreme:

> A trackless wilderness rolls north and west,
> Savannahs, savage woods, enormous mountains,
> Bleak uplands, black ravines with torrent fountains;
> And eastward rolls the shipless sea's unrest.
>
> ('The City of Dreadful Night', I)

There is no containing normality; instead the city has infected the land around with its empty desolation, and the last word of 'The City of Dreadful Night' is 'despair'.

Certainly there was little comfort for the city-dweller of the poorer class in this world; or in the next. In spite of vigorous attempts at revival by all the denominations, shown most dramatically by the Baptists under the inspiration of Charles Haddon Spurgeon, and the mission of William Booth which led to the foundation of the Salvation Army, religion in the cities was generally a pursuit of the middle and upper classes, of tradesmen rather than artisans. In religion, as in other matters, the student of the Victorian period finds himself in the presence of striking contrasts, for it was an age of great religious activity and also an age of growing disbelief. One of the things which Arnold, the agnostic, imagined that his portly jeweller might be going to do was to attend a service at Exeter Hall in the Strand, where the evangelicals held popular 'Preaching Services'. The project was typical of the energy expended in the propagation of the gospel, which was equalled only by the tension resulting from religious controversy, particularly between the Church of England and the Nonconformists, and by the Oxford Movement. But little of this penetrated to the poor; Dickens's crossing-sweeper Jo, in *Bleak House*, who was taught to say a few phrases of the Lord's Prayer on his death-bed, was only a dramatic instance of a formidable problem for the nineteenth-century churches. Yet more important as a problem, though it might not have

[1] *Conditions of the Working Class*, pp. 57–8.

seemed so at the time, was the spread of disbelief and uncertainty among the kind of people for whom Arnold spoke:

> The Sea of Faith
> Was once, too, at the full, and round earth's shore
> Lay like the folds of a bright girdle furl'd.
> But now I only hear
> Its melancholy, long, withdrawing roar,
> Retreating, to the breath
> Of the night-wind, down the vast edges drear
> And naked shingles of the world.
>
> ('Dover Beach')

Once again Clough, who resigned his Fellowship at Oriel because of his loss of faith, is a central figure. In 'Epi-Strauss-Ium' and the two 'Easter Day' poems he can be seen trying to grapple with the problems caused by the new discoveries put forward in Lyell's *Principles of Geology* (1830–33), which called into question the Biblical account of the Creation, and Strauss's *Das Leben Jesu* (1835), which questioned the authenticity of the gospels. *In Memoriam* is even more representative of a central problem of the time, with its moments of doubt leading to an uneasy hope. It asks the major questions: if there is no God, what is man, and the purpose of this life? Shall man

> Who loved, who suffered countless ills,
> Who battled for the True, the Just,
> Be blown about the desert dust,
> Or sealed within the iron hills?
>
> No more? A monster then, a dream,
> A discord. Dragons of the prime,
> That tare each other in their slime,
> Were mellow music matched with him.
>
> O life as futile, then, as frail!
> O for thy voice to soothe and bless!
> What hope of answer, or redress?
> Behind the veil, behind the veil.

Of the answers that were hidden behind the veil, the most pressing for the Victorians was the reply to the question of death. One celebrated picture, by Henry Alexander Bowler, put the question in its title: *The Doubt: Can these Dry Bones Live?* In the picture a young girl leans upon a gravestone and gazes at some bones and a skull; the contrast between the bones and the inscriptions on the headstones—'I am the Resurrection and the Life' and 'Resurgam'—suggests the two possible answers to the problem. The picture was directly inspired by *In Memoriam*, and Tennyson's poem is so central because it deals with death in an age of doubt. In an age of faith, it is possible to believe in a life after death and to think, with Christina Rossetti, that in the ultimate inn there will be beds for all who come; or like William Barnes, to pray to rejoin a loved one:

To goo where you do bide;
Above the tree an' bough, my love,
Where you be gone avore,
An' be a-waiten vor me now,
To come vor evermwore.

But if you lose your faith under the influence of the new scientific rational-
ism, if you find yourself convinced by Professors Huxley and Tyndall, then
death becomes a much more serious problem. For most people, as for
Tennyson, the answer was, as it is now, that they just did not know: as he
says in *In Memoriam*, Lazarus is the only man who can claim to have
experienced death and returned, but

> The rest remaineth unrevealed;
> He told it not; or something sealed
> The lips of that Evangelist.

Such an ignorance was painful to the Victorians, unless, like Swinburne,
they were able to respond with a jubilant and sensuous paganism. For
most it was an occasion for worry and sadness; and perhaps in compensa-
tion they clung to the beliefs they had with a tenacity and a beleaguered
vigour. The polemical nature of their attitudes is, to us, astonishing: when
Clough resigned his Fellowship and asked the Provost of Oriel to support
his application for a job as Principal of the University of Sydney, the
Provost refused on the grounds that 'no-one ought to be appointed to such
a situation who is at all in a state of doubt and difficulty as to his own
religious beliefs'. Similarly the authors of *Essays and Reviews* (1860), a
collection of rationalistic essays, were called the *Septem contra Christum*;
six of them were clergymen, and Dean Burgon wrote of 'the immoral
spectacle of six ministers of religion conspiring to assail the faith which
they outwardly professed'. The intensity and passion which marked
religious discussion from the time of the Oxford Movement onwards is a
phenomenon peculiar to the age, and has something melodramatic about
it; like the drama of the time, it flourished on strong attitudes and flam-
boyant gestures. When Newman, after preaching his last sermon as an
Anglican, took off his hood and threw it over the altar-rail, he was making
a gesture which was theatrical and powerful; powerful, too, were the
sermons of the great preachers, Spurgeon, Liddon, Dale of Birmingham,
F. W. Robertson of Brighton, all of whom drew huge crowds and produced
great effects upon their listeners; while from across the Atlantic came
Moody and Sankey, with their particular kind of catchy sacred song. There
is something curiously intense and excitable about all this expenditure of
energy, far removed from the seventeenth-century piety of a George
Herbert; like the constantly changing environment of the city in which it
flourished, it provided nothing simple and stable where the mind could
rest.

Rest for the mind was something which the Victorians hankered after
and did not find. In his essay on Byron, Matthew Arnold follows Goethe
who

INTRODUCTION

saw the constant state of warfare and combat, the 'negative and polemical working', which makes Byron's poetry a poetry in which we can so little find rest.[1]

Byron had something else, however, which particularly appealed to the Victorians (probably because of their own lack of opportunity for it) and that was heroism. In George Eliot's *Middlemarch*, Dorothea Brooke is a latter-day Saint Theresa, with no outlet for her energies and aspirations; and Carlyle saw heroism as linked to a period in which man saw a divinity in man and nature, whereas:

> I am well aware that in these days Hero-worship, the thing I call Hero-worship, professes to have gone-out, and finally ceased. This . . . is an age that as it were denies the existence of great men; denies the desirableness of great men. Show our critics a great man, a Luther for example, they begin to what they call 'account' for him; not to worship him, but take the dimensions of him,—and bring him out to be a little kind of man! He was the 'creature of the Time,' they say; the Time called him forth, the Time did everything, he nothing —but what the little critic could have done too! This seems to me but melancholy work.[2]

Carlyle saw this absence of hero-worship as connected with the 'unbelief and universal spiritual paralysis', in which nobility was no longer worshipped and modern history became 'bottomless and shoreless', lost in the chaos which was destroying religion; for 'The greatest of all Heroes is One—whom we do not name here!'[3] Certainly the reader of the poems in this anthology will find qualities—stoicism in particular—which might be called heroic, but never an active and martial heroism, except in the Arthurian poetry of William Morris.

Morris's mediaevalism was only one example of a widespread reaction against the confused and unspiritual nature of nineteenth-century ideas. In the place of unheroic and commercial patterns of living the Middle Ages offered magic, romance and nobility. The fashion for gothic architecture in buildings, secular as well as religious—Manchester Town Hall, the Prudential building in Holborn, St Pancras Station, the Houses of Parliament—was partly an attempt to inject something of the spirit of a nobler age into the body of national and corporate life. Aesthetic and spiritual concerns joined hands: Pugin, in *Contrasts*, put side by side the picture of a nineteenth-century town full of factories with a picture of the same town as he visualized it in the fourteenth century, full of the spires of churches. William Morris opened *The Earthly Paradise* with the admonition to his readers to—

[1] *Essays in Criticism* (second series, 1891), p. 184.
[2] *On Heroes, Hero-Worship, and the Heroic in History* (London, edition of 1858), pp. 193–4.
[3] *Ibid.*, p. 193.

xvii

> Forget six counties overhung with smoke,
> Forget the snorting steam and piston stroke,
> Forget the spreading of the hideous town;
> Think rather of the pack-horse on the down,
> And dream of London, small, and white, and clean,
> The clear Thames bordered by its gardens green; ...

which obliquely attacks the materialism of his own day through a sweet nostalgia. The Middle Ages had churches, cleanliness (it was thought) and God; the Victorians built and restored churches by the thousand, but they could do little about cleanliness or God, and they looked back with longing to an earlier age. Nor was this just an aesthetic and spiritual longing; facing the problems of a complex industrial society as they were, the feudalism of the Middle Ages seemed to the nineteenth century to be simpler and more humane, an age in which master and man knew one another and worked together in a spirit of mutual responsibility. It seemed a better age in economic and social terms, in which the peasants were better off than the workers of the nineteenth century; if not financially, then in the close-knit paternalism of the mediaeval village. The most notable text of this idea was Carlyle's *Past and Present*, written in 1842 and directly inspired by a visit to a workhouse followed by a visit to the ruins of the abbey at Bury St Edmunds. With its bitter account of poverty and squalor in modern England, Carlyle contrasted the England of Landlord Edmund; and although he acknowledged that it had its bad periods, the man could arise to set it right. This was Carlyle's hero, Abbot Samson, and it is noteworthy that, in Carlyle's eyes, his economic and social reforms were the result of his spiritual strength. Such personal endeavour and individual heroism were, as Scott had perceived, qualities which had room to flourish in feudal times; and another reason for the cultivation of mediaeval styles and values was that it supplied the heroism which was felt to be lacking. Hence the attraction of the Arthurian legends, parts of which were attempted by Hawker, Swinburne, Morris and Tennyson. In the pages of Malory they found beauty and passion, violence and subterfuge, but also daring and strength (as in Lancelot's rescue of Guenevere) and, above all, perhaps, the sense of nobility and brotherhood in the service of a great English king. So mediaevalism became linked with patriotism, and the short-lived Prince Albert, in Tennyson's dedication, became 'Scarce other than my king's ideal knight'.

A local patriotism, in the form of regionalism, is an important factor in the widespread interest in nature at this time, which is as important as mediaevalism as a subject for Victorian poetry. Nature, like the cult of the Middle Ages, seemed to offer values which were in danger of being forgotten: stability, simplicity, beauty, good health and (following Wordsworth) spiritual uplift. In particular this was the great age of the regional poet. Not only were there experiments with dialect poetry by Tennyson and William Barnes, but poets such as Barnes, Hawker and Tennyson-Turner used local legends and celebrated old ways of life. Through them, remote areas of Victorian England found a voice to mourn their own passing. It is easy to sentimentalize rural, pre-industrial England, but it is also evident that much was sacrificed in the name of progress. One of James Thomson's most telling images of the weariness of city life is of a watch without dial or hands:

> The works proceed until run down; although
> Bereft of purpose, void of use, still go.

His shades drift endlessly through meaningless routines and recurring patterns like lost souls in limbo; like other poets of the time (and T. S. Eliot later) Thomson found in Dante's *Inferno* the true image of the sorrowful city, giving a new lease of life to the idea of hell in a secular age. The regionalists, on the other hand, celebrated what they saw as a work which had meaning, subject to the natural laws of time and season; like the mediaevalists who longed for a return to a paternalistic feudalism, they saw work as forging the community and the personal relationship within it. Courtship begins over the milking pails in Barnes's 'Milken Time', and in 'A Father Out, an' Mother Hwome' family ties and duties find practical demonstration throughout the working day. For all these writers, a landscape intimately known contains 'hallowed places', for it is these which help a man to retain his identity in a changing world. Men and things have a value which cannot be measured in material terms: in a small parish 'Old Stephen' will be missed, and grandmother's wedding shoes are reverently cherished. When change does threaten the village, Barnes protests, as in 'The Common a-Took In'; and he delights to remember the continuity of village life, as he does in 'Lydlinch Bells':

> Their sons did pull the bells that rung
> Their mothers' wedded peals avore, . . .

Tennyson-Turner writes of the old handicrafts:

> I love the spinning-wheel, which hums far down
> In yon lone valley, though, from day to day,
> The boom of Science shakes it from the town.

The work of these poets has a plangency, a dying fall, because 'old ruralities' were being swept away by enclosure, new farming methods, the railways and the new board schools; and this note of sadness is part of their charm. It may be said that they idealized; but their work has more social awareness than is sometimes acknowledged. Barnes makes an unfallen Eden of the Vale of Blackmore, and obliquely criticizes the evils of modern industrial economics. His prose work, *Views of Labour and Gold*, anticipates the critiques of Ruskin and Morris, and it is these considered social and political views which give coherence and direction to much of his poetry. Similarly a scarecrow, to Tennyson-Turner, is a grim reminder of some poor city clerk left derelict after the collapse of his firm, and Hawker sighs

> for the poor man's church again
> With one roof over all.

The conservatism of these poets is seen also in their confidence in tradi-
tional poetic forms, and in their ways of life as clergymen. All three
carried out their pastoral duties with exemplary, if eccentric, care, as if to
emphasize their commitment to the local community; they nurtured, too,
an older kind of faith, in the new dark age. William Allingham records in
his diaries a meeting between Barnes and Tennyson:

> Tennyson now took Barnes and me to his top room. Darwinism.
> Man from Ape. Would that make any difference? 'Time is nothing,'
> said Tennyson. 'Are we not all part of Deity?' 'Pantheism,' hinted
> Barnes, who was not at ease in this sort of speculation. 'Well,' said
> Tennyson, 'I think I believe in Pantheism of a sort.' Barnes to bed.
> Tennyson and I up a ladder to the roof and looked at Orion. Then to
> my room where more talk. He liked Barnes, he said, but he is not
> accustomed to strong views theologic.

Thus these poets gave themselves a measure of protection from the 'doubts,
disputes, distractions, fears' of Tennyson, Arnold and Clough, and from
the despair of Thomson. And although we cannot be sure that Barnes's
village congregation did indeed move serenely to church in the manner
described in 'Lydlinch Bells', Barnes's idyll makes a startling contrast to
the overwhelming sense of desolation and loss that Clough experienced in
'the great sinful streets of Naples', which hardens in Thomson into a
militant scepticism, and the doctrine of 'Necessity Supreme'.

Surrounded by the influences of nature, the parson-poets of the regions
preserved their faith and celebrated the old order of community life. From
the cities, the nature poetry of the age was different: in Meredith and
Morris, nature is recreative, a therapy to be sought rather than a normal
way of life. Morris watches the changing seasons through the months with
an eye which is vividly pictorial, but he stands outside the scene, and never
becomes part of the rhythm it depicts:

> the shepherd binds
> The withy round the hurdles of his fold,
> Down in the foss the river fed of old,
> That through long lapse of time has grown to be
> The little grassy valley that you see.

The way to the Georgians was open: the country becomes the delight of
the senses, rather than the place where old customs and values are pre-
served. Even more dedicated to the senses is the individual nature poetry
of Swinburne, which delights in physical sensation, as Swinburne himself
loved to plunge in the sea. But a new kind of urban sensibility and a new
city lyricism may be seen emerging in Henley's 'In Hospital'; though
Henley professes a nostalgia for the spring in his hospital bed, the poetry
is particularly unconvincing:

> Pageants of colour and fragrance,
> Pass the sweet meadows, and viewless
> Walks the mild spirit of May,
> Visibly blessing the world.

Whereas the city, which was for Thomson the source of all death, is to Henley the source of regeneration and life:

> O, the wonder, the spell of the streets!
> The stature and strength of the horses,
> The rustle and echo of footfalls,
> The flat roar and rattle of wheels!
> A swift tram floats huge on us . . .
> It's a dream?
> The smell of the mud in my nostrils
> Blows brave—like the breath of the sea!

With his question 'It's a dream?' Henley catches an unusual moment in Victorian poetry. Usually the dream-world of Victorian poetry is away from the city, the trams, the roar and rattle of wheels; Henley uses his special viewpoint, of a man newly risen from a hospital bed, to emphasize the delight of living. He finds his earthly paradise not in a garden or sea-girt city, or in the land of romance, or in a dying pattern of nature, but in Edinburgh in 1875. He is one of the most notable of the poets whom this anthology has seen as particularly significant because they do not reject their environment out-of-hand.

Henley, however, was unusual; for as a final reaction against the change-ful and indeterminate age, there is the consciousness of art, not as em-bodying life so much as distilling its finest moments. When this happens, the purity of art, the moment burning with its gem-like flame, begins to stand apart from the confusion and mediocrity of ordinary existence. This is an idea which can be found in Keats's 'Ode on Melancholy', and in those Victorian poems which celebrate the power of the moment—Browning's 'The Last Ride Together', Tennyson's 'Break, Break, Break', Christina Rossetti's 'A Birthday', D. G. Rossetti's 'Sudden Light'. It is also found in the Victorian mastery of technique: Browning thought that he could make a rhyme for every word in the English language, and Tennyson believed that he knew the quantity of every word in it except scissors. Coventry Patmore was an expert on metre, and Swinburne a master of rhythm and alliteration. And although Tennyson, in 'The Palace of Art', ostensibly rejected aestheticism, his soul acknowledged the power and fascination of the palace and longed to return to it.

The poetry of the distilled moment and the pursuit of technical perfec-tion led undeviatingly towards the doctrine of art for art's sake, and the aestheticism of the 'nineties. In a difficult and changing world, the poet could feel security in responding to the challenges of his art, and in attempting to preserve the moments of exquisite perception. Meanwhile, as Villiers de l'Isle Adam said, their servants would do the living for them. This anthology stops at this point, when the search for perfection and technical mastery becomes aestheticism and decadence. It presents—with some of the longer poems in full—what we consider to be the most significant and the best Victorian poetry from 1850 to 1890, with the exception of the major figures, Tennyson, Browning, Arnold and Hopkins. This is the period which begins after 1848, and the reforming 'thirties and disturbed 'forties, which moves with the Great Exhibition of 1851 into the high Victorian age, and which lasts until the crumbling of the fabric in the excesses and refinements of the 'nineties. To be fair to the earlier poets, we have allowed ourselves a good deal of leeway in respect of the earlier date: this is particularly the case with Barnes, Hawker, Mrs Browning and Clough.

Tennyson and Browning are the great poets of this age, and they are major in a particularly interesting way. Tennyson is the representative poet of the age, wrestling with the fundamental questions of faith, doubt and immortality in a style that was widely approved; Browning is the great individualist, with his astonishing techniques, his unusual subject matter, and his penetrating moral vision. Behind these two stand Arnold and Hopkins: Arnold the representative of an age unsure of itself and directionless, Hopkins the great original, forging his art in isolation from the pressures of the time. Behind these four poets there are a host of others, as representative of the age as their ideas allow, and as individual and original as their talent permits. We have tried to select the most important of them, without obscuring the great variety and range of Victorian poetry, and emphasizing its contribution to the life of the time; and as the problems of the Victorians are also our problems—faith, doubt, urban living, the power of the machine—their poetry makes its contribution to our own age, too.

September, 1973
N. P. MESSENGER
J. R. WATSON

William Barnes

William Barnes (1801–86), a remarkable and still undervalued writer, was born of humble parents near Sturminster Newton in the Vale of Blackmore, Dorset. As schoolmaster, poet, and finally clergyman, his life and work were dedicated to this corner of what was then remote and retarded pre-industrial England. Despite his fierce, regional loyalty and his uncompromising efforts to 're-saxonize' the language in his *Poems of Rural Life in the Dorset Dialect*, Barnes was a deft, sophisticated and, above all, 'celebratory' poet, who preferred the elaborate bardic devices of celtic and oriental poetry to the expressive romanticism of many of his Victorian contemporaries.

EVENEN IN THE VILLAGE

Now the light o' the west is a-turn'd to gloom,
    An' the men be at hwome vrom ground;
An' the bells be a-zenden all down the Coombe
    From tower, their mwoansome sound.
5   An' the wind is still,
        An' the house-dogs do bark,
An' the rooks be a-vled to the elems high an' dark,
    An' the water do roar at mill.

An' the flickeren light drough the window-peäne
10   Vrom the candle's dull fleäme do shoot,
An' young Jemmy the smith is a-gone down leäne,
    A-playen his shrill-vaïced flute.
        An' the miller's man
        Do zit down at his ease
15 On the seat that is under the cluster o' trees,
    Wi' his pipe an' his cider can.

WOODLEY

Sweet Woodley! oh! how fresh an' gaÿ
Thy leänes an' vields be now in Maÿ,

The while the broad-leav'd clotes do zwim
In brooks wi' gil'cups at the brim;
5   An' yollow cowslip-beds do grow
By thorns in blooth so white as snow;
An' win' do come vrom copse wi' smells
O' grægles wi' their hangen bells!

Though time do dreve me on, my mind
10   Do turn in love to thee behind,
The seäme's a bulrush that's a-shook
By wind a-blowen up the brook:
The curlen stream would dreve en down,
But plaÿsome aïr do turn en roun',
15   An' meäke en seem to bend wi' love
To zunny hollows up above.

Thy tower still do overlook
The woody knaps an' winden brook,
An' leänes wi' here an' there a hatch,
20   An' house wi' elem sheäded thatch,
An' vields where chaps do vur outdo
The Zunday sky, wi' cwoats o' blue;
An' maïdens' frocks do vur surpass
The whitest deäises in the grass.

25   What peals to-day from thy wold tow'r
Do strike upon the zummer flow'r,
As all the club, wi' dousty lags,
Do walk wi' poles an' flappen flags,
An' wind, to music, roun' between
30   A zwarm o' vo'k upon the green!
Though time do dreve me on, my mind
Do turn wi' love to thee behind.

ECLOGUE: THE COMMON A-TOOK IN

THOMAS AN' JOHN

Thomas
Good morn t'ye, John. How b'ye? how b'ye?
Zoo you be gwaïn to market, I do zee.
Why, you be quite a-lwoaded wi' your geese.

2

John

Ees, Thomas, ees.
Why, I'm a-getten rid ov ev'ry goose
An' goslen I've a-got: an' what is woose,
I fear that I must zell my little cow.

Thomas

How zoo, then, John? Why, what's the matter now?
What, can't ye get along? B'ye run a-ground?
An' can't paÿ twenty shillens vor a pound?
What, can't ye put a lwoaf on shelf?

John

                                        Ees, now;
But I do fear I shan't 'ithout my cow.
No; they do meän to teäke the moor in, I do hear,
An' 'twill be soon begun upon;
Zoo I must zell my bit o' stock to-year,
Because they woon't have any groun' to run upon.

Thomas

Why, what d'ye tell o'? I be very zorry
To hear what they be gwaïn about;
But yet I s'pose there'll be a 'lotment vor ye,
When they do come to mark it out.

John

No; not vor me, I fear. An' if there should,
Why 'twoulden be so handy as 'tis now;
Vor 'tis the common that do do me good,
The run vor my vew geese, or vor my cow.

Thomas

Ees, that's the job; why 'tis a handy thing
To have a bit o' common, I do know,
To put a little cow upon in Spring,
The while woone's bit ov orcha'd grass do grow.

John

Aye, that's the thing, you zee. Now I do mow
My bit o' grass, an' meäke a little rick;
An' in the zummer, while do grow,
My cow do run in common vor to pick
A bleäde or two o' grass, if she can vind em,
Vor tother cattle don't leäve much behind em.

3

35 Zoo in the evenen, we do put a lock
O' nice fresh grass avore the wicket;
An' she do come at vive or zix o'clock,
As constant as the zun, to pick it.
An' then, bezides the cow, why we do let
40 Our geese run out among the emmet hills;
An' then when we do pluck em, we do get
Vor zeäle zome veathers an' zome quills;
An' in the winter we do fat em well,
An' car em to the market vor to zell
45 To gentlevo'ks, vor we don't oft avvword
To put a goose a-top ov ouer bwoard;
But we do get our feäst,—vor we be eäble
To clap the giblets up a-top o' teäble.

Thomas

An' I don't know o' many better things,
50 Than geese's heads and gizzards, lags an' wings.

John

An' then, when I ha' nothen else to do,
Why I can teäke my hook an' gloves, an' goo
To cut a lot o' vuzz and briars
Vor heten ovens, or vor lighten viers.
55 An' when the children be too young to eärn
A penny, they can g'out in zunny weather,
An' run about, an' get together
A bag o' cow-dung vor to burn.

Thomas

'Tis handy to live near a common;
60 But I've a-zeed, an' I've a-zaid,
That if a poor man got a bit o' bread,
They'll try to teäke it vrom en.
But I wer twold back tother day,
That they be got into a way
65 O' letten bits o' groun' out to the poor.

John

Well, I do hope 'tis true, I'm sure;
An' I do hope that they will do it here,
Or I must goo to workhouse, I do fear.

GRAMMER'S SHOES

I do seem to zee Grammer as she did use
Vor to show us, at Chris'mas, her wedden shoes,
An' her flat spreaden bonnet so big an' roun'
As a girt pewter dish a-turn'd upside down;
    5   When we all did draw near
            In a cluster to hear
O' the merry wold soul how she did use
To walk an' to dance wi' her high-heel shoes.

She'd a gown wi' girt flowers lik' hollyhocks,
An' zome stockens o' gramfer's a-knit wi' clocks,
An' a token she kept under lock an' key,—
A small lock ov his heäir off avore 't wer grey.
            An' her eyes wer red,
            An' she shook her head,
When we'd all a-look'd at it, an' she did use
To lock it away wi' her wedden shoes.

She could tell us such teäles about heavy snows,
An' o' raïns an' o' floods when the waters rose
All up into the housen, an' carr'd awoy
All the bridge wi' a man an' his little bwoy;
            An' o' vog an' vrost,
            An' o' vo'k a-lost,
An' o' peärties at Chris'mas, when she did use
Vor to walk hwome wi' gramfer in high-heel shoes.

Ev'ry Chris'mas she lik'd vor the bells to ring,
An' to have in the zingers to heär em zing
The wold carols she heärd many years a-gone,
While she warm'd em zome cider avore the bron';
            An' she'd look an' smile
            At our dancen, while
She did tell how her friends now a-gone did use
To reely wi' her in their high-heel shoes.

Ah! an' how she did like vor to deck wi' red
Holly-berries the window an' wold clock's head,
An' the clavy wi' boughs o' some bright green leaves,
An' to meäke twoast an' eäle upon Chris'mas eves;
            But she's now, drough greäce,
            In a better pleäce,
Though we'll never vorget her, poor soul, nor lose
Gramfer's token ov heäir, nor her wedden shoes.

A FATHER OUT, AN' MOTHER HWOME

The snow-white clouds did float on high
In shoals avore the sheenen sky,
An' runnen weäves in pon' did cheäse
Each other on the water's feäce,
5   As hufflen win' did blow between
The new-leav'd boughs o' sheenen green.
An' there, the while I walked along
The path, drough leäze, above the drong,
A little maïd, wi' bloomen feäce,
10   Went on up hill wi' nimble peäce,
A-leänen to the right-han' zide,
To car a basket that did ride,
A-hangen down, wi' all his heft,
Upon her elbow at her left.
15   An' yet she hardly seem'd to bruise
The grass-bleädes wi' her tiny shoes,
That pass'd each other, left an' right,
In steps a'most too quick vor zight.
But she'd a-left her mother's door
20   A-bearen vrom her little store
Her father's welcome bit o' food,
Where he wer out at work in wood;
An' she wer bless'd wi' mwore than zome—
A father out, an' mother hwome.

25   An' there, a-vell'd 'ithin the copse,
Below the timber's new-leav'd tops,
Wer ashen poles, a-casten straïght,
On primrwose beds, their langthy waïght;
Below the yollow light, a-shed
30   Drough boughs upon the vi'let's head,
By climen ivy, that did reach,
A-sheenen roun' the dead-leav'd beech.
An' there her father zot, an' meäde
His hwomely meal bezide a gleäde;
35   While she, a-croopen down to ground,
Did pull the flowers, where she vound
The droopen vi'let out in blooth,
Or yollow primrwose in the lewth,
That she mid car em proudly back,
40   An' zet em on her mother's tack;
Vor she wer bless'd wi' mwore than zome—
A father out, an' mother hwome.

6

A father out, an' mother hwome,
Be blessens soon a-lost by zome;
A-lost by me, an' zoo I pray'd
They mid be speär'd the little maïd.

DAY'S WORK A-DONE

An' oh! the jaÿ our rest did yield,
    At evenen by the mossy wall,
When we'd a-work'd all day a-vield,
    While zummer zuns did rise an' vall,
      As there a-letten
      Goo all fretten,
An' vorgetten all our tweils,
We zot among our childern's smiles.

An' under skies that glitter'd white,
    The while our smoke, arisèn blue,
Did melt in aïr, out o' zight,
    Above the trees that kept us lew,
      Wer birds a-zingen,
      Tongues a-ringen,
Childern springen, vull o' jaÿ,
A-finishen the day in plaÿ.

An' back behind, a-stannen tall,
    The cliff did sheen to western light;
An' while avore the watervall,
    A-rottlen loud, an' foamen white,
      The leaves did quiver,
      Gnots did whiver,
By the river, where the pool,
In evenen aïr did glissen cool.

An' childern there, a-runnen wide,
    Did plaÿ their geämes along the grove,
Vor though to us 'twer jaÿ to bide
    At rest, to them 'twer jaÿ to move,
      The while my smilen
      Jeäne, beguilen
All my tweilen, wi' her ceäre,
Did call me to my evenen feäre.

HALLOWED PLEACES

At Woodcombe farm, wi' ground an' tree
Hallow'd by times o' youthvul glee,
At Chris'mas time I spent a night
Wi' feäces dearest to my zight;
5   An' took my wife to tread, woonce mwore,
Her maïden hwome's vorseäken vloor;
An' under stars that slowly wheel'd
Aloft, above the keen-aïr'd vield,
While night bedimm'd the rus'len copse,
10   An' darken'd all the ridges' tops,
The hall, a-hung wi' holly, rung
Wi' many a tongue o' wold an' young.

There, on the he'th's well-hetted ground,
Hallow'd by times o' zitten round,
15   The brimvul mug o' cider stood
An' hiss'd avore the bleäzen wood;
An' zome, a-zitten knee by knee,
Did tell their teäles wi' hearty glee,
An' others gamboll'd in a roar
20   O' laughter on the stwonen vloor;
An' while the moss o' winter-tide
Clung chilly roun' the house's zide,
The hall, a-hung wi' holly, rung
Wi' many a tongue o' wold an' young.

25   There, on the pworches bench o' stwone,
Hallow'd by times o' youthvul fun,
We laugh'd an' sigh'd to think o' neämes
That rung there woonce, in evenen geämes;
An' while the swaÿen cypress bow'd,
30   In chilly wind, his darksome sh'oud,
An' honeyzuckles, beäre o' leaves,
Still reach'd the window-sheädèn eaves
Up where the clematis did trim
The stwonen arches mossy rim,
35   The hall, a-hung wi' holly, rung
Wi' many a tongue o' wold an' young.

There, in the geärden's wall-bound square,
Hallow'd by times o' strollen there,
The winter wind, a-hufflen loud,
40   Did swaÿ the pear-tree's leafless sh'oud,
An' beät the bush that woonce did bear
The damask rwose vor Jenny's heäir;

An' there the walk o' peäven stwone
That burn'd below the zummer zun,
45   Struck icy-cwold drough shoes a-wore
By maïdens vrom the hetted vloor
In hall, a-hung wi' holm, where rung
Vull many a tongue o' wold an' young.

There at the geäte that woonce wer blue,
50   Hallow'd by times o' passen drough,
Light strawmotes rose in flaggen flight,
A-floated by the winds o' night,
Where leafy ivy-stems did crawl
In moonlight on the windblown wall,
55   An' merry maïdens' vaïces vled
In echoes sh'ill, vrom wall to shed,
As shiv'ren in their frocks o' white
They come to bid us there 'Good night,'
Vrom hall, a-hung wi' holm, that rung
60   Wi' many a tongue o' wold an' young.

There in the narrow leäne an' drong
Hallow'd by times o' gwaïn along,
The lofty ashes' leafless sh'ouds
Rose dark avore the clear-edged clouds,
65   The while the moon, at girtest height,
Bespread the pooly brook wi' light,
An' as our child, in loose-limb'd rest,
Lay peäle upon her mother's breast,
Her waxen eyelids seal'd her eyes
70   Vrom darksome trees, an' sheenen skies,
An' halls a-hung wi' holm, that rung
Wi' many a tongue, o' wold an' young.

MILKEN TIME

'Twer when the busy birds did vlee,
Wi' sheenen wings, vrom tree to tree,
To build upon the mossy lim',
Their hollow nestes' rounded rim;
5   The while the zun, a-zinken low,
Did roll along his evenen bow,
I come along where wide-horn'd cows,
'Ithin a nook, a-screen'd by boughs,
Did stan' an' flip the white-hoop'd païls
10   Wi' heäiry tufts o' swingen taïls;

An' there wer Jenny Coom a-gone
Along the path a vew steps on,
A-bearen on her head, upstraïght,
Her païl, wi' slowly-riden waïght,
15   An' hoops a-sheenen, lily-white,
Ageän the evenen's slanten light;
An' zoo I took her païl, an' left
Her neck a-freed vrom all his heft;
An' she a-looken up an' down,
20   Wi' sheäpely head an' glossy crown,
Then took my zide, an' kept my peäce
A-talken on wi' smilen feäce,
An' zetten things in sich a light,
I'd faïn ha' heärd her talk all night;
25   An' when I brought her milk avore
The geäte, she took it in to door,
An' if her païl had but allow'd
Her head to vall, she would ha' bow'd,
An' still, as 'twer, I had the zight
30   Ov her sweet smile droughout the night.

THE WATER CROWVOOT

O small-feäc'd flow'r that now dost bloom
To stud wi' white the shallow Frome,
An' leäve the clote to spread his flow'r
On darksome pools o' stwoneless Stour,
5   When sof'ly-rizèn aïrs do cool
The water in the sheenen pool,
Thy beds o' snow-white buds do gleam
So feäir upon the sky-blue stream,
As whitest clouds, a-hangen high
10   Avore the blueness o' the sky;
An' there, at hand, the thin-heäir'd cows,
In aïry sheädes o' withy boughs,
Or up bezide the mossy raïls,
Do stan' an' zwing their heavy taïls,
15   The while the ripplen stream do flow
Below the dousty bridge's bow;
An' quiv'ren water-gleams do mock
The weäves, upon the sheäded rock;
An' up athirt the copen stwone
20   The laïtren bwoy do leän alwone,
A-watchen, wi' a stedvast look,
The vallèn waters in the brook,

10

The while the zand o' time do run
An' leäve his errand still undone.
25 An' oh! as long's thy buds would gleam
Above the softly-sliden stream,
While sparklen zummer-brooks do run
Below the lofty-climen zun,
I only wish that thou could'st staÿ
30 Vor noo man's harm, an' all men's jaÿ.
But no, the waterman 'ull weäde
Thy water wi' his deadly bleäde,
To slaÿ thee even in thy bloom,
Fair small-feäc'd flow'r o' the Frome.

LYDLINCH BELLS

When skies wer peäle wi' twinklen stars,
An' whislen aïr a-risèn keen;
An' birds did leäve the icy bars
To vind, in woods, their mossy screen;
5 When vrozen grass, so white's a sheet,
Did scrunchy sharp below our veet,
An' water, that did sparkle red
At zunzet, wer a-vrozen dead;
The ringers then did spend an hour
10 A-ringen changes up in tow'r;
Vor Lydlinch bells be good vor sound,
An' liked by all the naïghbours round.

An' while along the leafless boughs
O' ruslen hedges, win's did pass,
15 An' orts ov haÿ, a-left by cows,
Did russle on the vrozen grass,
An' maïdens' païls, wi' all their work
A-done, did hang upon their vurk,
An' they, avore the fleämen brand,
20 Did teäke their needle-work in hand,
The men did cheer their heart an hour
A-ringen changes up in tow'r;
Vor Lydlinch bells be good vor sound,
An' liked by all the naïghbours round.

25 Their sons did pull the bells that rung
Their mothers' wedden peals avore,
The while their fathers led em young
An' blushen vrom the churches door,

11

An' still did cheem, wi' happy sound,
30 As time did bring the Zundays round,
An' call em to the holy pleäce
Vor heav'nly gifts o' peace an' greäce;
An' vo'k did come, a-streamen slow
Along below the trees in row,
35 While they, in merry peals, did sound
The bells vor all the naïghbours round.

An' when the bells, wi' changen peal,
Did smite their own vo'k's window-peänes,
Their sof'en'd sound did often steal
40 Wi' west winds drough the Bagber leänes;
Or, as the win' did shift, mid goo
Where woody Stock do nessle lew,
Or where the risèn moon did light
The walls o' Thornhill on the height;
45 An' zoo, whatever time mid bring
To meäke their vive clear vaïces zing,
Still Lydlinch bells wer good vor sound,
An' liked by all the naïghbours round.

THE WIFE A-LOST

Since I noo mwore do zee your feäce,
    Up steäirs or down below,
I'll zit me in the lwonesome pleäce,
    Where flat-bough'd beech do grow;
5 Below the beeches' bough, my love,
    Where you did never come,
An' I don't look to meet ye now,
    As I do look at hwome.

Since you noo mwore be at my zide,
10   In walks in zummer het,
I'll goo alwone where mist do ride,
    Drough trees a-drippen wet;
Below the raïn-wet bough, my love,
    Where you did never come,
15 An' I don't grieve to miss ye now,
    As I do grieve at hwome.

Since now bezide my dinner-bwoard
    Your vaïce do never sound,
I'll eat the bit I can avvword,
20   A-yield upon the ground;

12

Below the darksome bough, my love,
    Where you did never dine,
An' I don't grieve to miss ye now,
    As I at hwome do pine.

25   Since I do miss your vaïce an' feäce
    In praÿer at eventide,
I'll praÿ wi' woone sad vaïce vor greäce
    To goo where you do bide;
Above the tree an' bough, my love,
30   Where you be gone avore,
An' be a-waïten vor me now,
    To come vor evermwore.

NAIGHBOUR PLAYMEATES

O jaÿ betide the dear wold mill,
    My naïghbour plaÿmeätes' happy hwome,
Wi' rollen wheel, an' leäpen foam,
    Below the overhangen hill,
5   Where, wide an' slow,
          The stream did flow,
An' flags did grow, an' lightly vlee
Below the grey-leav'd withy tree,
While clack, clack, clack, vrom hour to hour,
10   Wi' whirlen stwone, an' streamen flour,
Did goo the mill by cloty Stour.

An' there in geämes by evenen-skies,
    When Meäry zot her down to rest,
The broach upon her panken breast,
15   Did quickly vall an' lightly rise,
          While swans did zwim
          In steätely trim,
An' swifts did skim the water, bright
Wi' whirlen froth, in western light;
20   An' clack, clack, clack, that happy hour,
Wi' whirlen stwone, an' streamen flour,
Did goo the mill by cloty Stour.

Now mortery jeints, in streaks o' white,
    Along the geärden wall do show
25   In Maÿ, an' cherry boughs do blow,
        Wi' bloomen tutties, snowy white,
          Where rollen round,
          Wi' rumblen sound,

The wheel woonce drown'd the vaïce so dear
30   To me. I faïn would goo to hear
The clack, clack, clack, vor woone short hour,
Wi' whirlen stwone, an' streamen flour,
Bezide the mill on cloty Stour.

But should I vind a-heaven now
35   Her breast wi' aïr o' thik dear pleäce?
Or zee dark locks by such a brow,
        Or het o' plaÿ on such a feäce?
            No! She's now staïd,
            An' where she plaÿ'd,
40   There's noo such maïd that now ha' took
The pleäce that she ha' long vorsook,
Though clack, clack, clack, vrom hour to hour,
Wi' whirlen stwone an' streamen flour,
Do goo the mill by cloty Stour.

45   An' still the pulley rwope do heist
        The wheat vrom red-wheeled waggon beds,
An' ho'ses there wi' lwoads ov grist,
        Do stand an' toss their heavy heads;
            But on the vloor,
50   Or at the door,
Do show noo mwore the kindly feäce
Her father show'd about the pleäce,
As clack, clack, clack, vrom hour to hour,
Wi' whirlen stwone, an' streamen flour,
55   Did goo his mill by cloty Stour.

WOAK HILL

When sycamore leaves wer a-spreaden,
        Green-ruddy, in hedges,
Bezide the red doust o' the ridges,
        A-dried at Woak Hill;

5   I packed up my goods all a-sheenen
        Wi' long years o' handlen,
On dousty red wheels ov a waggon,
        To ride at Woak Hill.

The brown thatchen ruf o' the dwellen
10   I then wer a-leäven,
Had shelter'd the sleek head o' Meäry,
        My bride at Woak Hill.

14

But now vor zome years, her light voot-vall
    'S a-lost vrom the vlooren.
15 Too soon vor my jaÿ an' my childern,
    She died at Woak Hill.

But still I do think that, in soul,
    She do hover about us;
To ho vor her motherless childern,
20   Her pride at Woak Hill.

Zoo—lest she should tell me hereafter
    I stole off 'ithout her,
An' left her, uncall'd at house-ridden,
    To bide at Woak Hill—

25 I call'd her so fondly, wi' lippens
    All soundless to others,
An' took her wi' aïr-reachen hand,
    To my zide at Woak Hill.

On the road I did look round, a-talken
30   To light at my shoulder,
An' then led her in at the door-way,
    Miles wide vrom Woak Hill.

An' that's why vo'k thought, vor a season,
    My mind wer a-wandren
35 Wi' sorrow, when I wer so sorely
    A-tried at Woak Hill.

But no; that my Meäry mid never
    Behold herzelf slighted,
I wanted to think that I guided
40   My guide vrom Woak Hill.

R. S. Hawker

Robert Stephen Hawker (1803–75) was for most of his life vicar of Morwenstow, a country parish in north-east Cornwall. There he became known as 'the sailor's friend', partly because he would pay for the burial of sailors drowned near by. His poetry was considerably influenced by local legend and feeling; and his best-known poems (though not, we think, his best) is probably 'The Song of the Western Men', with its defiant use of an old refrain:

> And shall Trelawny die?
> Here's twenty thousand Cornish men
> Will know the reason why!

Like other nineteenth-century poets, Hawker was also very interested in the Arthurian legends, and wrote a long poem, 'The Quest of the Sangraal'. But perhaps his most remarkable achievement, combining Christianity with ancient customs, was the invention of the Harvest Festival.

FEATHERSTONE'S DOOM

> Twist thou and twine! in light and gloom
>   A spell is on thine hand;
> The wind shall be thy changeful loom,
>   Thy web the shifting sand.

5
> Twine from this hour, in ceaseless toil,
>   On Blackrock's sullen shore;
> Till cordage of the sand shall coil
>   Where crested surges roar.

> 'Tis for that hour, when, from the wave,
10
>   Near voices wildly cried;
> When thy stern hand no succour gave,
>   The cable at thy side.

> Twist thou and twine! in light and gloom
>   The spell is on thine hand;
15
> The wind shall be thy changeful loom,
>   Thy web the shifting sand.

THE SILENT TOWER OF BOTTREAU

I

Tintadgel bells ring o'er the tide,
The boy leans on his vessel side;
He hears that sound, and dreams of home
Soothe the wild orphan of the foam.
    'Come to thy God in time!'
    Thus saith their pealing chime:
    Youth, manhood, old age past,
    'Come to thy God at last.'

II

But why are Bottreau's echoes still?
Her tower stands proudly on the hill;
Yet the strange chough that home hath found:
The lamb lies sleeping on the ground.
    'Come to thy God in time!'
    Should be her answering chime:
    'Come to thy God at last!'
    Should echo on the blast.

III

The ship rode down with courses free,
The daughter of a distant sea:
Her sheet was loose, her anchor stored,
The merry Bottreau bells on board.
    'Come to thy God in time!'
    Rung out Tintadgel chime;
    Youth, manhood, old age past,
    'Come to thy God at last!'

IV

The pilot heard his native bells
Hang on the breeze in fitful swells;
'Thank God,' with reverent brow he cried,
'We make the shore with evening's tide.'
    'Come to thy God in time!'
    It was his marriage chime:
    Youth, manhood, old age past,
    His bell must ring at last.

V

'Thank God, thou whining knave, on land,
But thank, at sea, the steersman's hand,'
The captain's voice above the gale:
'Thank the good ship and ready sail.'

'Come to thy God in time!'
Sad grew the boding chime:
'Come to thy God at last!'
40 Boomed heavy on the blast.

VI

Uprose that sea! as if it heard
The mighty Master's signal-word:
What thrills the captain's whitening lip?
The death-groans of his sinking ship.
45   'Come to thy God in time!'
Swung deep the funeral chime:
Grace, mercy, kindness past,
'Come to thy God at last!'

VII

Long did the rescued pilot tell—
50 When gray hairs o'er his forehead fell,
While those around would hear and weep—
That fearful judgment of the deep.
'Come to thy God in time!'
He read his native chime:
55   Youth, manhood, old age past,
His bell rung out at last.

VIII

Still when the storm of Bottreau's waves,
Is wakening in his weedy caves:
Those bells, that sullen surges hide,
60 Peal their deep notes beneath the tide:
'Come to thy God in time!'
Thus saith the ocean chime:
Storm, billow, whirlwind past,
'Come to thy God at last!'

THE POOR MAN AND HIS PARISH CHURCH
A TRUE TALE

I

The poor have hands, and feet, and eyes,
Flesh, and a feeling mind:
They breathe the breath of mortal sighs,
They are of human kind.
5 They weep such tears as others shed,
And now and then they smile:—
For sweet to them is that poor bread,
They win with honest toil.

II

The poor men have their wedding-day:
    And children climb their knee:
They have not many friends, for they
    Are in such misery.
They sell their youth, their skill, their pains,
    For hire in hill and glen:
The very blood within their veins,
    It flows for other men.

III

They should have roofs to call their own,
    When they grow old and bent:
Meek houses built of dark gray stone,
    Worn labour's monument.
There should they dwell, beneath the thatch,
    With threshold calm and free:
No stranger's hand should lift the latch,
    To mark their poverty.

IV

Fast by the church those walls should stand,
    Her aisles in youth they trod:—
They have no home in all the land,
    Like that old House of God.
There, there, the Sacrament was shed,
    That gave them heavenly birth;
And lifted up the poor man's head
    With princes of the earth.

V

There in the chancel's voice of praise,
    Their simple vows were pour'd;
And angels looked with equal gaze
    On Lazarus and his Lord.
There, too, at last, they calmly sleep,
    Where hallowed blossoms bloom;
And eyes as fond and faithful weep,
    As o'er the rich man's tomb.

VI

They told me of an ancient home,
    Beside a churchyard wall,
Where roses round the porch would roam,
    And gentle jasmines fall:
There dwelt an old man, worn and blind,
    Poor, and of lowliest birth;
He seemed the last of all his kind,—
    He had no friend on earth.

VII

Men saw him till his eyes grew dim,
    At morn and evening tide
Pass, 'mid the graves, with tottering limb
    To the gray chancel's side:
There knelt he down, and meekly prayed
    The prayer his youth had known;
Words by the old Apostles made,
    In tongues of ancient tone.

VIII

At Matin-time, at evening hour,
    He bent with reverent knee:
The dial carved upon the tower,
    Was not more true than he.
This lasted till the blindness fell
    In shadows round his bed;
And on those walls he loved so well,
    He looked and they were fled.

IX

Then would he watch, and fondly turn,
    If feet of men were there,
To tell them how his soul would yearn,
    For the old place of prayer:
And some would lead him on, to stand,
    While fast their tears would fall,
Until he felt beneath his hand
    The long-accustomed wall.

X

Then joy in those dim eyes would melt,
    Faith found the former tone;
His heart within his bosom felt
    The touch of every stone.
He died—he slept beneath the dew,
    In his own grassy mound:
The corpse, within the coffin, knew
    That calm, that holy ground.

XI

I know not why—but when they tell
    Of houses fair and wide,
Where troops of poor men go to dwell
    In chambers side by side:—
I dream of that old cottage door,
    With garlands overgrown,
And wish the children of the poor
    Had flowers to call their own.

XII

And when they vaunt, that in those walls
    They have their worship day,
Where the stern signal coldly calls
    The prisoned poor to pray,—
I think upon that ancient home,
    Beside the churchyard wall,
Where roses round the porch would roam,
    And gentle jasmines fall.

XIII

I see the old man of my lay,
    His gray head bowed and bare:
He kneels by one dear wall to pray,
    The sunlight in his hair.
Well! they may strive, as wise men will,
    To work with wit and gold;
I think my own dear Cornwall still,
    Was happier of old.

XIV

O! for the poor man's church again,
    With one roof over all;
Where the true hearts of Cornish men,
    Might beat beside the wall:
The altars where, in holier days,
    Our fathers were forgiven;
Who went with meek and faithful ways,
    Through the old aisles to heaven.

THE BURIAL HOUR

I

'At eve should be the time,' they said,
'To close their brother's narrow bed:'
'Tis at that pleasant hour of day
The labourer treads his homeward way.

II

His work was o'er, his toil was done,
And therefore, with the set of sun,
To wait the wages of the dead
We laid our hireling in his bed.

A LEGEND OF THE HIVE

Behold those wingèd images,
    Bound for their evening bowers:
They are the nation of the bees,
    Born from the breath of flowers.
5   Strange people they! a mystic race,
In life, in food, and dwelling-place.

They first were seen on earth, 'tis said,
    When the rose breathes in spring:
Men thought her blushing bosom shed
10   These children of the wing.
But lo! their hosts went down the wind,
Filled with the thoughts of God's own mind.

They built them houses made with hands,
    And there alone they dwell:
15   No man to this day understands
    The mystery of their cell.
Your mighty sages cannot see
The deep foundations of the bee.

Low in the violet's breast of blue,
20   For treasured food they sink;
They know the flowers that hold the dew,
    For their small race to drink.
They glide—King Solomon might gaze
With wonder on their awful ways.

25   And once—it is a grandame's tale,
    Yet filled with secret lore—
There dwelt within a woodland vale,
    Fast by old Cornwall's shore,
An ancient woman, worn and bent,
30   Fallen nature's mournful monument.

A home had they, the clustering race,
    Beside her garden wall:
All blossoms breathed around the place,
    And sunbeams fain would fall.
35   The lily loved that combe the best
Of all the valleys of the west.

But so it was, that on a day
    When summer built her bowers,
The waxen wanderers ceased to play
40   Around the cottage flowers.
No hum was heard, no wing would roam:
They dwelt within their cloister'd home.

This lasted long—no tongue could tell
    Their pastime or their toil;
45 What binds the soldier to his cell?
    Who should divide the spoil?
It lasted long—it fain would last,
Till autumn rustled on the blast.

Then sternly went that woman old,
50   She sought the chancel floor,
And there, with purpose bad and bold,
    Knelt down amid the poor.
She took—she hid—that blessèd bread,
Whereon the Invisible is shed.

55 She bore it to her distant home,
    She laid it by the hive:
To lure the wanderers forth to roam,
    That so her store might thrive.
'Twas a wild wish, a thought unblest,
60 Some evil legend of the west.

But lo! at morning tide, a sign
    For wondering eyes to trace:
They found above that bread, a shrine
    Reared by the harmless race.
65 They brought their walls from bud and flower,
They built bright roof and beamy tower.

Was it a dream? or did they hear,
    Float from those golden cells,
A sound as of some psaltery near,
70   Or soft and silvery bells;
A low sweet psalm that grieved within,
In mournful memory of the sin.

Was it a dream? 'tis sweet no less:
    Set not the vision free,
75 Long let the lingering legend bless
    The nation of the bee.
So shall they bear upon their wings
A parable of sacred things.

So shall they teach, when men blaspheme
80   Or sacrament or shrine,
That humbler things may fondly dream
    Of mysteries divine;
And holier hearts than his may beat
Beneath the bold blasphemer's feet.

THE FATAL SHIP

Down the deep sea, full fourscore fathoms down,
    An iron vault hath clutched five hundred men!
They died not, like the nations, one by one:
    A thrill! a bounding pulse! a shout! and then
5   Five hundred hearts stood still, at once, nor beat again!

That night the Angel of the Lord beheld
    A vast battalion of the gliding dead:
Souls that came up where seething surges quelled
    Their stately ship—their throne—and now the bed
10   Where they shall wait, in shrouded sleep, the Morn of
    Dread!

Fast slept the sailor boy! A silent dream
    Soften'd his brow with smiles—his mother's face
Droops over him—and her soft kisses seem
    Warm on his cheek: what severs that embrace?
15   Death! strangling death!—alive—a conscious burial-
    place!

And he, the kingly mind, whose skill had planned
    That lordly bastion of the world of wave?
But yesterday he stood, in proud command,
    And now a thing of nought, where ocean raves
20   Above his shuddering sepulchre in the weedy caves!

The monsters of the sea will glide and glare:
    Baffled Leviathan shall roar in vain:
The Sea Kings of the Isles are castled there:
    They man that silent fortress of the main:
25   Yea! in the realms of death their dust shall rule and reign!

Lord Yahvah of the Waters! Thou wert there!
    They presence shone throughout that dark abode:
Thy mighty touch assuaged the last despair:
    Their pulses paused in the calm midst of God:
30   Their souls, amid surrounding Angels, went abroad!

Elizabeth Barrett Browning

Elizabeth Barrett Browning (1806–61) was the central figure in the most celebrated elopement in the history of English letters, when she married Robert Browning in 1846. Until that date she had been a writer and a semi-invalid in the house in Wimpole Street presided over by her over-protective father. After the marriage the Brownings lived mainly in Italy, where Mrs Browning's health improved under the influence of her new-found happiness. She had established a reputation as a poet before 1846, and throughout her lifetime she continued to be more successful and famous than her husband: her particular blend of conventional moralizing and emotional expressiveness suited the Victorian public better than his original and sometimes quirky technique.

THE CRY OF THE CHILDREN

Φεῦ, φεῦ· τί προσδέρκεσθέ μ' ὄμμασιν, τέκνα;

Medea

I

Do ye hear the children weeping, O my brothers,
    Ere the sorrow comes with years?
They are leaning their young heads against their mothers,
    And *that* cannot stop their tears.
5   The young lambs are bleating in the meadows,
        The young birds are chirping in the nest,
The young fawns are playing with the shadows,
        The young flowers are blowing toward the west—
But the young, young children, O my brothers,
10   They are weeping bitterly!
They are weeping in the playtime of the others,
    In the country of the free.

II

Do you question the young children in the sorrow,
    Why their tears are falling so?
15   The old man may weep for his to-morrow
    Which is lost in Long Ago;

The old tree is leafless in the forest,
    The old year is ending in the frost,
The old wound, if stricken, is the sorest,
20   The old hope is hardest to be lost.
But the young, young children, O my brothers,
    Do you ask them why they stand
Weeping sore before the bosoms of their mothers,
    In our happy Fatherland?

III

25 They look up with their pale and sunken faces,
    And their looks are sad to see,
For the man's hoary anguish draws and presses
    Down the cheeks of infancy.
'Your old earth,' they say, 'is very dreary;
30   Our young feet,' they say, 'are very weak!
Few paces have we taken, yet are weary—
    Our grave-rest is very far to seek.
Ask the aged why they weep, and not the children;
    For the outside earth is cold;
35 And we young ones stand without, in our bewildering,
    And the graves are for the old.'

IV

'True,' say the children, 'it may happen
    That we die before our time;
Little Alice died last year—her grave is shapen
40   Like a snowball, in the rime.
We looked into the pit prepared to take her:
    Was no room for any work in the close clay!
From the sleep wherein she lieth none will wake her,
    Crying, "Get up, little Alice! it is day."
45 If you listen by that grave, in sun and shower,
    With your ear down, little Alice never cries;
Could we see her face, be sure we should not know her,
    For the smile has time for growing in her eyes:
And merry go her moments, lulled and stilled in
50   The shroud by the kirk-chime!
It is good when it happens,' say the children,
    'That we die before our time.'

V

Alas, alas, the children! they are seeking
    Death in life, as best to have;
55 They are binding up their hearts away from breaking,
    With a cerement from the grave.
Go out, children, from the mine and from the city,
    Sing out, children, as the little thrushes do;

Pluck you handfuls of the meadow cowslips pretty,
60   Laugh aloud, to feel your fingers let them through!
But they answer, 'Are your cowslips of the meadows
        Like our weeds anear the mine?
Leave us quiet in the dark of the coal-shadows,
        From your pleasures fair and fine!

VI

65 'For oh,' say the children, 'we are weary,
        And we cannot run or leap;
If we cared for any meadows, it were merely
        To drop down in them and sleep.
Our knees tremble sorely in the stooping,
70   We fall upon our faces, trying to go;
And, underneath our heavy eyelids drooping,
        The reddest flower would look as pale as snow;
For, all day, we drag our burden tiring
        Through the coal-dark, underground—
75 Or, all day, we drive the wheels of iron,
        In the factories, round and round.

VII

'For, all day, the wheels are droning, turning,—
        Their wind comes in our faces,—
Till our hearts turn,—our head, with pulses burning,
80   And the walls turn in their places:
Turns the sky in the high window blank and reeling,
        Turns the long light that drops adown the wall,
Turn the black flies that crawl along the ceiling,
        All are turning, all the day, and we with all.
85 And all day, the iron wheels are droning,
        And sometimes we could pray,
"O ye wheels" (breaking out in a mad moaning),
        "Stop! be silent for to-day!"'

VIII

Aye! be silent! Let them hear each other breathing
90   For a moment, mouth to mouth!
Let them touch each other's hands, in a fresh wreathing
        Of their tender human youth!
Let them feel that this cold metallic motion
        Is not all the life God fashions or reveals:
95 Let them prove their living souls against the notion
        That they live in you, or under you, O wheels!—
Still, all day, the iron wheels go onward,
        Grinding life down from its mark;
And the children's souls, which God is calling sunward,
100   Spin on blindly in the dark.

27

IX

Now tell the poor young children, O my brothers,
    To look up to Him and pray;
So the blessèd One who blesseth all the others,
    Will bless them another day.
105 They answer, 'Who is God that He should hear us,
    While the rushing of the iron wheels is stirred?
When we sob aloud, the human creatures near us
    Pass by, hearing not, or answer not a word.
And *we* hear not (for the wheels in their resounding)
110   Strangers speaking at the door:
Is it likely God, with angels singing round Him,
    Hears our weeping any more?

X

'Two words, indeed, of praying we remember,
    And at midnight's hour of harm,
115 "Our Father," looking upward in the chamber,
    We say softly for a charm.
We know no other words, except "Our Father,"
    And we think that, in some pause of angels' song,
God may pluck them with the silence sweet to gather,
120   And hold both within His right hand which is strong.
"Our Father!" If He heard us, He would surely
    (For they call Him good and mild)
Answer, smiling down the steep world very purely,
    "Come and rest with Me, My child."

XI

125 'But, no!' say the children, weeping faster,
    'He is speechless as a stone;
And they tell us, of His image is the master
    Who commands us to work on.
Go to!' say the children,—'up in Heaven,
130   Dark, wheel-like, turning clouds are all we find.
Do not mock us; grief has made us unbelieving—
    We look up for God, but tears have made us blind.'
Do you hear the children weeping and disproving,
    O my brothers, what ye preach?
135 For God's possible is taught by His world's loving,
    And the children doubt of each.

XII

And well may the children weep before you!
    They are weary ere they run;
They have never seen the sunshine, nor the glory
140   Which is brighter than the sun.

They know the grief of man, without its wisdom;
    They sink in man's despair, without its calm;
Are slaves, without the liberty in Christdom,
    Are martyrs, by the pang without the palm,—
145 Are worn, as if with age, yet unretrievingly
    The harvest of its memories cannot reap,—
Are orphans of the earthly love and heavenly.
    Let them weep! let them weep!

XIII

They look up, with their pale and sunken faces,
150   And their look is dread to see,
For they mind you of their angels in high places,
    With eyes turned on Deity!—
'How long,' they say, 'how long, O cruel nation,
    Will you stand, to move the world, on a child's heart,—
155 Stifle down with a mailed heel its palpitation,
    And tread onward to your throne amid the mart?
Our blood splashes upward, O gold-heaper,
    And your purple shows your path!
But the child's sob in the silence curses deeper
160   Than the strong man in his wrath.'

From SONNETS FROM THE PORTUGUESE

I

I thought once how Theocritus had sung
Of the sweet years, the dear and wished-for years,
Who each one in a gracious hand appears
To bear a gift for mortals, old or young:
5 And, as I mused it in his antique tongue,
I saw, in gradual vision through my tears,
The sweet, sad years, the melancholy years,
Those of my own life, who by turns had flung
A shadow across me. Straightway I was 'ware,
10 So weeping, how a mystic Shape did move
Behind me, and drew me backward by the hair,
And a voice said in mastery while I strove, . . .
'Guess now who holds thee?'—'Death,' I said. But, there,
The silver answer rang, . . . 'Not Death, but Love.'

29

XVIII

I never gave a lock of hair away
To a man, dearest, except this to thee,
Which now upon my fingers thoughtfully
I ring out to the full brown length and say
5   'Take it.' My day of youth went yesterday;
My hair no longer bounds to my foot's glee,
Nor plant I it from rose or myrtle-tree,
As girls do, any more. It only may
Now shade on two pale cheeks, the mark of tears,
10 Taught drooping from the head that hangs aside
Through sorrow's trick. I thought the funeral-shears
Would take this first, but Love is justified,—
Take it, thou, . . . finding pure, from all those years,
The kiss my mother left here when she died.

XLIII

How do I love thee? Let me count the ways.
I love thee to the depth and breadth and height
My soul can reach, when feeling out of sight
For the ends of Being and ideal Grace.
5   I love thee to the level of every day's
Most quiet need, by sun and candlelight.
I love thee freely, as men strive for Right;
I love thee purely, as they turn from Praise.
I love thee with the passion put to use
10 In my old griefs, and with my childhood's faith.
I love thee with a love I seemed to lose
With my lost saints,—I love thee with the breath,
Smiles, tears, of all my life!—and, if God choose,
I shall but love thee better after death.

XLIV

Belovèd, thou hast brought me many flowers
Plucked in the garden, all the summer through
And winter, and it seemed as if they grew
In this close room, nor missed the sun and showers.
5   So, in the like name of that love of ours,
Take back these thoughts which here unfolded too,
And which on warm and cold days I withdrew
From my heart's ground. Indeed, those beds and bowers
Be overgrown with bitter weeds and rue,
10 And wait thy weeding; yet here's eglantine,
Here's ivy!—take them, as I used to do
Thy flowers, and keep them where they shall not pine.
Instruct thine eyes to keep their colours true,
And tell thy soul, their roots are left in mine.

A MUSICAL INSTRUMENT

I

What was he doing, the great god Pan,
    Down in the reeds by the river?
Spreading ruin and scattering ban,
Splashing and paddling with hoofs of a goat,
And breaking the golden lilies afloat
    With the dragon-fly on the river.

II

He tore out a reed, the great god Pan,
    From the deep cool bed of the river:
The limpid water turbidly ran,
And the broken lilies a-dying lay,
And the dragon-fly had fled away,
    Ere he brought it out of the river.

III

High on the shore sate the great god Pan,
    While turbidly flowed the river;
And hacked and hewed as a great god can,
With his hard bleak steel at the patient reed,
Till there was not a sign of a leaf indeed
    To prove it fresh from the river.

IV

He cut it short, did the great god Pan
    (How tall it stood in the river!),
Then drew the pith, like the heart of a man,
Steadily from the outside ring,
And notched the poor dry empty thing
    In holes, as he sate by the river.

V

'This is the way,' laughed the great god Pan
    (Laughed while he sate by the river),
'The only way, since gods began
To make sweet music, they could succeed.'
Then, dropping his mouth to a hole in the reed,
    He blew in power by the river.

VI

Sweet, sweet, sweet, O Pan!
    Piercing sweet by the river!
Blinding sweet, O great god Pan!

The sun on the hill forgot to die,
35 And the lilies revived, and the dragon-fly
        Came back to dream on the river.

VII

Yet half a beast is the great god Pan,
    To laugh as he sits by the river,
Making a poet out of a man:
40 The true gods sigh for the cost and pain,—
For the reed which grows nevermore again
        As a reed with the reeds in the river.

Charles Tennyson-Turner

Charles Tennyson-Turner (1808–79) was the elder and favourite brother of Alfred Tennyson, who changed his name to Turner in 1837 on receipt of a legacy from his great uncle. He grew up with Alfred at Somersby, and shared the authorship of *Poems of Two Brothers* (1827). He graduated from Trinity College, Cambridge, in 1832, and was ordained in 1835. In 1836 he married Louisa Sellwood, sister of Emily, Alfred's future wife, and spent the rest of his life as vicar of Grasby, a remote Lincolnshire village.

Charles Tennyson-Turner shared something of his brother's lyrical gifts together with the inherited Tennysonian melancholy. His sonnets afford a vivid insight into the quality of rural parish life in the middle of the nineteenth century.

WIND ON THE CORN

Full often as I rove by path or stile,
To watch the harvest ripening in the vale,
Slowly and sweetly, like a growing smile—
A smile that ends in laughter—the quick gale
5   Upon the breadths of gold-green wheat descends;
While still the swallow, with unbaffled grace,
About his viewless quarry dips and bends—
And all the fine excitement of the chase
Lies in the hunter's beauty: In the eclipse
10   Of that brief shadow, how the barley's beard
Tilts at the passing gloom, and wild-rose dips
Among the white-tops in the ditches rear'd:
And hedgerow's flowery breast of lacework stirs
Faintly in that full wind that rocks the outstanding firs.

MARY—A REMINISCENCE

She died in June, while yet the woodbine sprays
Waved o'er the outlet of this garden-dell;
Before the advent of these Autumn days
And dark unblossom'd verdure. As befel,

5 I from my window gazed, yearning to forge
 Some comfort out of anguish so forlorn;
 The dull rain stream'd before the bloomless gorge,
 By which, erewhile, on each less genial morn,
 Our Mary pass'd, to gain her shelter'd lawn,
10 With Death's disastrous rose upon her cheek.
 How often had I watched her, pale and meek,
 Pacing the sward! and now I daily seek
 The track, by those slow pausing footsteps worn,
 How faintly worn! though trodden week by week.

EUSTACE AND EDITH
OR THE OLD ROCKING-HORSE

 Poor rocking-horse! Eustace, and Edith too,
 Mount living steeds: she leans her dainty whip
 Across thy smooth-worn flank, and feels thee dip
 Beneath the pressure, while she dons a shoe,
5 Or lifts a glove, and thinks 'My childhood's gone!'
 While the young statesman, with high hopes possest,
 Lays a light hand upon thy yielding crest,
 And rocks thee vacantly and passes on.
 Yet they both love thee—nor would either brook
10 Thine absence from this hall, tho' other aims
 And interests have supplanted thy mute claims,
 And thou must be content with casual look
 From those, who sought thee once with earnest will,
 And gallop'd thee with all their might and skill.

THE STEAM THRESHING-MACHINE
WITH THE STRAW CARRIER

 Flush with the pond the lurid furnace burn'd
 At eve, while smoke and vapour fill'd the yard;
 The gloomy winter sky was dimly starr'd,
 The fly-wheel with a mellow murmur turn'd;
5 While, ever rising on its mystic stair
 In the dim light, from secret chambers borne,
 The straw of harvest, sever'd from the corn,
 Climb'd, and fell over, in the murky air.
 I thought of mind and matter, will and law,
10 And then of him, who set his stately seal
 Of Roman words on all the forms he saw
 Of old-world husbandry: *I* could but feel
 With what a rich precision *he* would draw
 The endless ladder, and the booming wheel!

THE DRUNKARD'S LAST MARKET

The taper wastes within yon window-pane,
And the blind flutters, where his fever'd hand
Has raised the sash, to cool his burning brain;
But he has pass'd away from house and land.
5 Cheerly and proudly through the gusty dark
The red cock crows! the new-dropt lambkin tries
His earliest voice in the home-field, while stark
And stiff, on his own bed, the drunkard lies;
O'erdone by that steep ride, his weary horse
10 Poises his batter'd feet and cannot feed;
From the near moorland hill, the brawling force
Calls loudly—but the dead man takes no heed;
While Keeper howls his notice of alarm,
And thrills with awe the dusky mountain farm.

ON THE ECLIPSE OF THE MOON OF OCTOBER 1865

One little noise of life remain'd—I heard
The train pause in the distance, then rush by,
Brawling and hushing, like some busy fly
That murmurs and then settles; nothing stirr'd
5 Beside. The shadow of our travelling earth
Hung on the silver moon, which mutely went
Through that grand process, without token sent,
Or any sign to call a gazer forth,
Had I not chanced to see; dumb was the vault
10 Of heaven, and dumb the fields—no zephyr swept
The forest walks, or through the coppice crept;
Nor other sound the stillness did assault,
Save that faint-brawling railway's move and halt;
So perfect was the silence Nature kept.

THE SEASIDE
IN AND OUT OF THE SEASON

In summer-time it was a paradise
Of mountain, frith, and bay, and shining sand;
Our outward rowers sang towards the land,
Follow'd by waving hands and happy cries:
5 By the full flood the groups no longer roam;
And when, at ebb, the glistening beach grows wide,

35

No barefoot children race into the foam,
But passive jellies wait the turn of tide.
Like some forsaken lover, lingering there,
10   The boatman stands; the maidens trip no more
With loosen'd locks; far from the billows' roar
The Mauds and Maries knot their tresses fair,
Where not a foam-flake from th' enamour'd shore
Comes down the sea-wind on the golden hair.

OLD RURALITIES
A REGRET

With joy all relics of the past I hail;
The heath-bell, lingering in our cultured moor,
Or the dull sound of the slip-shoulder'd flail,
Still busy on the poor man's threshing-floor:
5   I love this unshorn hedgerow, which survives
Its stunted neighbours, in this farming age:
The thatch and house-leek, where old Alice lives
With her old herbal, trusting every page;
I love the spinning-wheel, which hums far down
10   In yon lone valley, though, from day to day,
The boom of Science shakes it from the town.
Ah! sweet old world! thou speedest fast away!
My boyhood's world! but all last looks are dear;
More touching is the death-bed than the bier!

TO A RED-WHEAT FIELD

O rich red wheat! thou wilt not long defer
Thy beauty, though thou art not wholly grown;
The fair blue distance and the moorland fir
Long for thy golden laughter! Four years gone,
5   How oft! with eager foot, I scaled the top
Of this long rise, to give mine eye full range;
And, now again, rotation brings the change
From seeds and clover, to my favourite crop;
How oft I've watch'd thee from my garden, charm'd
10   With thy noon-stillness, or thy morning tears!
Or, when the wind clove and the sunset warm'd
Thine amber-shafted depths and russet ears;
O! all ye cool green stems! improve the time,
Fulfil your beauty! justify my rhyme!

36

CHARLES TENNYSON-TURNER

TO A SCARECROW, OR MALKIN, LEFT LONG
AFTER HARVEST

Poor malkin, why hast thou been left behind?
The wains long since have carted off the sheaves,
And keen October, with his whistling wind,
Snaps all the footstalks of the crisping leaves;
5 Methinks thou art not wholly make-believe;
Thy posture, hat, and coat, are human still;
Could'st thou but push a hand from out thy sleeve!
Or smile on me! but ah! thy face is nil!
The stubbles darken round thee, lonely one!
10 And man has left thee, all this dreary term,
No mate beside thee—far from social joy;
As some poor clerk survives his ruin'd firm,
And, in a napless hat, without employ,
Stands, in the autumn of his life, alone.

AN EVENING IN HARVEST TIME

On goes the age with footsteps fleet and strong,
And we have seen a wondrous sight to-day;
The mighty Chariot-reaper forced its way
Where erst the half-hidden scythes-man stoop'd along.
5 Another tale of harvest hours is o'er,
With all its great, and all its little gains,
And poor old Ailsie piles her wheaten store,
And feels as rich as all the rolling wains.
The moonrise seems to burn a golden oil
10 To light a world of plenty, while it shows
The woodland, listening in its dark repose
To many a voice and homeward step of toil,
Till all have pass'd beyond the forest bound,
And not a footfall chafes it into sound.

AFTER THE SCHOOL-FEAST

The Feast is o'er—the music and the stir—
The sound of bat and ball, the mimic gun;
The lawn grows darker, and the setting sun
Has stolen the flash from off the gossamer,

37

5   And drawn the midges westward; youth's glad cry—
    The smaller children's fun-exacting claims,
    Their merry raids across the graver games,
    Their ever-crossing paths of restless joy,
    Have ceased—And, ere a new Feast-day shall shine,
10 Perchance my soul to other worlds may pass;
    Another head in childhood's cause may plot,
    Another Pastor muse in this same spot,
    And the fresh dews, that gather on the grass
    Next morn, may gleam in every track but mine!

TO A 'TENTING' BOY

    Early thou goest forth, to put to rout
    The thievish rooks, that all about thee sail;
    While thy tin tube, and monitory shout
    Report thy lonely function to the vale;
5   From spot to spot thou rovest far and near,
    While the sick ewe in the next pasture ground
    Lifts her white eyelash, points her languid ear,
    And turns her pensive face towards the sound;
    All day thy little trumpet wails about
10 The great brown field, and, whilst I slowly climb
    The grassy slope, with ready watch drawn out,
    To meet thy constant question of the time,
    Methinks I owe thee much, my little boy,
    For this new duty, and its quiet joy.

OLD STEPHEN

    He served his master well from youth to age;
    Who gave him then a little plot of land,
    Enough a busy spirit to engage,
    Too small to overtax an aged hand.
5   Old Stephen's memory hallows all the ground;
    He made this thrifty lawn so spruce and small,
    Dial and seat within its narrow bound,
    And both half-hid with woodbine from the Hall.
    But he is gone at last: how meek he lay
10 That night, and pray'd his dying hours away—
    When the sun rose he ceased to breathe and feel:
    Day broke—his eyes were on a lovelier dawn,
    While ours beheld the sweet May morning steal
    Across his dial and his orphan lawn.

THE QUIET TIDE NEAR ARDROSSAN

On to the beach the quiet waters crept:
But, though I stood not far within the land,
No tidal murmur reach'd me from the strand.
The mirror'd clouds beneath old Arran slept.
5 I look'd again across the watery waste:
The shores were full, the tide was near its height,
Though scarcely heard: the reefs were drowning fast,
And an imperial whisper told the might
Of the outer floods, that press'd into the bay,
10 Though all besides was silent. I delight
In the rough billows, and the foam-ball's flight:
I love the shore upon a stormy day;
But yet more stately were the power and ease
That with a whisper deepen'd all the seas.

A COUNTRY DANCE

He has not woo'd, but he has lost his heart.
That country dance is a sore test for him;
He thinks her cold; his hopes are faint and dim;
But though with seeming mirth she takes her part
5 In all the dances and the laughter there,
And though to many a youth, on brief demand,
She gives a kind assent and courteous hand,
She loves but him, for him is all her care.
With jealous heed her lessening voice he hears
10 Down that long vista, where she seems to move
Among fond faces and relays of love,
And sweet occasion, full of tender fears:
Down those long lines he watches from above,
Till with the refluent dance she reappears.

Arthur Hugh Clough

Arthur Hugh Clough (1819–61) was born at Liverpool, the son of a cotton merchant who later emigrated to America. The boy returned to England in 1828, and spent his schooldays at Rugby School, where he was Dr Arnold's prize pupil, and wholly identified with the prevailing tone of moral scrupulousness. This placed a great strain upon him when he went up to Oxford in 1837 at the height of the Tractarian controversy, and though he later became a Fellow of Oriel, religious doubt led to his resignation in 1848. Clough's sense of release led to the composition of *The Bothie of Tober-na-Vuolich* and the publication of *Ambarvalia*, together with the drafting of his masterpiece, 'Amours de Voyage', and several fine shorter poems which remained unpublished until after his death. Thereafter his gifts suffered a slow eclipse. His most ambitious poem, 'Dipsychus' (written during a miserable stay in London as Principal of University Hall), remained unfinished. More travelling, indecision and financial anxiety followed; he wrote little poetry of distinction after his marriage in 1854 to Blanche Smith, a cousin of Florence Nightingale, and his taking up of a settled and arduous occupation in the Civil Service.

Clough's poetry was not popular in his own day; his preference for a plain style, and his probing and questioning mind with its bent towards satire, were found to be too deficient in 'the beautiful' and the elevated for contemporary taste.

DUTY

Duty—that's to say, complying,
    With whate'er's expected here;
On your unknown cousin's dying,
    Straight be ready with the tear;
5   Upon etiquette relying,
Unto usage nought denying,
Lend your waist to be embraced,
    Blush not even, never fear;
Claims of kith and kin connection,
10   Claims of manners honour still,
Ready money of affection
    Pay, whoever drew the bill.

With the form conforming duly,
Senseless what it meaneth truly,
15   Go to church—the world require you,
    To balls—the world require you too,
And marry—papa and mamma desire you,
    And your sisters and schoolfellows do.
Duty—'tis to take on trust
20   What things are good, and right, and just;
    And whether indeed they be or be not,
    Try not, test not, feel not, see not:
    'Tis walk and dance, sit down and rise
    By leading, opening ne'er your eyes;
25   Stunt sturdy limbs that Nature gave,
And be drawn in a Bath chair along to the grave.
'Tis the stern and prompt suppressing,
    As an obvious deadly sin,
All the questing and the guessing
30   Of the soul's own soul within:
'Tis the coward acquiescence
    In a destiny's behest,
To a shade by terror made,
Sacrificing, aye, the essence
35   Of all that's truest, noblest, best:
'Tis the blind non-recognition
    Or of goodness, truth, or beauty,
Save by precept and submission;
    Moral blank, and moral void,
40   Life at very birth destroyed.
Atrophy, exinanition!
Duty!
Yea, by duty's prime condition
    Pure nonentity of duty!

'IS IT TRUE, YE GODS'

Is it true, ye gods, who treat us
As the gambling fool is treated;
O ye, who ever cheat us,
And let us feel we're cheated!
5   Is it true that poetical power,
The gift of heaven, the dower
Of Apollo and the Nine,
The inborn sense, 'the vision and
    the faculty divine,'
All we glorify and bless
10   In our rapturous exaltation,

All invention, and creation,
Exuberance of fancy, and sublime
    imagination,
All a poet's fame is built on,
The fame of Shakespeare, Milton,
15   Of Wordsworth, Byron, Shelley,
Is in reason's grave precision,
Nothing more, nothing less,
Than a peculiar conformation,
Constitution, and condition
20   Of the brain and of the belly?
Is it true, ye gods who cheat us?
And that's the way ye treat us?

Oh say it, all who think it,
Look straight, and never blink it!
25   If it is so, let it be so,
And we will all agree so;
But the plot has counterplot,
It may be, and yet be not.

QUI LABORAT, ORAT

O only Source of all our light and life,
    Whom as our truth, our strength, we see and feel,
But whom the hours of mortal moral strife
    Alone aright reveal!

5   Mine inmost soul, before Thee inly brought,
    Thy presence owns ineffable, divine;
Chastised each rebel self-encentered thought,
    My will adoreth Thine.

With eye down-dropt, if then this earthly mind
10   Speechless remain, or speechless e'en depart;
Nor seek to see—for what of earthly kind
    Can see Thee as Thou art?—

If well-assured 'tis but profanely bold
    In thought's abstractest forms to seem to see,
15   It dare not dare the dread communion hold
    In ways unworthy Thee,

O not unowned, thou shalt unnamed forgive,
    In worldly walks the prayerless heart prepare;
And if in work its life it seem to live,
20   Shalt make that work be prayer.

Nor times shall lack, when while the work it plies,
　　Unsummoned powers the blinding film shall part,
And scarce by happy tears made dim, the eyes
　　In recognition start.

25　But, as thou willest, give or e'en forbear
　　　The beatific supersensual sight,
　　So, with Thy blessing blest, that humbler prayer
　　　Approach Thee morn and night.

QUA CURSUM VENTUS

As ships, becalmed at eve, that lay
　　With canvas drooping, side by side,
Two towers of sail at dawn of day
　　Are scarce long leagues apart descried;

5　When fell the night, upsprung the breeze,
　　　And all the darkling hours they plied,
　　Nor dreamt but each the self-same seas
　　　By each was cleaving, side by side:

　E'en so—but why the tale reveal
10　　　Of those, whom year by year unchanged,
　　Brief absence joined anew to feel,
　　　Astounded, soul from soul estranged?

　At dead of night their sails were filled,
　　　And onward each rejoicing steered—
15　Ah, neither blame, for neither willed,
　　　Or wist, what first with dawn appeared!

　To veer, how vain! On, onward strain,
　　　Brave barks! In light, in darkness too,
　Through winds and tides one compass guides—
20　　　To that, and your own selves, be true.

　But O blithe breeze! and O great seas,
　　　Though ne'er, that earliest parting past,
　On your wide plain they join again,
　　　Together lead them home at last.

25　One port, methought, alike they sought,
　　　One purpose hold where'er they fare,—
　O bounding breeze, O rushing seas!
　　　At last, at last, unite them there!

43

EPI-STRAUSS-IUM

Matthew and Mark and Luke and holy John
Evanished all and gone!
Yea, he that erst his dusky curtains quitting,
Thro' Eastern pictured panes his level beams transmitting,
5   With gorgeous portraits blent,
On them his glories intercepted spent.
Southwestering now, thro' windows plainly glassed,
On the inside face his radiance keen hath cast,
And in the lustre lost, invisible and gone,
10   Are, say you, Matthew, Mark and Luke and holy John?
Lost, is it, lost, to be recovered never?
However,
The place of worship the meantime with light
Is, if less richly, more sincerely bright,
15   And in blue skies the Orb is manifest to sight.

NATURA NATURANS

Beside me,—in the car,—she sat,
    She spake not, no, nor looked to me:
From her to me, from me to her,
    What passed so subtly, stealthily?
5   As rose to rose that by it blows
    Its interchanged aroma flings;
Or wake to sound of one sweet note
    The virtues of disparted strings.

Beside me, nought but this!—but this,
10   That influent as within me dwelt
Her life, mine too within her breast,
    Her brain, her every limb she felt:
We sat; while o'er and in us, more
    And more, a power unknown prevailed,
15   Inhaling, and inhaled,—and still
    'Twas one, inhaling or inhaled.

Beside me, nought but this;—and passed;
    I passed; and know not to this day
If gold or jet her girlish hair,
20   If black, or brown, or lucid-grey
Her eye's young glance: the fickle chance
    That joined us, yet may join again;
But I no face again could greet
    As her's, whose life was in me then.

25   As unsuspecting mere a maid
            As, fresh in maidhood's bloomiest bloom,
        In casual second-class did e'er
            By casual youth her seat assume;
        Or vestal, say, of saintliest clay,
30   For once by balmiest airs betrayed
        Unto emotions too, too sweet
            To be unlingeringly gainsaid:

        Unowning then, confusing soon
            With dreamier dreams that o'er the glass
35   Of shyly ripening woman-sense
            Reflected, scarce reflected, pass,
        A wife may-be, a mother she
            In Hymen's shrine recals not now,
        She first in hour, ah, not profane,
40   With me to Hymen learnt to bow.

        Ah no!—Yet owned we, fused in one,
            The Power which e'en in stones and earths
        By blind elections felt, in forms
            Organic breeds to myriad births;
45   By lichen small on granite wall
            Approved, its faintest feeblest stir
        Slow-spreading, strengthening long, at last
            Vibrated full in me and her.

        In me and her—sensation strange!
50   The lily grew to pendent head,
        To vernal airs the mossy bank
            Its sheeny primrose spangles spread,
        In roof o'er roof of shade sun-proof
            Did cedar strong itself outclimb,
55   And altitude of aloe proud
            Aspire in floreal crown sublime;

        Flashed flickering forth fantastic flies,
            Big bees their burly bodies swung,
        Rooks roused with civic din the elms,
60   And lark its wild reveillez rung;
        In Libyan dell the light gazelle,
            The leopard lithe in Indian glade,
        And dolphin, brightening tropic seas,
            In us were living, leapt and played:

65   Their shells did slow crustacea build,
            Their gilded skins did snakes renew,
        While mightier spines for loftier kind
            Their types in amplest limbs outgrew;

45

Yea, close comprest in human breast,
70 What moss, and tree, and livelier thing,
What Earth, Sun, Star of force possest,
  Lay budding, burgeoning forth for Spring.

Such sweet preluding sense of old
  Led on in Eden's sinless place
75 The hour when bodies human first
  Combined the primal prime embrace,
Such genial heat the blissful seat
  In man and woman owned unblamed,
When, naked both, its garden paths
80 They walked unconscious, unashamed:

Ere, clouded yet in mistiest dawn,
  Above the horizon dusk and dun,
One mountain crest with light had tipped
  That Orb that is the Spirit's Sun;
85 Ere dreamed young flowers in vernal showers
  Of fruit to rise the flower above,
Or ever yet to young Desire
  Was told the mystic name of Love.

EASTER DAY
NAPLES, 1849

Through the great sinful streets of Naples as I past,
  With fiercer heat than flamed above my head
My heart was hot within me; till at last
  My brain was lightened when my tongue had said—
  Christ is not risen!

  Christ is not risen, no—
  He lies and moulders low;
5 Christ is not risen!

What though the stone were rolled away, and though
10 The grave found empty there?—
  If not there, then elsewhere;
If not where Joseph laid Him first, why then
  Where other men
Translaid Him after, in some humbler clay.
15 Long ere to-day
Corruption that sad perfect work hath done,
Which here she scarcely, lightly had begun:

46

The foul engendered worm
Feeds on the flesh of the life-giving form
20   Of our most Holy and Anointed One.
        He is not risen, no—
        He lies and moulders low;
          Christ is not risen!

What if the women, ere the dawn was grey,
25   Saw one or more great angels, as they say
(Angels, or Him himself)? Yet neither there, nor then,
Nor afterwards, nor elsewhere, nor at all,
Hath He appeared to Peter or the Ten;
Nor, save in thunderous terror, to blind Saul;
30   Save in an after Gospel and late Creed,
        He is not risen, indeed,—
          Christ is not risen!

Or, what if e'en, as runs a tale, the Ten
Saw, heard, and touched, again and yet again?
35   What if at Emmaüs inn, and by Capernaum's Lake,
        Came One, the bread that brake—
Came One that spake as never mortal spake,
And with them ate, and drank, and stood, and walked about?
        Ah! 'some' did well to 'doubt!'
40   Ah! the true Christ, while these things came to pass,
Nor heard, nor spake, nor walked, nor lived, alas!
        He was not risen, no—
        He lay and mouldered low,
          Christ was no risen!

45   As circulates in some great city crowd
A rumour changeful, vague, importunate, and loud,
From no determined centre, or of fact
        Or authorship exact,
        Which no man can deny
50   Nor verify;
        So spread the wondrous fame;
          He all the same
        Lay senseless, mouldering, low:
        He was not risen, no—
55   Christ was not risen!

Ashes to ashes, dust to dust;
As of the unjust, also of the just—
        Yea, of that Just One, too!
This is the one sad Gospel that is true—
60   Christ is not risen!

Is He not risen, and shall we not rise?
      Oh, we unwise!
What did we dream, what wake we to discover?
Ye hills, fall on us, and ye mountains, cover!
65   In darkness and great gloom
Come ere we thought it is *our* day of doom;
From the cursed world, which is one tomb,
      Christ is not risen!

Eat, drink, and play, and think that this is bliss:
70 There is no heaven but this;
      There is no hell,
Save earth, which serves the purpose doubly well,
      Seeing it visits still
With equalest apportionment of ill
75 Both good and bad alike, and brings to one same dust
      The unjust and the just
      With Christ, who is not risen.

Eat, drink, and die, for we are souls bereaved:
      Of all the creatures under heaven's wide cope
80   We are most hopeless, who had once most hope,
And most beliefless, that had most believed.
      Ashes to ashes, dust to dust;
      As of the unjust, also of the just—
      Yea, of that Just One too!
85   It is the one sad Gospel that is true—
      Christ is not risen!

      Weep not beside the tomb,
      Ye women, unto whom
He was great solace while ye tended Him;
90   Ye who with napkin o'er the head
And folds of linen round each wounded limb
      Laid out the Sacred Dead;
And thou that bar'st Him in thy wondering womb;
Yea, Daughters of Jerusalem, depart,
95 Bind up as best ye may your own sad bleeding heart:
Go to your homes, your living children tend,
      Your earthly spouses love;
      Set your affections *not* on things above,
Which moth and rust corrupt, which quickliest come to end:
100 Or pray, if pray ye must, and pray, if pray ye can,
For death; since dead is He whom ye deemed more than man,
      Who is not risen: no—
      But lies and moulders low—
      Who is not risen!

105   Ye men of Galilee!
Why stand ye looking up to heaven, where Him ye ne'er
  may see,
Neither ascending hence, nor returning hither again?
    Ye ignorant and idle fishermen!
Hence to your huts, and boats, and inland native shore,
110   And catch not men, but fish;
    Whate'er things ye might wish,
Him neither here nor there ye e'er shall meet with more.
    Ye poor deluded youths, go home,
    Mend the old nets ye left to roam,
115   Tie the split oar, patch the torn sail:
    It was indeed an 'idle tale'—
     He was not risen!

And, oh, good men of ages yet to be,
Who shall believe *because* ye did not see—
120   Oh, be ye warned, be wise!
    No more with pleading eyes,
    And sobs of strong desire,
   Unto the empty vacant void aspire,
Seeking another and impossible birth
125 That is not of your own, and only mother earth.
But if there is no other life for you,
Sit down and be content, since this must even do:
    He is not risen!

    One look, and then depart,
130   Ye humble and ye holy men of heart;
And ye! ye ministers and stewards of a Word
Which ye would preach, because another heard—
   Ye worshippers of that ye do not know,
    Take these things hence and go:—
135   He is not risen!

    Here, on our Easter Day
We rise, we come, and lo! we find Him not,
Gardener nor other, on the sacred spot:
Where they have laid Him there is none to say;
140 No sound, nor in, nor out—no word
Of where to seek the dead or meet the living Lord.
There is no glistering of an angel's wings,
There is no voice of heavenly clear behest:
Let us go hence, and think upon these things
145   In silence, which is best.
    Is He not risen? No—
    But lies and moulders low?
    Christ is not risen?

EASTER DAY
II

So in the sinful streets, abstracted and alone,
I with my secret self held communing of mine own.
   So in the southern city spake the tongue
   Of one that somewhat overwildly sung,
5   But in a later hour I sat and heard
Another voice that spake—another graver word.
Weep not, it bade, whatever hath been said,
Though He be dead, He is not dead.
     In the true creed
10   He is yet risen indeed;
         Christ is yet risen.

Weep not beside His tomb,
Ye women unto whom
He was great comfort and yet greater grief;
15   Nor ye, ye faithful few that went with Him to roam,
Seek sadly what for Him ye left, go hopeless to your home;
Nor ye despair, ye sharers yet to be of their belief;
       Though He be dead, He is not dead,
       Nor gone, though fled,
20   Not lost, though vanished;
       Though He return not, though
       He lies and moulders low;
       In the true creed
       He is yet risen indeed;
25   Christ is yet risen.

Sit if ye will, sit down upon the ground,
Yet not to weep and wail, but calmly look around.
       Whate'er befel,
       Earth is not hell;
30   Now, too, as when it first began,
Life is yet life, and man is man.
For all that breathe beneath the heaven's high cope,
Joy with grief mixes, with despondence hope.
Hope conquers cowardice, joy grief;
35   Or at least, faith unbelief.
       Though dead, not dead;
       Not gone, though fled;
       Not lost, though vanished.
       In the great gospel and true creed,
40   He is yet risen indeed;
         Christ is yet risen.

SAY NOT THE STRUGGLE NOUGHT AVAILETH

Say not, the struggle nought availeth,
    The labour and the wounds are vain,
The enemy faints not, nor faileth,
    And as things have been they remain.

5   If hopes were dupes, fears may be liars;
        It may be, in yon smoke concealed,
Your comrades chase e'en now the fliers,
    And, but for you, possess the field.

For while the tired waves, vainly breaking,
10   Seem here no painful inch to gain,
Far back, through creeks and inlets making,
    Comes silent, flooding in, the main,

And not by eastern windows only,
    When daylight comes, comes in the light,
15   In front, the sun climbs slow, how slowly,
    But westward, look, the land is bright.

From AMOURS DE VOYAGE

CANTO I

I. *Claude to Eustace*

Dear Eustatio, I write that you may write me an answer,
Or at the least to put us again *en rapport* with each other.
Rome disappoints me much,—St. Peter's, perhaps, in especial;
Only the Arch of Titus and view from the Lateran please me:
5   This, however, perhaps is the weather, which truly is horrid.
Greece must be better, surely; and yet I am feeling so spiteful,
That I could travel to Athens, to Delphi, and Troy, and
    Mount Sinai,
Though but to see with my eyes that these are vanity also.
    Rome disappoints me much; I hardly as yet understand, but
10   *Rubbishy* seems the word that most exactly would suit it.
All the foolish destructions, and all the sillier savings,
All the incongruous things of past incompatible ages,
Seem to be treasured up here to make fools of present and future.
Would to Heaven the old Goths had made a cleaner sweep of it!
15   Would to Heaven some new ones would come and destroy
    these churches!
However, one can live in Rome as also in London.

It is a blessing, no doubt, to be rid, at least for a time, of
All one's friends and relations,—yourself (forgive me!)
      included,—
All the *assujettissement* of having been what one has been,
20   What one thinks one is, or thinks that others suppose one;
Yet, in despite of all, we turn like fools to the English.
Vernon has been my fate; who is here the same that you
      knew him,—
Making the tour, it seems, with friends of the name of Trevellyn.

II. *Claude to Eustace*

Rome disappoints me still; but I shrink and adapt myself to it.
25   Somehow a tyrannous sense of a superincumbent oppression
Still, wherever I go, accompanies ever, and makes me
Feel like a tree (shall I say?) buried under a ruin of brickwork.
Rome, believe me, my friend, is like its own Monte Testaceo,
Merely a marvellous mass of broken and castaway wine-pots.
30   Ye gods! what do I want with this rubbish of ages departed,
Things that nature abhors, the experiments that she has failed in?
What do I find in the Forum? An archway and two or three
      pillars.
Well, but St. Peter's? Alas, Bernini has filled it with sculpture!
No one can cavil, I grant, at the size of the great Coliseum.
35   Doubtless the notion of grand and capacious and massive
      amusement,
This the old Romans had; but tell me, is this an idea?
Yet of solidity much, but of splendour little is extant:
'Brickwork I found thee, and marble I left thee!' their
      Emperor vaunted;
'Marble I thought thee, and brickwork I find thee!' the
      Tourist may answer.

III. *Georgina Trevellyn to Louisa* ——

40   At last, dearest Louisa, I take up my pen to address you.
Here we are, you see, with the seven-and-seventy boxes,
Courier, Papa and Mamma, the children, and Mary and Susan:
Here we all are at Rome, and delighted of course with
      St. Peter's,
And very pleasantly lodged in the famous Piazza di Spagna.
45   Rome is a wonderful place, but Mary shall tell you about it;
Not very gay, however; the English are mostly at Naples;
There are the A.'s, we hear, and most of the W. party.
    George, however, is come; did I tell you about his mustachios?
Dear, I must really stop, for the carriage, they tell me, is waiting;
50   Mary will finish; and Susan is writing, they say, to Sophia.
Adieu, dearest Louise,—evermore your faithful Georgina.
Who can a Mr. Claude be whom George has taken to be with?
Very stupid, I think, but George says so *very* clever.

IV. *Claude to Eustace*

No, the Christian faith, as at any rate I understood it,
55   With its humiliations and exaltations combining,
Exaltations sublime, and yet diviner abasements,
Aspirations from something most shameful here upon
    earth and
In our poor selves to something most perfect above in the
    heavens,—
No, the Christian faith, as I, at least, understood it,
60   Is not here, O Rome, in any of these thy churches;
Is not here, but in Freiburg, or Rheims, or Westminster
    Abbey.
What in thy Dome I find, in all thy recenter efforts,
Is a something, I think, more *rational* far, more earthly,
Actual, less ideal, devout not in scorn and refusal,
65   But in a positive, calm, Stoic-Epicurean acceptance.
This I begin to detect in St. Peter's and some of the churches,
Mostly in all that I see of the sixteenth-century masters;
Overlaid of course with infinite gauds and gewgaws,
Innocent, playful follies, the toys and trinkets of childhood,
70   Forced on maturer years, as the serious one thing needful,
By the barbarian will of the rigid and ignorant Spaniard.
    Curious work, meantime, re-entering society: how we
Walk a livelong day, great Heaven, and watch our shadows!
What our shadows seem, forsooth, we will ourselves be.
75   Do I look like that? you think me that: then I *am* that.

V. *Claude to Eustace*

Luther, they say, was unwise; like a half-taught German, he
    could not
See that old follies were passing most tranquilly out of
    remembrance;
Leo the Tenth was employing all efforts to clear out abuses;
Jupiter, Juno, and Venus, Fine Arts, and Fine Letters, the
    Poets,
80   Scholars, and Sculptors, and Painters, were quietly clearing
    away the
Martyrs, and Virgins, and Saints, or at any rate Thomas
    Aquinas:
He must forsooth make a fuss and distend his huge
    Wittenberg lungs, and
Bring back Theology once yet again in a flood upon Europe:
Lo you, for forty days from the windows of heaven it fell; the
85   Waters prevail on the earth yet more for a hundred and fifty;
Are they abating at last? the doves that are sent to explore are
Wearily fain to return, at the best with a leaflet of promise,—
Fain to return, as they went, to the wandering wave-tost
    vessel,—

Fain to re-enter the roof which covers the clean and the
    unclean,—
90   Luther, they say, was unwise; he didn't see how things were
    going;
Luther was foolish,—but, O great God! what call you
    Ignatius?
O my tolerant soul, be still! but you talk of barbarians,
Alaric, Attila, Genseric;—why, they came, they killed, they
Ravaged, and went on their way; but these vile, tyrannous
    Spaniards,
95   These are here still,—how long, O ye heavens, in the country
    of Dante?
These, that fanaticized Europe, which now can forget them,
    release not
This, their choicest of prey, this Italy; here you see them,—
Here, with emasculate pupils and gimcrack churches of Gesu,
Pseudo-learning and lies, confessional-boxes and postures,—
100   Here, with metallic beliefs and regimental devotions,—
Here, overcrusting with slime, perverting, defacing, debasing,
Michael Angelo's dome, that had hung the Pantheon in heaven,
Raphael's Joys and Graces, and thy clear stars, Galileo!

VI. Claude to Eustace

Which of three Misses Trevellyn it is that Vernon shall marry
105   Is not a thing to be known; for our friend is one of those
    natures
Which have their perfect delight in the general tender-domestic;
So that he trifles with Mary's shawl, ties Susan's bonnet,
Dances with all, but at home is most, they say, with Georgina,
Who is, however, *too* silly in my apprehension for Vernon.
110   I, as before when I wrote, continue to see them a little;
Not that I like them much or care a *bajocco* for Vernon,
But I am slow at Italian, have not many English acquaintance,
And I am asked, in short, and am not good at excuses.
Middle-class people these, bankers very likely, not wholly
115   Pure of the taint of the shop; will at table d'hôte and restaurant
Have their shilling's worth, their penny's pennyworth even:
Neither man's aristocracy this, nor God's, God knoweth!
Yet they are fairly descended, they give you to know, well
    connected;
Doubtless somewhere in some neighbourhood have, and are
    careful to keep, some
120   Threadbare-genteel relations, who in their turn are enchanted
Grandly among county people to introduce at assemblies
To the unpennied cadets our cousins with excellent fortunes.
Neither man's aristocracy this, nor God's, God knoweth!

VII. Claude to Eustace

Ah, what a shame, indeed, to abuse these most worthy people!
125 Ah, what a sin to have sneered at their innocent rustic
    pretensions!
Is it not laudable really, this reverent worship of station?
Is it not fitting that wealth should tender this homage to culture?
Is it not touching to witness these efforts, if little availing,
Painfully made, to perform the old ritual service of manners?
130 Shall not devotion atone for the absence of knowledge? and
    fervour
Palliate, cover, the fault of a superstitious observance?
Dear, dear, what do I say? but, alas! just now, like Iago,
I can be nothing at all, if it is not critical wholly;
So in fantastic height, in coxcomb exultation,
135 Here in the garden I walk, can freely concede to the Maker
That the works of His hand are all very good: His creatures,
Beast of the field and fowl, He brings them before me; I
    name them;
That which I name them, they are,—the bird, the beast, and
    the cattle.
But for Adam,—alas, poor critical coxcomb Adam!
140 But for Adam there is not found an help-meet for him.

VIII. Claude to Eustace

No, great Dome of Agrippa, thou art not Christian! canst not,
Strip and replaster and daub and do what they will with
    thee, be so!
Here underneath the great porch of colossal Corinthian
    columns,
Here as I walk, do I dream of the Christian belfries above
    them;
145 Or, on a bench as I sit and abide for long hours, till thy whole
    vast
Round grows dim as in dreams to my eyes, I repeople thy
    niches
Not with the Martyrs, and Saints, and Confessors, and
    Virgins, and children,
But with the mightier forms of an older, austerer worship;
And I recite to myself, how
150   Eager for battle here
    Stood Vulcan, here matronal Juno,
        And with the bow to his shoulder faithful
    He who with pure dew laveth of Castaly
    His flowing locks, who holdeth of Lycia
155   The oak forest and the wood that bore him,
        Delos' and Patara's own Apollo.

IX. Claude to Eustace

Yet it is pleasant, I own it, to be in their company; pleasant,
Whatever else it may be, to abide in the feminine presence.
Pleasant, but wrong, will you say? But this happy, serene
    coexistence
160 Is to some poor soft souls, I fear, a necessity simple,
Meat and drink and life, and music, filling with sweetness,
Thrilling with melody sweet, with harmonies strange
    overwhelming,
All the long-silent strings of an awkward, meaningless fabric.
Yet as for that, I could live, I believe, with children; to have
    those
165 Pure and delicate forms encompassing, moving about you,
This were enough, I could think; and truly with glad
    resignation
Could from the dream of Romance, from the fever of flushed
    adolescence,
Look to escape and subside into peaceful avuncular functions.
Nephews and nieces! alas, for as yet I have none! and,
    moreover,
170 Mothers are jealous, I fear me, too often, too rightfully;
    fathers
Think they have title exclusive to spoiling their own little
    darlings;
And by the law of the land, in despite of Malthusian doctrine,
No sort of proper provision is made for that most patriotic,
Most meritorious subject, the childless and bachelor uncle.

X. Claude to Eustace

175 Ye, too, marvellous Twain, that erect on the Monte Cavallo
Stand by your rearing steeds in the grace of your motionless
    movement,
Stand with your upstretched arms and tranquil regardant faces,
Stand as instinct with life in the might of immutable manhood,—
O ye mighty and strange, ye ancient divine ones of Hellas.
180 Are ye Christian too? to convert and redeem and renew you,
Will the brief form have sufficed, that a Pope has set up on
    the apex
Of the Egyptian stone that o'ertops you, the Christian symbol?
    And ye, silent, supreme in serene and victorious marble,
Ye that encircle the walls of the stately Vatican chambers,
185 Juno and Ceres, Minerva, Apollo, the Muses and Bacchus,
Ye unto whom far and near come posting the Christian pilgrims,
Ye that are ranged in the halls of the mystic Christian Pontiff,
Are ye also baptized; are ye of the kingdom of Heaven?
Utter, O some one, the word that shall reconcile Ancient and
    Modern!
190 Am I to turn me from this unto thee, great Chapel of Sixtus?

XI. Claude to Eustace

These are the facts. The uncle, the elder brother, the squire (a
Little embarrassed, I fancy), resides in the family place in
Cornwall, of course; 'Papa is in business,' Mary informs me;
He's a good sensible man, whatever his trade is. The mother
195 Is—shall I call it fine?—herself she would tell you refined, and
Greatly, I fear me, looks down on my bookish and maladroit
    manners;
Somewhat affecteth the blue; would talk to me often of poets;
Quotes, which I hate, Childe Harold; but also appreciates
    Wordsworth;
Sometimes adventures on Schiller; and then to religion diverges;
200 Questions me much about Oxford; and yet, in her loftiest
    flights still
Grates the fastidious ear with the slightly mercantile accent.

Is it contemptible, Eustace—I'm perfectly ready to think so,—
Is it,—the horrible pleasure of pleasing inferior people?
I am ashamed my own self; and yet true it is, if disgraceful,
205 That for the first time in life I am living and moving with
    freedom.
I, who never could talk to the people I meet with my uncle,—
I, who have always failed,—I, trust me, can suit the Trevellyns;
I, believe me,—great conquest, am liked by the country bankers.
And I am glad to be liked, and like in return very kindly.
210 So it proceeds; *Laissez faire, laissez aller,*—such is the
    watch-word.
Well, I know there are thousands as pretty and hundreds as
    pleasant,
Girls by the dozen as good, and girls in abundance with polish
Higher and manners more perfect than Susan or Mary Trevellyn.
Well, I know, after all, it is only juxtaposition,—
215 Juxtaposition, in short; and what is juxtaposition?

XII. Claude to Eustace

But I am in for it now,—*laissez faire*, of a truth, *laissez aller*.
Yes, I am going,—I feel it, I feel and cannot recall it,—
Fusing with this thing and that, entering into all sorts of
    relations,
Tying I know not what ties, which, whatever they are, I
    know one thing,
220 Will, and must, woe is me, be one day painfully broken,—
Broken with painful remorses, with shrinkings of soul, and
    relentings,
Foolish delays, more foolish evasions, most foolish renewals.
But I have made the step, have quitted the ship of Ulysses;
Quitted the sea and the shore, passed into the magical island;
225 Yet on my lips is the *moly*, medicinal, offered of Hermes.

I have come into the precinct, the labyrinth closes around me,
Path into path rounding slyly; I pace slowly on, and the fancy,
Struggling awhile to sustain the long sequences weary,
    bewildered,
Fain must collapse in despair; I yield, I am lost, and know
    nothing;
230 Yet in my bosom unbroken remaineth the clue; I shall use it.
Lo, with the rope on my loins I descend through the fissure;
    I sink, yet
Inly secure in the strength of invisible arms up above me;
Still, wheresoever I swing, wherever to shore, or to shelf, or
Floor of cavern untrodden, shell sprinkled, enchanting, I
    know I
235 Yet shall one time feel the strong cord tighten about me,—
Feel it, relentless, upbear me from spots I would rest in; and
    though the
Rope sway wildly, I faint, crags wound me, from crag unto
    crag re-
Bounding, or, wide in the void, I die ten deaths, ere the end I
Yet shall plant firm foot on the broad lofty spaces I quit, shall
240 Feel underneath me again the great massy strengths of
    abstraction,
Look yet abroad from the height o'er the sea whose salt
    wave I have tasted.

XIII. Georgina Trevellyn to Louisa ——

Dearest Louisa,—Inquire, if you please, about Mr. Claude ——.
He has been once at R., and remembers meeting the H.'s.
Harriet L., perhaps, may be able to tell you about him.
245 It is an awkward youth, but still with very good manners;
Not without prospects, we hear; and, George says, highly
    connected.
Georgy declares it absurd, but Mamma is alarmed, and
    insists he has
Taken up strange opinions, and may be turning a Papist.
Certainly once he spoke of a daily service he went to.
250 'Where?' we asked, and he laughed and answered, 'At the
    Pantheon.'
This was a temple, you know, and now is a Catholic church;
    and
Though it is said that Mazzini has sold it for Protestant
    service,
Yet I suppose this change can hardly as yet be effected.
Adieu again,—evermore, my dearest, your loving Georgina.

P.S. by Mary Trevellyn

255 I am to tell you, you say, what I think of our last new
    acquaintance.

Well, then, I think that George has a very fair right to be
    jealous.
I do not like him much, though I do not dislike being with him.
He is what people call, I suppose, a superior man, and
Certainly seems so to me; but I think he is terribly selfish.

CANTO II

I. Claude to Eustace

What do the people say, and what does the government do?—
    you
Ask, and I know not at all. Yet fortune will favour your
    hopes; and
I, who avoided it all, am fated, it seems, to describe it.
I, who nor meddle nor make in politics,—I who sincerely
5   Put not my trust in leagues nor any suffrage by ballot,
Never predicted Parisian millenniums, never beheld a
New Jerusalem coming down dressed like a bride out of
    heaven
Right on the Place de la Concorde,—I, nevertheless, let me
    say it,
Could in my soul of souls, this day, with the Gaul at the
    gates shed
10   One true tear for thee, thou poor little Roman Republic;
What, with the German restored, with Sicily safe to the
    Bourbon,
Not leave one poor corner for native Italian exertion?
France, it is foully done! and you, poor foolish England,—
You, who a twelvemonth ago said nations must choose for
    themselves, you
15   Could not, of course, interfere,—you, now, when a nation
    has chosen——
Pardon this folly! The *Times* will, of course, have announced
    the occasion,
Told you the news of to-day; and although it was slightly in
    error
When it proclaimed as a fact the Apollo was sold to a Yankee,
You may believe when it tells you the French are at Civita
    Vecchia.

II. Claude to Eustace

20   *Dulce* it is, and *decorum*, no doubt, for the country to fall,—to
Offer one's blood an oblation to Freedom, and die for the
    Cause; yet
Still, individual culture is also something, and no man
Finds quite distinct the assurance that he of all others is
    called on,

Or would be justified even, in taking away from the world that
25 Precious creature, himself. Nature sent him here to abide here;
Else why send him at all? Nature wants him still, it is likely;
On the whole, we are meant to look after ourselves; it is certain
Each has to eat for himself, digest for himself, and in general
Care for his own dear life, and see to his own preservation;
30 Nature's intentions, in most things uncertain, in this are
    decisive;
Which, on the whole, I conjecture the Romans will follow,
    and I shall.

    So we cling to our rocks like limpets; Ocean may bluster,
Over and under and round us; we open our shells to imbibe
    our
Nourishment, close them again, and are safe, fulfilling the
    purpose
35 Nature intended,—a wise one, of course, and a noble, we
    doubt not.
Sweet it may be and decorous, perhaps, for the country to
    die; but,
On the whole, we conclude the Romans won't do it, and I
    sha'n't.

III. Claude to Eustace

Will they fight? They say so. And will the French? I can
    hardly,
Hardly think so; and yet——He is come, they say, to Palo,
40 He is passed from Monterone, at Santa Severa
He hath laid up his guns. But the Virgin, the Daughter of
    Roma,
She hath despised thee and laughed thee to scorn,—the
    Daughter of Tiber,
She hath shaken her head and built barricades against thee!
Will they fight? I believe it. Alas! 'tis ephemeral folly,
45 Vain and ephemeral folly, of course, compared with pictures,
Statues, and antique gems!—Indeed: and yet indeed too,
Yet methought, in broad day did I dream,—tell it not in
    St. James's,
Whisper it not in thy courts, O Christ Church!—yet did I,
    waking,
Dream of a cadence that sings, *Si tombent nos jeunes héros, la*
50 *Terre en produit de nouveaux contre vous tous prêts à se battre*;
Dreamt of great indignations and angers transcendental,
Dreamt of a sword at my side and a battle-horse underneath me.

IV. Claude to Eustace

Now supposing the French or the Neapolitan soldier
Should by some evil chance come exploring the Maison Serny
55 (Where the family English are all to assemble for safety),

Am I prepared to lay down my life for the British female?
Really, who knows? One has bowed and talked, till, little by little,
All the natural heat has escaped of the chivalrous spirit.
Oh, one conformed, of course; but one doesn't die for good manners,
60 Stab or shoot, or be shot, by way of graceful attention.
No, if it should be at all, it should be on the barricades there;
Should I incarnadine ever this inky pacifical finger,
Sooner far should it be for this vapour of Italy's freedom,
Sooner far by the side of the d——d and dirty plebeians.
65 Ah, for a child in the street I could strike; for the full-blown lady——
Somehow, Eustace, alas! I have not felt the vocation.
Yet these people of course will expect, as of course, my protection,
Vernon in radiant arms stand forth for the lovely Georgina,
And to appear, I suppose, were but common civility. Yes, and
70 Truly I do not desire they should either be killed or offended.
Oh, and of course, you will say, 'When the time comes, you will be ready.'
Ah, but before it comes, am I to presume it will be so?
What I cannot feel now, am I to suppose that I shall feel?
Am I not free to attend for the ripe and indubious instinct?
75 Am I forbidden to wait for the clear and lawful perception?
Is it the calling of man to surrender his knowledge and insight,
For the mere venture of what may, perhaps, be the virtuous action?
Must we, walking our earth, discern a little, and hoping
Some plain visible task shall yet for our hands be assigned us,—
80 Must we abandon the future for fear of omitting the present,
Quit our own fireside hopes at the alien call of a neighbour,
To the mere possible shadow of Deity offer the victim?
And is all this, my friend, but a weak and ignoble refining,
Wholly unworthy the head or the heart of Your Own Correspondent?

V. Claude to Eustace

85 Yes, we are fighting at last, it appears. This morning, as usual,
Murray, as usual, in hand, I enter the Caffè Nuovo;
Seating myself with a sense as it were of a change in the weather,
Not understanding, however, but thinking mostly of Murray,
And, for to-day is their day, of the Campidoglio Marbles;
90 *Caffè-latte!* I call to the waiter,—and *Non c' è latte*,
This is the answer he makes me, and this is the sign of a battle.
So I sit; and truly they seem to think anyone else more
Worthy than me of attention. I wait for my milkless *nero*,
Free to observe undistracted all sorts and sizes of persons,

95   Blending civilian and soldier in strangest costume, coming in, and
Gulping in hottest haste, still standing, their coffee,—
    withdrawing
Eagerly, jangling a sword on the steps, or jogging a musket
Slung to the shoulder behind. They are fewer, moreover, than
    usual,
Much and silenter far; and so I begin to imagine
100   Something is really afloat. Ere I leave, the Caffè is empty,
Empty too the streets, in all its length the Corso
Empty, and empty I see to my right and left the Condotti.
        Twelve o'clock, on the Pincian Hill, with lots of English,
Germans, Americans, French,—the Frenchmen, too, are
    protected,—
105   So we stand in the sun, but afraid of a probable shower;
So we stand and stare, and see, to the left of St. Peter's,
Smoke, from the cannon, white,—but that is at intervals only,—
Black, from a burning house, we suppose, by the Cavalleggieri;
And we believe we discern some lines of men descending
110   Down through the vineyard-slopes, and catch a bayonet
    gleaming.
Every ten minutes, however,—in this there is no misconception,—
Comes a great white puff from behind Michael Angelo's dome,
    and
After a space the report of a real big gun,—not the
    Frenchman's!—
That must be doing some work. And so we watch and
    conjecture.
115   Shortly, an Englishman comes, who says he has been to
    St. Peter's,
Seen the Piazza and troops, but that is all he can tell us;
So we watch and sit, and, indeed, it begins to be tiresome.—
All this smoke is outside; when it has come to the inside,
It will be time, perhaps, to descend and retreat to our houses.
120   Half-past one, or two. The report of small arms frequent,
Sharp and savage indeed; that cannot all be for nothing:
So we watch and wonder; but guessing is tiresome, very.
Weary of wondering, watching, and guessing, and gossiping idly,
Down I go, and pass through the quiet streets with the knots of
125   National Guards patrolling, and flags hanging out at the windows,
English, American, Danish,—and, after offering to help an
Irish family moving *en masse* to the Maison Serny,
After endeavouring idly to minister balm to the trembling
Quinquagenarian fears of two lone British spinsters,
130   Go to make sure of my dinner before the enemy enter.
But by this there are signs of stragglers returning; and voices
Talk, though you don't believe it, of guns and prisoners taken;
And on the walls you read the first bulletin of the morning.—
This is all that I saw, and all I know of the battle.

VI. *Claude to Eustace*

135 Victory! Victory!—Yes! ah, yes, thou republican Zion,
Truly the kings of the earth are gathered and gone by together;
Doubtless they marvelled to witness such things, were
    astonished, and so forth.
Victory! Victory! Victory!—Ah, but it is, believe me,
Easier, easier far, to intone the chant of the martyr
140 Than to indite any pæan of any victory. Death may
Sometimes be noble; but life, at the best, will appear an illusion.
While the great pain is upon us, it is great; when it is over,
Why, it is over. The smoke of the sacrifice rises to heaven,
Of a sweet savour, no doubt, to Somebody; but on the altar,
145 Lo, there is nothing remaining but ashes and dirt and ill odour.
    So it stands, you perceive; the labial muscles that swelled
    with
Vehement evolution of yesterday Marseillaises,
Articulations sublime of defiance and scorning, to-day col-
Lapse and languidly mumble, while men and women and papers
150 Scream and re-scream to each other the chorus of Victory.
    Well, but
I am thankful they fought, and glad that the Frenchmen were
    beaten.

VII. *Claude to Eustace*

So, I have seen a man killed! An experience that, among others!
Yes, I suppose I have; although I can hardly be certain,
And in a court of justice could never declare I had seen it.
155 But a man was killed, I am told, in a place where I saw
Something; a man was killed, I am told, and I saw something.
    I was returning home from St. Peter's; Murray, as usual,
Under my arm, I remember; had crossed the St. Angelo
    bridge; and
Moving towards the Condotti, had got to the first barricade, when
160 Gradually, thinking still of St. Peter's, I became conscious
Of a sensation of movement opposing me,—tendency this way
(Such as one fancies may be in a stream when the wave of the
    tide is
Coming and not yet come,—a sort of poise and retention);
So I turned, and, before I turned, caught sight of stragglers
165 Heading a crowd, it is plain, that is coming behind that corner.
Looking up, I see windows filled with heads; the Piazza,
Into which you remember the Ponte St. Angelo enters,
Since I passed, has thickened with curious groups; and now the
Crowd is coming, has turned, has crossed that last barricade, is
170 Here at my side. In the middle they drag at something. What
    is it?
Ha! bare swords in the air, held up? There seem to be voices

Pleading and hands putting back; official, perhaps; but the
    swords are
Many, and bare in the air. In the air? they descend; they are
    smiting,
Hewing, chopping—At what? In the air once more
    upstretched? And—
175 Is it blood that's on them? Yes, certainly blood! Of whom,
    then?
Over whom is the cry of this furor of exultation?
    While they are skipping and screaming, and dancing their
      caps on the points of
Swords and bayonets, I to the outskirts back, and ask a
Mercantile-seeming bystander, 'What is it?' and he, looking
    always
180 That way, makes me answer, 'A Priest, who was trying to fly to
The Neapolitan army,'—and thus explains the proceeding.
    You didn't see the dead man? No;—I began to be doubtful;
I was in black myself, and didn't know what mightn't happen,—
But a National Guard close by me, outside of the hubbub,
185 Broke his sword with slashing a broad hat covered with
    dust,—and
Passing away from the place with Murray under my arm, and
Stooping, I saw through the legs of the people the legs of a
    body.
    You are the first, do you know, to whom I have mentioned
    the matter.
Whom should I tell it to else?—these girls?—the Heavens
    forbid it!—
190 Quidnuncs at Monaldini's?—idlers upon the Pincian?
    If I rightly remember, it happened on that afternoon when
Word of the nearer approach of a new Neapolitan army
First was spread. I began to bethink me of Paris Septembers,
Thought I could fancy the look of that Old 'Ninety-two. On
    that evening
195 Three or four, or, it may be, five, of these people were
    slaughtered.
Some declared they had, one of them, fired on a sentinel; others
Say they were only escaping; a Priest, it is currently stated,
Stabbed a National Guard on the very Piazza Colonna:
History, Rumour of Rumours, I leave it to thee to determine!
200 But I am thankful to say the government seems to have
    strength to
Put it down; it has vanished, at least; the place is most
    peaceful.
Through the Trastevere walking last night, at nine of the
    clock, I
Found no sort of disorder; I crossed by the Island-bridges,
So by the narrow streets to the Ponte Rotto, and onwards

205 Thence by the Temple of Vesta, away to the great Coliseum,
Which at the full of the moon is an object worthy a visit.

VIII. Georgina Trevellyn to Louisa ——
Only think, dearest Louisa, what fearful scenes we have
 witnessed!—
*   *   *   *   *

George has just seen Garibaldi, dressed up in a long white
 cloak, on
Horseback, riding by, with his mounted negro behind him:
210 This is a man, you know, who came from America with him,
Out of the woods, I suppose, and uses a *lasso* in fighting,
Which is, I don't quite know, but a sort of noose, I imagine;
This he throws on the heads of the enemy's men in a battle,
Pulls them into his reach, and then most cruelly kills them:
215 Mary does not believe, but we heard it from an Italian.
Mary allows she was wrong about Mr. Claude *being selfish*;
He was *most* useful and kind on the terrible thirtieth of April.
Do not write here any more; we are starting directly for
 Florence:
We should be off to-morrow, if only Papa could get horses;
220 All have been seized everywhere for the use of this dreadful
 Mazzini.

P.S.
 Mary has seen thus far.—I am really so angry, Louisa,—
Quite out of patience, my dearest! What can the man be
 intending?
I am quite tired; and Mary, who might bring him to in a
 moment,
Lets him go on as he likes, and neither will help nor dismiss him.

IX. Claude to Eustace
225 It is most curious to see what a power a few calm words (in
Merely a brief proclamation) appear to possess on the people.
Order is perfect, and peace; the city is utterly tranquil;
And one cannot conceive that this easy and *nonchalant* crowd,
 that
Flows like a quiet stream through street and market-place,
 entering
230 Shady recesses and bays of church, *osteria*, and *caffè*,
Could in a moment be changed to a flood as of molten lava,
Boil into deadly wrath and wild homicidal delusion.
 Ah, 'tis an excellent race,—and even in old degradation,
Under a rule that enforces to flattery, lying, and cheating,
235 E'en under Pope and Priest, a nice and natural people.
Oh, could they but be allowed this chance of redemption!—
 but clearly

That is not likely to be. Meantime, notwithstanding all journals,
Honour for once to the tongue and the pen of the eloquent
    writer!
Honour to speech! and all honour to thee, thou noble Mazzini!

X. Claude to Eustace

240 I am in love, meantime, you think; no doubt you would
    think so.
I am in love, you say; with those letters, of course, you would
    say so.
I am in love, you declare. I think not so; yet I grant you
It is a pleasure indeed to converse with this girl. Oh, rare gift,
Rare felicity, this! she can talk in a rational way, can
245 Speak upon subjects that really are matters of mind and of
    thinking,
Yet in perfection retain her simplicity; never, one moment,
Never, however you urge it, however you tempt her, consents to
Step from ideas and fancies and loving sensations to those vain
Conscious understandings that vex the minds of mankind.
250 No, though she talk, it is music; her fingers desert not the
    keys; 'tis
Song, though you hear in the song the articulate vocables
    sounded,
Syllabled singly and sweetly the words of melodious meaning.
I am in love, you say; I do not think so, exactly.

XI. Claude to Eustace

There are two different kinds, I believe, of human attraction:
255 One which simply disturbs, unsettles, and makes you uneasy,
And another that poises, retains, and fixes and holds you.
I have no doubt, for myself, in giving my voice for the latter.
I do not wish to be moved, but growing where I was growing,
There more truly to grow, to live where as yet I had languished.
260 I do not like being moved: for the will is excited; and action
Is a most dangerous thing; I tremble for something factitious,
Some malpractice of heart and illegitimate process;
We are so prone to these things, with our terrible notions of
    duty.

XII. Claude to Eustace

Ah, let me look, let me watch, let me wait, unhurried,
    unprompted!
265 Bid me not venture on aught that could alter or end what is
    present!
Say not, Time flies, and Occasion, that never returns, is
    departing!
Drive me not out, ye ill angels with fiery swords, from my Eden,

Waiting, and watching, and looking! Let love be its own
    inspiration!
Shall not a voice, if a voice there must be, from the airs that
    environ,
270 Yea, from the conscious heavens, without our knowledge or
    effort,
Break into audible words? And love be its own inspiration?

XIII. Claude to Eustace

Wherefore and how I am certain, I hardly can tell; but it *is* so.
She doesn't like me, Eustace; I think she never will like me.
Is it my fault, as it is my misfortune, my ways are not her ways?
275 Is it my fault, that my habits and modes are dissimilar wholly?
'Tis not her fault; 'tis her nature, her virtue, to misapprehend
    them:
'Tis not her fault; 'tis her beautiful nature, not ever to know me.
Hopeless it seems,—yet I cannot, though hopeless, determine
    to leave it:
She goes—therefore I go; she moves,—I move, not to lose her.

From DIPSYCHUS

'There is no God,' the wicked saith,
    'And truly it's a blessing,
For what He might have done with us
    It's better only guessing.'

5 'There is no God,' a youngster thinks,
    'Or really, if there may be,
He surely didn't mean a man
    Always to be a baby.'

'There is no God, or if there is,'
10   The tradesman thinks, ''twere funny
If He should take it ill in me
    To make a little money.'

'Whether there be,' the rich man says,
    'It matters very little,
15 For I and mine, thank somebody,
    Are not in want of victual.'

Some others, also, to themselves,
    Who scarce so much as doubt it,
Think there is none, when they are well,
20   And do not think about it.

But country folks who live beneath
    The shadow of the steeple;
The parson and the parson's wife,
    And mostly married people;

25   Youths green and happy in first love,
    So thankful for illusion;
And men caught out in what the world
    Calls guilt, in first confusion;

And almost every one when age,
30   Disease, or sorrows strike him,
Inclines to think there is a God,
    Or something very like Him.

As I sat at the café, I said to myself,
They may talk as they please about what they call pelf,
They may sneer as they like about eating and drinking,
But help it I cannot, I cannot help thinking,
5   How pleasant it is to have money, heigh ho!
    How pleasant it is to have money.

I sit at my table *en grand seigneur*,
And when I have done, throw a crust to the poor;
Not only the pleasure, one's self, of good living,
10   But also the pleasure of now and then giving.
        So pleasant it is to have money, heigh ho!
    So pleasant it is to have money.

It was but last winter I came up to town,
But already I'm getting a little renown;
15   I make new acquaintance where'er I appear;
I am not too shy, and have nothing to fear.
        So pleasant it is to have money, heigh ho!
    So pleasant it is to have money.

I drive through the streets, and I care not a d——n;
20   The people they stare, and they ask who I am;
And if I should chance to run over a cad,
I can pay for the damage if ever so bad.
        So pleasant it is to have money, heigh ho!
    So pleasant it is to have money.

25 We stroll to our box and look down on the pit,
    And if it weren't low should be tempted to spit;
    We loll and we talk until people look up,
    And when it's half over we go out to sup.
        So pleasant it is to have money, heigh ho!
30   So pleasant it is to have money.

    The best of the tables and the best of the fare——
    And as for the others, the devil may care;
    It isn't our fault if they dare not afford
    To sup like a prince and be drunk as a lord.
35   So pleasant it is to have money, heigh ho!
            So pleasant it is to have money.

    We sit at our tables and tipple champagne;
    Ere one bottle goes, comes another again;
    The waiters they skip and they scuttle about,
40 And the landlord attends us so civilly out.
            So pleasant it is to have money, heigh ho!
            So pleasant it is to have money.

    It was but last winter I came up to town,
    But already I'm getting a little renown;
45 I get to good houses without much ado,
    Am beginning to see the nobility too.
            So pleasant it is to have money, heigh ho!
            So pleasant it is to have money.

    O dear! what a pity they ever should lose it!
50 For they are the gentry that know how to use it;
    So grand and so graceful, such manners, such dinners,
    But yet, after all, it is we are the winners.
            So pleasant it is to have money, heigh ho!
            So pleasant it is to have money.

55 Thus I sat at my table *en grand seigneur*,
    And when I had done threw a crust to the poor;
    Not only the pleasure, one's self, of good eating.
    But also the pleasure of now and then treating,
            So pleasant it is to have money, heigh ho!
60   So pleasant it is to have money.

    They may talk as they please about what they call pelf,
    And how one ought never to think of one's self,
    And how pleasures of thought surpass eating and drinking—
    My pleasure of thought is the pleasure of thinking
65   How pleasant it is to have money, heigh ho!
            How pleasant it is to have money.

THE LATEST DECALOGUE

Thou shalt have one God only; who
Would be at the expense of two?
No graven images may be
Worshipped, except the currency:
5   Swear not at all; for, for thy curse
Thine enemy is none the worse:
At church on Sunday to attend
Will serve to keep the world thy friend:
Honour thy parents; that is, all
10   From whom advancement may befall;
Thou shalt not kill; but need'st not strive
Officiously to keep alive:
Do not adultery commit;
Advantage rarely comes of it:
15   Thou shalt not steal; an empty feat,
When it's so lucrative to cheat:
Bear not false witness; let the lie
Have time on its own wings to fly:
Thou shalt not covet, but tradition
20   Approves all forms of competition.

IN THE GREAT METROPOLIS

Each for himself is still the rule:
We learn it when we go to school—
   The devil take the hindmost, O!

And when the schoolboys grow to men,
5   In life they learn it o'er again—
   The devil take the hindmost, O!

For in the church, and at the bar,
On 'Change, at court, where'er they are,
   The devil takes the hindmost, O!

10   Husband for husband, wife for wife,
Are careful that in married life
   The devil takes the hindmost, O!

From youth to age, whate'er the game,
The unvarying practice is the same—
15   The devil take the hindmost, O!

And after death, we do not know,
But scarce can doubt, where'er we go,
The devil takes the hindmost, O!

20

Ti rol de rol, ti rol de ro,
The devil take the hindmost, O!

Coventry Patmore

Coventry Patmore (1823–96) was the son of Peter George Patmore, a prominent literary figure in the 1820s and a friend of Hazlitt. In 1847 he married Emily Augusta Andrews, and the marriage was a very happy one; during it Patmore worked in the library of the British Museum, became a friend and associate of the Pre-Raphaelite Brotherhood, and published *The Angel in the House*, his poem celebrating the delights of married love and domestic happiness. His wife died in 1862. Patmore married twice more, becoming a wealthy gentleman-farmer in Sussex and later a man of leisure.

Patmore's poetry is individual and original; in *The Angel in the House* he combines a sublime and mystical view of love with an abundance of domestic detail (as B. Ifor Evans has written, 'the spirit of Dante was to be expressed in the setting of the Trollope novels'). The later odes are also original, particularly in their metre, a subject in which Patmore was an expert. Only occasionally (as in '1867') does the reactionary and abrasive side of his character emerge.

From THE ANGEL IN THE HOUSE

THE CATHEDRAL CLOSE

I

Once more I came to Sarum Close,
    With joy half memory, half desire,
And breathed the sunny wind that rose
    And blew the shadows o'er the Spire,
5   And toss'd the lilac's scented plumes,
    And sway'd the chestnut's thousand cones,
And fill'd my nostrils with perfumes,
    And shaped the clouds in waifs and zones,
And wafted down the serious strain
10   Of Sarum bells, when, true to time,
I reach'd the Dean's, with heart and brain
    That trembled to the trembling chime.

II

'Twas half my home, six years ago.
　　The six years had not alter'd it:
Red-brick and ashlar, long and low,
　　With dormers and with oriels lit.
Geranium, lychnis, rose array'd
　　The windows, all wide open thrown;
And some one in the Study play'd
　　The Wedding-March of Mendelssohn.
And there it was I last took leave:
　　'Twas Christmas: I remember'd now
The cruel girls, who feign'd to grieve,
　　Took down the evergreens; and how
The holly into blazes woke
　　The fire, lighting the large, low room
A dim, rich lustre of old oak
　　And crimson velvet's glowing gloom.

III

No change had touch'd Dean Churchill: kind,
　　By widowhood more than winters bent,
And settled in a cheerful mind,
　　As still forecasting heaven's content.
Well might his thoughts be fix'd on high,
　　Now she was there! Within her face
Humility and dignity
　　Were met in a most sweet embrace.
She seem'd expressly sent below
　　To teach our erring minds to see
The rhythmic change of time's swift flow
　　As part of still eternity.
Her life, all honour, observed, with awe
　　Which cross experience could not mar,
The fiction of the Christian law
　　That all men honourable are;
And so her smile at once conferr'd
　　High flattery and benign reproof;
And I, a rude boy, strangely stirr'd,
　　Grew courtly in my own behoof.
The years, so far from doing her wrong,
　　Anointed her with gracious balm,
And made her brows more and more young
　　With wreaths of amaranth and palm.

LOVE AT LARGE

Whene'er I come where ladies are,
  How sad soever I was before,
Though like a ship frost-bound and far
  Withheld in ice from the ocean's roar,
Third-winter'd in that dreadful dock,
  With stiffen'd cordage, sails decay'd,
And crew that care for calm and shock
  Alike, too dull to be dismay'd,
Yet, if I come where ladies are,
  How sad soever I was before,
Then is my sadness banish'd far,
  And I am like that ship no more;
Or like that ship if the ice-field splits,
  Burst by the sudden polar Spring,
And all thank God with their warming wits,
  And kiss each other and dance and sing,
And hoist fresh sails, that make the breeze
  Blow them along the liquid sea,
Out of the North, where life did freeze,
  Into the haven where they would be.

THE COUNTY BALL

I

Well, Heaven be thank'd my first-love fail'd,
  As, Heaven be thank'd, our first-loves do!
Thought I, when Fanny past me sail'd,
  Loved once, for what I never knew,
Unless for colouring in her talk,
  When cheeks and merry mouth would show
Three roses on a single stalk,
  The middle wanting room to blow,
And forward ways, that charm'd the boy
  Whose love-sick mind, misreading fate,
Scarce hoped that any Queen of Joy
  Could ever stoop to be his mate.

II

But there danced she, who from the leaven
  Of ill preserv'd my heart and wit
All unawares, for she was heaven,
  Others at best but fit for it.
One of those lovely things she was
  In whose least action there can be

Nothing so transient but it has
    An air of immortality.
I mark'd her step, with peace elate,
    Her brow more beautiful than morn,
Her sometime look of girlish state
    Which sweetly waived its right to scorn;
The giddy crowd, she grave the while,
    Although, as 'twere beyond her will,
Around her mouth the baby smile,
    That she was born with, linger'd still.
Her ball-dress seem'd a breathing mist,
    From the fair form exhaled and shed,
Raised in the dance with arm and wrist
    All warmth and light, unbraceleted.
Her motion, feeling 'twas beloved,
    The pensive soul of tune express'd,
And, oh, what perfume, as she moved,
    Came from the flowers in her breast!
How sweet a tongue the music had!
    'Beautiful Girl,' it seem'd to say,
'Though all the world were vile and sad,
    'Dance on; let innocence be gay.'
Ah, none but I discern'd her looks,
    When in the throng she pass'd me by,
For love is like a ghost, and brooks
    Only the chosen seer's eye;
And who but she could e'er divine
    The halo and the happy trance,
When her bright arm reposed on mine,
    In all the pauses of the dance!

III

Whilst so her beauty fed my sight,
    And whilst I lived in what she said,
Accordant airs, like all delight
    Most sweet when noted least, were play'd;
And was it like the Pharisee
    If I in secret bow'd my face
With joyful thanks that I should be,
    Not as were many, but with grace,
And fortune of well-nurtured youth,
    And days no sordid pains defile,
And thoughts accustom'd to the truth,
    Made capable of her fair smile?

IV

Charles Barton follow'd down the stair,
    To talk with me about the Ball,

75

And carp at all the people there.
  The Churchills chiefly stirr'd his gall:
65 'Such were the Kriemhilds and Isondes
  'You storm'd about at Trinity!
'Nothing at heart but handsome Blondes!
  'Folk say that you and Fanny Fry—'
'They err! Good-night! Here lies my course,
70   'Through Wilton.' Silence blest my ears,
And, weak at heart with vague remorse,
  A passing poignancy of tears
Attack'd mine eyes. By pale and park
  I rode, and ever seem'd to see,
75 In the transparent starry dark,
  That splendid brow of chastity,
That soft and yet subduing light,
  At which, as at the sudden moon,
I held my breath, and thought 'how bright!'
80   That guileless beauty in its noon,
Compelling tribute of desires
  Ardent as day when Sirius reigns,
Pure as the permeating fires
  That smoulder in the opal's veins.

From THE UNKNOWN EROS

THE TOYS

My little Son, who look'd from thoughtful eyes
And moved and spoke in quiet grown-up wise,
Having my law the seventh time disobey'd,
I struck him, and dismiss'd
5 With hard words and unkiss'd,
His Mother, who was patient, being dead.
Then, fearing lest his grief should hinder sleep,
I visited his bed,
But found him slumbering deep,
10 With darken'd eyelids, and their lashes yet
From his late sobbing wet.
And I, with moan,
Kissing away his tears, left others of my own;
For, on a table drawn beside his head,
15 He had put, within his reach,
A box of counters and a red-vein'd stone,
A piece of glass abraded by the beach

76

And six or seven shells,
A bottle with bluebells
20 And two French copper coins, ranged there with
            careful art,
To comfort his sad heart.
So when that night I pray'd
To God, I wept, and said:
Ah, when at last we lie with tranced breath,
25 Not vexing Thee in death,
And Thou rememberest of what toys
We made our joys,
How weakly understood,
Thy great commanded good,
30 Then, fatherly not less
Than I whom Thou hast moulded from the clay,
Thou'lt leave Thy wrath, and say,
'I will be sorry for their childishness.'

MAGNA EST VERITAS

Here, in this little Bay,
Full of tumultuous life and great repose,
Where, twice a day,
The purposeless, glad ocean comes and goes,
5 Under high cliffs, and far from the huge town,
I sit me down.
For want of me the world's course will not fail:
When all its work is done, the lie shall rot;
The truth is great, and shall prevail,
10 When none cares whether it prevail or not.

1867

In the year of the great crime,
When the false English Nobles and their Jew,
By God demented, slew
The Trust they stood twice pledged to keep from wrong,
5 One said, Take up thy Song,
That breathes the mild and almost mythic time
Of England's prime!
But I, Ah, me,
The freedom of the few
10 That, in our free Land, were indeed the free,
Can song renew?

Ill singing 'tis with blotting prison-bars,
How high soe'er, betwixt us and the stars;
Ill singing 'tis when there are none to hear;
15 And days are near
When England shall forget
The fading glow which, for a little while,
Illumes her yet,
The lovely smile
20 That grows so faint and wan,
Her people shouting in her dying ear,
Are not two daws worth two of any swan!
    Ye outlaw'd Best, who yet are bright
With the sunken light,
25 Whose common style
Is Virtue at her gracious ease,
The flower of olden sanctities,
Ye haply trust, by love's benignant guile,
To lure the dark and selfish brood
30 To their own hated good;
Ye haply dream
Your lives shall still their charmful sway sustain,
Unstifled by the fever'd steam
That rises from the plain.
35 Know, 'twas the force of function high,
In corporate exercise, and public awe
Of Nature's, Heaven's, and England's Law
That Best, though mix'd with Bad, should reign,
Which kept you in your sky!
40 But, when the sordid Trader caught
The loose-held sceptre from your hands distraught,
And soon, to the Mechanic vain,
Sold the proud toy for nought,
Your charm was broke, your task was sped,
45 Your beauty, with your honour, dead,
And though you still are dreaming sweet
Of being even now not less
Than Gods and Goddesses, ye shall not long so cheat
Your hearts of their due heaviness.
50 Go, get you for your evil watching shriven!
Leave to your lawful Master's itching hands
Your unking'd lands,
But keep, at least, the dignity
Of deigning not, for his smooth use, to be,
55 Voteless, the voted delegates
Of his strange interests, loves and hates.
In sackcloth, or in private strife
With private ill, ye may please Heaven,
And soothe the coming pangs of sinking life;

60   And prayer perchance may win
        A term to God's indignant mood
    And the orgies of the multitude,
    Which now begin;
    But do not hope to wave the silken rag
65   Of your unsanction'd flag,
    And so to guide
    The great ship, helmless on the swelling tide
    Of that presumptuous Sea,
    Unlit by sun or moon, yet inly bright
70   With lights innumerable that give no light,
    Flames of corrupted will and scorn of right,
    Rejoicing to be free.
        And, now, because the dark comes on apace
    When none can work for fear,
75   And Liberty in every Land lies slain,
    And the two Tyrannies unchallenged reign,
    And heavy prophecies, suspended long
    At supplication of the righteous few,
    And so discredited, to fulfilment throng,
80   Restrain'd no more by faithful prayer or tear,
    And the dread baptism of blood seems near
    That brings to the humbled Earth the Time of Grace,
    Breathless be song,
    And let Christ's own look through
85   The darkness, suddenly increased,
    To the gray secret lingering in the East.

NIGHT AND SLEEP

I

How strange at night to wake
    And watch, while others sleep,
Till sight and hearing ache
    For objects that may keep
5   The awful inner sense
    Unroused, lest it should mark
The life that haunts the emptiness
    And horror of the dark!

II

How strange at night the bay
10   Of dogs, how wild the note
Of cocks that scream for day,
    In homesteads far remote;

How strange and wild to hear
    The old and crumbling tower,
15   Amid the darkness, suddenly
       Take tongue and speak the hour!

III

Albeit the love-sick brain
    Affects the dreary moon,
Ill things alone refrain
20   From life's nocturnal swoon:
Men melancholy mad,
    Beasts ravenous and sly,
The robber, and the murderer,
    Remorse, with lidless eye.

IV

25   The nightingale is gay,
    For she can vanquish night;
Dreaming, she sings of day
    Notes that make darkness bright;
But when the refluent gloom
30   Saddens the gaps of song,
Men charge on her the dolefulness,
    And call her crazed with wrong.

A LONDON FÊTE

All night fell hammers, shock on shock;
With echoes Newgate's granite clang'd:
The scaffold built, at eight o'clock
They brought the man out to be hang'd.
5   Then came from all the people there
A single cry, that shook the air;
Mothers held up their babes to see,
Who spread their hands, and crow'd for glee;
Here a girl from her vesture tore
10   A rag to wave with, and join'd the roar;
There a man, with yelling tired,
Stopp'd, and the culprit's crime inquired;
A sot, below the doom'd man dumb,
Bawl'd his health in the world to come;
15   These blasphemed and fought for places;
Those, half-crush'd, cast frantic faces,
To windows, where, in freedom sweet,
Others enjoy'd the wicked treat.

At last, the show's black crisis pended;
20   Struggles for better standings ended;
The rabble's lips no longer curst,
But stood agape with horrid thirst;
Thousands of breasts beat horrid hope;
Thousands of eyeballs, lit with hell,
25   Burnt one way all, to see the rope
Unslacken as the platform fell.
The rope flew tight; and then the roar
Burst forth afresh; less loud, but more
Confused and affrighting than before.
30   A few harsh tongues for ever led
The common din, the chaos of noises,
But ear could not catch what they said.
As when the realm of the damn'd rejoices
At winning a soul to its will,
35   That clatter and clangour of hateful voices
Sicken'd and stunn'd the air, until
The dangling corpse hung straight and still.
The show complete, the pleasure past,
The solid masses loosen'd fast:
40   A thief slunk off, with ample spoil,
To ply elsewhere his daily toil;
A baby strung its doll to a stick;
A mother praised the pretty trick;
Two children caught and hang'd a cat;
45   Two friends walk'd on, in lively chat;
And two, who had disputed places,
Went forth to fight, with murderous faces.

George Meredith

George Meredith (1828–1909) was the son of a naval outfitter in Portsmouth, and educated in England and Germany. He was articled to a London solicitor, but preferred literature as a profession, publishing poems and novels and also working as a journalist. In 1849 he married Mary Ellen Nicholls, the widowed daughter of the novelist Thomas Love Peacock. The marriage was a failure, and she left him in 1858; the unhappiness of the experience is reflected in *Modern Love*, published in 1862, a year after his wife's death. A second marriage was much happier, and apart from a period as a war correspondent in the Italian-Austrian war of 1866, Meredith settled in Surrey and lived the life of a busy literary man.

Meredith's poetry is very varied, dealing with nature, history and politics, and love. His nature poetry owes much to the romantics, and especially to Wordsworth; his love poetry, with its fine exaltation ('Love in the Valley') or its unflinching description of misery (*Modern Love*) is his most interesting and individual work.

THE OLD CHARTIST

I

Whate'er I be, old England is my dam!
    So there's my answer to the judges, clear
I'm nothing of a fox, nor of a lamb;
    I don't know how to bleat nor how to leer:
5   I'm for the nation!
    That's why you see me by the wayside here,
      Returning home from transportation.

II

It's Summer in her bath this morn, I think.
    I'm fresh as dew, and chirpy as the birds:
10 And just for joy to see old England wink
      Thro' leaves again, I could harangue the herds:
          Isn't it something
    To speak out like a man when you've got words,
      And prove you're not a stupid dumb thing?

III

15

They shipp'd me off for it; I'm here again.
Old England is my dam, whate'er I be!
Says I, I'll tramp it home, and see the grain:
If you see well, you're king of what you see:
Eyesight is having,
20
If you're not given, I said, to gluttony.
Such talk to ignorance sounds as raving.

IV

You dear old brook, that from his Grace's park
Come bounding! on you run near my old town
My lord can't lock the water; nor the lark,
25
Unless he kills him, can my lord keep down.
Up, is the song-note!
I've tried it, too:—for comfort and renown,
I rather pitch'd upon the wrong note.

V

I'm not ashamed: Not beaten's still my boast:
30
Again I'll rouse the people up to strike.
But home's where different politics jar most.
Respectability the women like.
This form, or that form,—
The Government may be hungry pike,
35
But don't you mount a Chartist platform!

VI

Well, well! Not beaten—spite of them, I shout;
And my estate is suffering for the Cause.—
Now, what is yon brown water-rat about,
Who washes his old poll with busy paws?
40
What does he mean by 't?
It's like defying all our natural laws,
For him to hope that he'll get clean by 't.

VII

His seat is on a mud-bank, and his trade
Is dirt:—he's quite contemptible; and yet
45
The fellow's all as anxious as a maid
To show a decent dress, and dry the wet.
Now it's his whisker,
And now his nose, and ear: he seems to get
Each moment at the motion brisker!

VIII

50 To see him squat like little chaps at school,
I could let fly a laugh with all my might.
He peers, hangs both his fore-paws:—bless that fool,
He's bobbing at his frill now!—what a sight!
Licking the dish up,
55 As if he thought to pass from black to white,
Like parson into lawny bishop.

IX

The elms and yellow reed-flags in the sun
Look on quite grave:—the sunlight flecks his side;
And links of bindweed-flowers round him run,
60 And shine up doubled with him in the tide.
*I'm nearly splitting,
But nature seems like seconding his pride,
And thinks that his behaviour's fitting.

X

That isle o' mud looks baking dry with gold,
65 His needle-muzzle still works out and in.
It really is a wonder to behold,
And makes me feel the bristles of my chin;
Judged by appearance,
I fancy of the two I'm nearer Sin,
70 And might as well commence a clearance.

XI

And that's what my fine daughter said:—she meant:
Pray, hold your tongue, and wear a Sunday face.
Her husband, the young linendraper, spent
Much argument thereon:—I'm their disgrace.
75 Bother the couple!
I feel superior to a chap whose place
Commands him to be neat and supple.

XII

But if I go and say to my old hen:
I'll mend the gentry's boots, and keep discreet,
80 Until they grow *too* violent,—why, then,
A warmer welcome I might chance to meet:
Warmer and better.
And if she fancies her old cock is beat,
And drops upon her knees—so let her!

84

XIII

85 She suffered for me:—women, you'll observe,
Don't suffer for a Cause, but for a man.
When I was in the dock she show'd her nerve:
I saw beneath her shawl my old tea-can
Trembling ... she brought it
90 To screw me for my work: she loath'd my plan,
And therefore doubly kind I thought it.

XIV

I've never lost the taste of that same tea:
That liquor on my logic floats like oil,
When I state facts, and fellows disagree.
95 For human creatures all are in a coil:
All may want pardon.
I see a day when every pot will boil
Harmonious in one great Tea-garden!

XV

We wait the setting of the Dandy's day,
100 Before that time!—He's furbishing his dress,—
He *will* be ready for it!—and I say,
That yon old dandy rat amid the cress,—
Thanks to hard labour!—
If cleanliness is next to godliness,
105 The old fat fellow's heaven's neighbour!

XVI

You teach me a fine lesson, my old boy!
I've looked on my superiors far too long,
And small has been my profit as my joy.
You've done the right while I've denounced the
wrong.
110 Prosper me later!
Like you I will despise the sniggering throng,
And please myself and my Creator.

XVII

I'll bring the linendraper and his wife
Some day to see you; taking off my hat.
115 Should they ask why, I'll answer: in my life
I never found so true a democrat.
Base occupation
Can't rob you of your own esteem, old rat!
I'll preach you to the British nation.

From MODERN LOVE

I

By this he knew she wept with waking eyes:
That, at his hand's light quiver by her head,
The strange low sobs that shook their common bed
Were called into her with a sharp surprise,
5   And strangled mute, like little gaping snakes,
Dreadfully venomous to him. She lay
Stone-still, and the long darkness flowed away
With muffled pulses. Then, as midnight makes
Her giant heart of Memory and Tears
10 Drink the pale drug of silence, and so beat
Sleep's heavy measure, they from head to feet
Were moveless, looking through their dead black years,
By vain regret scrawled over the blank wall.
Like sculptured effigies they might be seen
15 Upon their marriage-tomb, the sword between;
Each wishing for the sword that severs all.

XII

Not solely that the Future she destroys,
And the fair life which in the distance lies
For all men, beckoning out from dim rich skies:
Nor that the passing hour's supporting joys
5   Have lost the keen-edged flavour, which begat
Distinction in old times, and still should breed
Sweet Memory, and Hope,—earth's modest seed,
And heaven's high-prompting: not that the world is flat
Since that soft-luring creature I embraced
10 Among the children of Illusion went:
Methinks with all this loss I were content,
If the mad Past, on which my foot is based,
Were firm, or might be blotted: but the whole
Of life is mixed: the mocking Past will stay:
15 And if I drink oblivion of a day,
So shorten I the stature of my soul.

XIII

'I play for Seasons; not Eternities!'
Says Nature, laughing on her way. 'So must
All those whose stake is nothing more than dust!'
And lo, she wins, and of her harmonies
5   She is full sure! Upon her dying rose
She drops a look of fondness, and goes by,

Scarce any retrospection in her eye;
For she the laws of growth most deeply knows,
Whose hands bear, here, a seed-bag—there, an urn.
10 Pledged she herself to aught, 'twould mark her end!
This lesson of our only visible friend
Can we not teach our foolish hearts to learn?
Yes! yes!—but, oh, our human rose is fair
Surpassingly! Lose calmly Love's great bliss,
15 When the renewed for ever of a kiss
Whirls life within the shower of loosened hair!

XXX

What are we first? First, animals; and next
Intelligences at a leap; on whom
Pale lies the distant shadow of the tomb,
And all that draweth on the tomb for text.
5 Into which state comes Love, the crowning sun:
Beneath whose light the shadow loses form.
We are the lords of life, and life is warm.
Intelligence and instinct now are one.
But nature says: 'My children most they seem
10 When they least know me: therefore I decree
That they shall suffer.' Swift doth young Love flee,
And we stand wakened, shivering from our dream.
Then if we study Nature we are wise.
Thus do the few who live but with the day:
15 The scientific animals are they.—
Lady, this is my sonnet to your eyes.

XXXVI

My Lady unto Madam makes her bow.
The charm of women is, that even while
You're probed by them for tears, you yet may smile,
Nay, laugh outright, as I have done just now.
5 The interview was gracious: they anoint
(To me aside) each other with fine praise:
Discriminating compliments they raise,
That hit with wondrous aim on the weak point:
My Lady's nose of Nature might complain.
10 It is not fashioned aptly to express
Her character of large-browed steadfastness.
But Madam says: Thereof she may be vain!
Now, Madam's faulty feature is a glazed
And inaccessible eye, that has soft fires,
15 Wide gates, at love-time, only. This admires
My Lady. At the two I stand amazed.

XLIII

Mark where the pressing wind shoots javelin-like
Its skeleton shadow on the broad-backed wave!
Here is a fitting spot to dig Love's grave;
Here where the ponderous breakers plunge and strike,
5   And dart their hissing tongues high up the sand:
In hearing of the ocean, and in sight
Of those ribbed wind-streaks running into white.
If I the death of Love had deeply planned,
I never could have made it half so sure,
10   As by the unblest kisses which upbraid
The full-waked sense; or failing that, degrade!
'Tis morning: but no morning can restore
What we have forfeited. I see no sin:
The wrong is mixed. In tragic life, God wot,
15   No villain need be! Passions spin the plot:
We are betrayed by what is false within.

XLIX

He found her by the ocean's moaning verge,
Nor any wicked change in her discerned;
And she believed his old love had returned,
Which was her exultation, and her scourge.
5   She took his hand, and walked with him, and seemed
The wife he sought, though shadow-like and dry.
She had one terror, lest her heart should sigh,
And tell her loudly she no longer dreamed.
She dared not say, 'This is my breast: look in.'
10   But there's a strength to help the desperate weak
That night he learned how silence best can speak
The awful things when Pity pleads for Sin.
About the middle of the night her call
Was heard, and he came wondering to the bed.
15   'Now kiss me, dear! it may be, now!' she said.
Lethe had passed those lips, and he knew all.

L

Thus piteously Love closed what he begat:
The union of this ever-diverse pair!
These two were rapid falcons in a snare,
Condemned to do the flitting of the bat.
5   Lovers beneath the singing sky of May,
They wandered once; clear as the dew on flowers:
But they fed not on the advancing hours:
Their hearts held cravings for the buried day.
Then each applied to each that fatal knife,
10   Deep questioning, which probes to endless dole.

Ah, what a dusty answer gets the soul
When hot for certainties in this our life!—
In tragic hints here see what evermore
Moves dark as yonder midnight ocean's force,
Thundering like ramping hosts of warrior horse,
To throw that faint thin line upon the shore!

LUCIFER IN STARLIGHT

On a starred night Prince Lucifer uprose.
Tired of his dark dominion swung the fiend
Above the rolling ball in cloud part screened,
Where sinners hugged their spectre of repose.
Poor prey to his hot fit of pride were those.
And now upon his western wing he leaned,
Now his huge bulk o'er Afric's sands careened,
Now the black planet shadowed Arctic snows.
Soaring through wider zones that pricked his scars
With memory of the old revolt from Awe,
He reached a middle height, and at the stars,
Which are the brain of heaven, he looked, and sank.
Around the ancient track marched, rank on rank,
The army of unalterable law.

LOVE IN THE VALLEY

Under yonder beech-tree single on the green-sward,
    Couched with her arms behind her golden head,
Knees and tresses folded to slip and ripple idly,
    Lies my young love sleeping in the shade.
Had I the heart to slide an arm beneath her,
    Press her parting lips as her waist I gather slow,
Waking in amazement she could not but embrace me:
    Then would she hold me and never let me go?

Shy as the squirrel and wayward as the swallow,
    Swift as the swallow along the river's light
Circleting the surface to meet his mirrored winglets,
    Fleeter she seems in her stay than in her flight.
Shy as the squirrel that leaps among the pine-tops,
    Wayward as the swallow overhead at set of sun,
She whom I love is hard to catch and conquer,
    Hard, but O the glory of the winning were she won!

89

When her mother tends her before the laughing mirror,
 Tying up her laces, looping up her hair,
Often she thinks, were this wild thing wedded,
20   More love should I have, and much less care.
When her mother tends her before the lighted mirror,
 Loosening her laces, combing down her curls,
Often she thinks, were this wild thing wedded,
 I should miss but one for many boys and girls.

25 Heartless she is as the shadow in the meadows
 Flying to the hills on a blue and breezy noon.
No, she is athirst and drinking up her wonder:
 Earth to her is young as the slip of the new moon.
Deals she an unkindness, 'tis but her rapid measure,
30   Even as in a dance; and her smile can heal no less:
Like the swinging May-cloud that pelts the flowers with
  hailstones
 Off a sunny border, she was made to bruise and bless.

Lovely are the curves of the white owl sweeping
 Wavy in the dusk lit by one large star.
35 Lone on the fir-branch, his rattle-note unvaried,
 Brooding o'er the gloom, spins the brown eve-jar.
Darker grows the valley, more and more forgetting:
 So were it with me if forgetting could be willed.
Tell the grassy hollow that holds the bubbling well-spring
40 Tell it to forget the source that keeps it filled.

Stepping down the hill with her fair companions,
 Arm in arm, all against the raying West,
Boldly she sings, to the merry tune she marches,
 Brave in her shape, and sweeter unpossessed.
45 Sweeter, for she is what my heart first awaking
 Whispered the world was; morning light is she.
Love that so desires would fain keep her changeless;
 Fain would fling the net, and fain have her free.

Happy happy time, when the white star hovers
50 Low over dim fields fresh with bloomy dew,
Near the face of dawn, that draws athwart the darkness,
 Threading it with colour, like yewberries the yew.
Thicker crowd the shades as the grave East deepens
 Glowing, and with crimson a long cloud swells.
55 Maiden still the morn is; and strange she is, and secret;
 Strange her eyes; her cheeks are cold as cold sea-shells.

Sunrays, leaning on our southern hills and lighting
    Wild cloud-mountains that drag the hills along,
Oft ends the day of your shifting brilliant laughter
60   Chill as a dull face frowning on a song.
Ay, but shows the South-West a ripple-feathered bosom
    Blown to silver while the clouds are shaken and ascend
Scaling the mid-heavens as they stream, there comes a sunset
    Rich, deep like love in beauty without end.

65 When at dawn she sighs, and like an infant to the window
    Turns grave eyes craving light, released from dreams,
Beautiful she looks, like a white water-lily
    Bursting out of bud in havens of the streams.
When from bed she rises clothed from neck to ankle
70   In her long nightgown sweet as boughs of May,
Beautiful she looks, like a tall garden lily
    Pure from the night, and splendid for the day.

Mother of the dews, dark eye-lashed twilight,
    Low-lidded twilight, o'er the valley's brim,
75 Rounding on thy breast sings the dew-delighted skylark,
    Clear as though the dewdrops had their voice in him.
Hidden where the rose-flush drinks the rayless planet,
    Fountain-full he pours the spraying fountain-showers.
Let me hear her laughter, I would have her ever
80   Cool as dew in twilight, the lark above the flowers.

All the girls are out with their baskets for the primrose;
    Up lanes, woods through, they troop in joyful bands.
My sweet leads: she knows not why, but now she loiters,
    Eyes the bent anemones, and hangs her hands.
85 Such a look will tell that the violets are peeping,
    Coming the rose: and unaware a cry
Springs in her bosom for odours and for colour,
    Covert and the nightingale; she knows not why.

Kerchiefed head and chin she darts between her tulips,
90   Streaming like a willow grey in arrowy rain:
Some bend beaten cheek to gravel, and their angel
    She will be; she lifts them, and on she speeds again.
Black the driving raincloud breasts the iron gateway:
    She is forth to cheer a neighbour lacking mirth.
95 So when sky and grass met rolling dumb for thunder
    Saw I once a white dove, sole light of earth.

Prim little scholars are the flowers of her garden,
    Trained to stand in rows, and asking if they please.
I might love them well but for loving more the wild ones:
100   O my wild ones! they tell me more than these.

You, my wild one, you tell of honied field-rose,
    Violet, blushing eglantine in life; and even as they,
They by the wayside are earnest of your goodness,
    You are of life's on the banks that line the way.

105 Peering at her chamber the white crowns the red rose,
    Jasmine winds the porch with stars two and three.
Parted is the window; she sleeps; the starry jasmine
    Breathes a falling breath that carries thoughts of me.
Sweeter unpossessed, have I said of her my sweetest?
110   Not while she sleeps: while she sleeps the jasmine
      breathes,
Luring her to love; she sleeps; the starry jasmine
    Bears me to her pillow under white rose-wreaths.

Yellow with birdfoot-trefoil are the grass-glades;
    Yellow with cinquefoil of the dew-grey leaf;
115 Yellow with stonecrop; the moss-mounds are yellow;
    Blue-necked the wheat sways, yellowing to the sheaf.
Green-yellow bursts from the copse the laughing yaffle;
    Sharp as a sickle is the edge of shade and shine:
Earth in her heart laughs looking at the heavens,
120   Thinking of the harvest: I look and think of mine.

This I may know: her dressing and undressing
    Such a change of light shows as when the skies in sport
Shift from cloud to moonlight; or edging over thunder
    Slips a ray of sun; or sweeping into port
125 White sails furl; or on the ocean borders
    White sails lean along the waves leaping green.
Visions of her shower before me, but from eyesight
    Guarded she would be like the sun were she seen.

Front door and back of the mossed old farmhouse
130   Open with the morn, and in a breezy link
Freshly sparkles garden to stripe-shadowed orchard,
    Green across a rill where on sand the minnows wink.
Busy in the grass the early sun of summer
    Swarms, and the blackbird's mellow fluting notes
135 Call my darling up with round and roguish challenge:
    Quaintest, richest carol of all the singing throats!

Cool was the woodside; cool as her white dairy
    Keeping sweet the cream-pan; and there the boys
      from school,
Cricketing below, rushed brown and red with sunshine;
140   O the dark translucence of the deep-eyed cool!

Spying from the farm, herself she fetched a pitcher
    Full of milk, and tilted for each in turn the beak.
Then a little fellow, mouth up and on tiptoe,
    Said, 'I will kiss you': she laughed and leaned her cheek.

145 Doves of the fir-wood walling high our red roof
    Through the long noon coo, crooning through the coo.
Loose droop the leaves, and down the sleepy roadway
    Sometimes pipes a chaffinch; loose droops the blue.
Cows flap a slow tail knee-deep in the river,
150   Breathless, given up to sun and gnat and fly.
Nowhere is she seen; and if I see her nowhere,
    Lightning may come, straight rains and tiger sky.

O the golden sheaf, the rustling treasure-armful!
    O the nutbrown tresses nodding interlaced!
155 O the treasure-tresses one another over
    Nodding! O the girdle slack about the waist!
Slain are the poppies that shot their random scarlet
    Quick amid the wheatears: wound about the waist,
Gathered, see these brides of Earth one blush of ripeness!
160   O the nutbrown tresses nodding interlaced!

Large and smoky red the sun's cold disk drops,
    Clipped by naked hills, on violet shaded snow:
Eastward large and still lights up a bower of moonrise,
    Whence at her leisure steps the moon aglow
165 Nightlong on black print-branches our beech-tree
    Gazes in this whiteness: nightlong could I.
Here may life on death or death on life be painted.
    Let me clasp her soul to know she cannot die!

Gossips count her faults; they scour a narrow chamber
170   Where there is no window, read not heaven or her.
'When she was a tiny,' one aged woman quavers,
    Plucks at my heart and leads me by the ear.
Faults she had once as she learnt to run and tumbled:
    Faults of feature some see, beauty not complete.
175 Yet, good gossips, beauty that makes holy
    Earth and air, may have faults from head to feet.

Hither she comes; she comes to me; she lingers,
    Deepens her brown eyebrows, while in new surprise
High rise the lashes in wonder of a stranger;
180   Yet am I the light and living of her eyes.
Something friends have told her fills her heart to brimming,
    Nets her in her blushes, and wounds her, and tames.—
Sure of her haven, O like a dove alighting,
    Arms up, she dropped: our souls were in our names.

185   Soon will she lie like a white-frost sunrise.
        Yellow oats and brown wheat, barley pale as rye,
    Long since your sheaves have yielded to the thresher,
        Felt the girdle loosened, seen the tresses fly.
    Soon will she lie like a blood-red sunset.
190   Swift with the to-morrow, green-winged Spring!
    Sing from the South-West, bring her back the truants,
        Nightingale and swallow, song and dipping wing.

    Soft new beech-leaves, up to beamy April
        Spreading bough on bough a primrose mountain, you,
195   Lucid in the moon, raise lilies to the skyfields,
        Youngest green transfused in silver shining through:
    Fairer than the lily, than the wild white cherry:
        Fair as in image my seraph love appears
    Borne to me by dreams when dawn is at my eyelids:
200   Fair as in the flesh she swims to me on tears.

    Could I find a place to be alone with heaven,
        I would speak my heart out: heaven is my need.
    Every woodland tree is flushing like the dogwood,
        Flashing like the whitebeam, swaying like the reed.
205   Flushing like the dogwood crimson in October;
        Streaming like the flag-reed South-West blown;
    Flashing as in gusts the sudden-lighted whitebeam:
        All seem to know what is for heaven alone.

Dante Gabriel Rossetti

Dante Gabriel Rossetti (1828–82) was the son of an Italian living in London, and elder brother of Christina. In 1848, as a young art student, he joined Holman Hunt, Millais and four others to form the Pre-Raphaelite Brotherhood. This movement called for a return to nature in English art, preferring the simplicity and purity of the early Italian painters to the academic style derived from Raphael. It was a literary as well as a pictorial movement,[1] and its short-lived magazine, *The Germ*, contained poems (notably 'The Blessed Damozel') by Rossetti and his sister in its four numbers published in 1850. In the same year Rossetti met Elizabeth Siddal, a beautiful girl who became his model and later his wife. She died, probably by her own hand, in 1862, and Rossetti, grief-stricken, placed his poems in her grave. In 1869 they were disinterred, and formed part of the volume of poems published by Rossetti in 1870. In these years Rossetti was profoundly affected by his love for Jane Morris, the wife of his friend William Morris. During the last ten years of his life he suffered from depression and insomnia.

Rossetti's great fault as a painter was his failure to discipline himself to undergo a formal technical training. This is not so evident in his poetry, where he has less difficulty in expressing his particular kind of dreamy sensuality, and the poignancy of passing time and human regret; though the studied vagueness of his imagery is often enlivened by moments of sharp precision, and an accurate and wakeful observation.

THE BLESSED DAMOZEL

The blessed damozel leaned out
    From the gold bar of Heaven;
Her eyes were deeper than the depth
    Of waters stilled at even;
5   She had three lilies in her hand,
    And the stars in her hair were seven.

[1] See *Pre-Raphaelite Writing* (Dent, 1973), ed. Derek Stanford.

Her robe, ungirt from clasp to hem,
    No wrought flowers did adorn,
But a white rose of Mary's gift,
10   For service meetly worn;
Her hair that lay along her back
    Was yellow like ripe corn.

Herseemed she scarce had been a day
    One of God's choristers;
15   The wonder was not yet quite gone
    From that still look of hers;
Albeit, to them she left, her day
    Had counted as ten years.

(To one, it is ten years of years.
20   . . . Yet now, and in this place,
Surely she leaned o'er me—her hair
    Fell all about my face. . . .
Nothing: the autumn-fall of leaves.
    The whole year sets apace.)

25 It was the rampart of God's house
    That she was standing on;
By God built over the sheer depth
    The which is Space begun;
So high, that looking downward thence
30   She scarce could see the sun.

It lies in Heaven, across the flood
    Of ether, as a bridge.
Beneath, the tides of day and night
    With flame and darkness ridge
35 The void, as low as where this earth
    Spins like a fretful midge.

Around her, lovers, newly met
    'Mid deathless love's acclaims,
Spoke evermore among themselves
40   Their heart-remembered names;
And the souls mounting up to God
    Went by her like thin flames.

And still she bowed herself and stooped
    Out of the circling charm;
45 Until her bosom must have made
    The bar she leaned on warm,
And the lilies lay as if asleep
    Along her bended arm.

From the fixed place of Heaven she saw
    Time like a pulse shake fierce
Through all the worlds. Her gaze still strove
    Within the gulf to pierce
Its path; and now she spoke as when
    The stars sang in their spheres.

The sun was gone now; the curled moon
    Was like a little feather
Fluttering far down the gulf; and now
    She spoke through the still weather.
Her voice was like the voice the stars
    Had when they sang together.

(Ah sweet! Even now, in that bird's song,
    Strove not her accents there,
Fain to be hearkened? When those bells
    Possessed the mid-day air,
Strove not her steps to reach my side
    Down all the echoing stair?)

'I wish that he were come to me,
    For he will come,' she said.
'Have I not prayed in Heaven?—on earth,
    Lord, Lord, has he not pray'd?
Are not two prayers a perfect strength?
    And shall I feel afraid?

'When round his head the aureole clings,
    And he is clothed in white,
I'll take his hand and go with him
    To the deep wells of light;
As unto a stream we will step down,
    And bathe there in God's sight.

'We two will stand beside that shrine,
    Occult, withheld, untrod,
Whose lamps are stirred continually
    With prayer sent up to God;
And see our old prayers, granted, melt
    Each like a little cloud.

'We two will lie i' the shadow of
    That living mystic tree
Within whose secret growth the Dove
    Is sometimes felt to be,
While every leaf that His plumes touch
    Saith His Name audibly.

'And I myself will teach to him,
    I myself, lying so,
The songs I sing here; which his voice
    Shall pause in, hushed and slow,
95   And find some knowledge at each pause,
    Or some new thing to know.'

(Alas! we two, we two, thou say'st!
    Yea, one wast thou with me
That once of old. But shall God lift
100   To endless unity
The soul whose likeness with thy soul
    Was but its love for thee?)

'We two,' she said, 'will seek the groves
    Where the lady Mary is,
105   With her five handmaidens, whose names
    Are five sweet symphonies,
Cecily, Gertrude, Magdalen,
    Margaret and Rosalys.

'Circlewise sit they, with bound locks
110   And foreheads garlanded;
Into the fine cloth white like flame
    Weaving the golden thread,
To fashion the birth-robes for them
    Who are just born, being dead.

115   'He shall fear, haply, and be dumb:
    Then will I lay my cheek
To his, and tell about our love,
    Not once abashed or weak:
And the dear Mother will approve
120   My pride, and let me speak.

'Herself shall bring us, hand in hand,
    To Him round whom all souls
Kneel, the clear-ranged unnumbered heads
    Bowed with their aureoles:
125   And angels meeting us shall sing
    To their citherns and citoles.

'There will I ask of Christ the Lord
    Thus much for him and me:—
Only to live as once on earth
130   With Love,—only to be,
As then awhile, for ever now
    Together, I and he.'

She gazed and listened and then said,
　　Less sad of speech than mild,—
'All this is when he comes.' She ceased.
　　The light thrilled towards her, fill'd
With angels in strong level flight.
　　Her eyes prayed, and she smil'd.

(I saw her smile.) But soon their path
　　Was vague in distant spheres:
And then she cast her arms along
　　The golden barriers,
And laid her face between her hands,
　　And wept. (I heard her tears.)

JENNY

*Vengeance of Jenny's case! Fie on her! Never name
　　her, child!—(Mrs. Quickly)*

Lazy laughing languid Jenny,
Fond of a kiss and fond of a guinea,
Whose head upon my knee to-night
Rests for a while, as if grown light
With all our dances and the sound
To which the wild tunes spun you round:
Fair Jenny mine, the thoughtless queen
Of kisses which the blush between
Could hardly make much daintier;
Whose eyes are as blue skies, whose hair
Is countless gold incomparable:
Fresh flower, scarce touched with signs that tell
Of Love's exuberant hotbed:—Nay,
Poor flower left torn since yesterday
Until to-morrow leave you bare;
Poor handful of bright spring-water
Flung in the whirlpool's shrieking face;
Poor shameful Jenny, full of grace
Thus with your head upon my knee;—
Whose person or whose purse may be
The lodestar of your reverie?

This room of yours, my Jenny, looks
A change from mine so full of books,
Whose serried ranks hold fast, forsooth,
So many captive hours of youth,—

The hours they thieve from day and night
To make one's cherished work come right,
And leave it wrong for all their theft,
Even as to-night my work was left:
30 Until I vowed that since my brain
And eyes of dancing seemed so fain,
My feet should have some dancing too:—
And thus it was I met with you.
Well, I suppose 'twas hard to part,
35 For here I am. And now, sweetheart,
You seem too tired to get to bed.

It was a careless life I led
When rooms like this were scarce so strange
Not long ago. What breeds the change,—
40 The many aims or the few years?
Because to-night it all appears
Something I do not know again.

The cloud's not danced out of my brain,—
The cloud that made it turn and swim
45 While hour by hour the books grew dim.
Why, Jenny, as I watch you there,—
For all your wealth of loosened hair,
Your silk ungirdled and unlac'd
And warm sweets open to the waist,
50 All golden in the lamplight's gleam,—
You know not what a book you seem,
Half-read by lightning in a dream!
How should you know, my Jenny? Nay,
And I should be ashamed to say:—
55 Poor beauty, so well worth a kiss!
But while my thought runs on like this
With wasteful whims more than enough,
I wonder what you're thinking of.

If of myself you think at all,
60 What is the thought?—conjectural
On sorry matters best unsolved?—
Or inly is each grace revolved
To fit me with a lure?—or (sad
To think!) perhaps you're merely glad
65 That I'm not drunk or ruffianly
And let you rest upon my knee.

For sometimes, were the truth confess'd,
You're thankful for a little rest,—

Glad from the crush to rest within,
From the heart-sickness and the din
Where envy's voice at virtue's pitch
Mocks you because your gown is rich;
And from the pale girl's dumb rebuke,
Whose ill-clad grace and toil-worn look
Proclaim the strength that keeps her weak,
And other nights than yours bespeak;
And from the wise unchildish elf,
To schoolmate lesser than himself
Pointing you out, what thing you are:—
Yes, from the daily jeer and jar,
From shame and shame's outbraving too,
Is rest not sometimes sweet to you?—
But most from the hatefulness of man,
Who spares not to end what he began,
Whose acts are ill and his speech ill,
Who, having used you at his will,
Thrusts you aside, as when I dine
I serve the dishes and the wine.

Well, handsome Jenny mine, sit up:
I've filled our glasses, let us sup,
And do not let me think of you,
Lest shame of yours suffice for two.
What, still so tired? Well, well then, keep
Your head there, so you do not sleep;
But that the weariness may pass
And leave you merry, take this glass.
Ah! lazy lily hand, more bless'd
If ne'er in rings it had been dress'd
Nor ever by a glove conceal'd!

Behold the lilies of the field,
They toil not neither do they spin;
(So doth the ancient text begin,—
Not of such rest as one of these
Can share). Another rest and ease
Along each summer-sated path
From its new lord the garden hath,
Than that whose spring in blessings ran
Which praised the bounteous husbandman,
Ere yet, in days of hankering breath,
The lilies sickened unto death.

What, Jenny, are your lilies dead?
Aye, and the snow-white leaves are spread
Like winter on the garden-bed.

But you had roses left in May,—
115 They were not gone too. Jenny, nay,
But must your roses die, and those
Their purfled buds that should unclose?
Even so; the leaves are curled apart,
Still red as from the broken heart,
120 And here's the naked stem of thorns.

Nay, nay, mere words. Here nothing warns
As yet of winter. Sickness here
Or want alone could waken fear,—
Nothing but passion wrings a tear.
125 Except when there may rise unsought
Haply at times a passing thought
Of the old days which seem to be
Much older than any history
That is written in any book;
130 When she would lie in fields and look
Along the ground through the blown grass,
And wonder where the city was,
Far out of sight, whose broil and bale
They told her then for a child's tale.

135 Jenny, you know the city now.
A child can tell the tale there, how
Some things which are not yet enroll'd
In market-lists are bought and sold
Even till the early Sunday light,
140 When Saturday night is market-night
Everywhere, be it dry or wet,
And market-night in the Haymarket.
Our learned London children know,
Poor Jenny, all your pride and woe;
145 Have seen your lifted silken skirt
Advertise dainties through the dirt;
Have seen your coach-wheels splash rebuke
On virtue; and have learned your look
When, wealth and health slipped past, you stare
150 Along the streets alone, and there,
Round the long park, across the bridge,
The cold lamps at the pavement's edge
Wind on together and apart,
A fiery serpent for your heart.

155 Let the thoughts pass, an empty cloud!
Suppose I were to think aloud,—
What if to her all this were said?
Why, as a volume seldom read

102

Being opened halfway shuts again,
160   So might the pages of her brain
Be parted at such words, and thence
Close back upon the dusty sense.
For is there hue or shape defin'd
165   In Jenny's desecrated mind,
Where all contagious currents meet,
A Lethe of the middle street?
Nay, it reflects not any face,
Nor sound is in its sluggish pace,
170   But as they coil those eddies clot,
And night and day remember not.

Why, Jenny, you're asleep at last!—
Asleep, poor Jenny, hard and fast,—
So young and soft and tired; so fair,
With chin thus nestled in your hair,
175   Mouth quiet, eyelids almost blue
As if some sky of dreams shone through!

Just as another woman sleeps!
Enough to throw one's thoughts in heaps
Of doubt and horror,—what to say
180   Or think,—this awful secret sway,
The potter's power over the clay!
Of the same lump (it has been said)
For honour and dishonour made,
Two sister vessels. Here is one.

185   My cousin Nell is fond of fun,
And fond of dress, and change, and praise,
So mere a woman in her ways:
And if her sweet eyes rich in youth
Are like her lips that tell the truth,
190   My cousin Nell is fond of love.
And she's the girl I'm proudest of.
Who does not prize her, guard her well?
The love of change, in cousin Nell,
Shall find the best and hold it dear:
195   The unconquered mirth turn quieter
Not through her own, through others' woe:
The conscious pride of beauty glow
Beside another's pride in her,
One little part of all they share.
200   For Love himself shall ripen these
In a kind soil to just increase
Through years of fertilizing peace.

Of the same lump (as it is said)
For honour and dishonour made,
205   Two sister vessels. Here is one.

It makes a goblin of the sun.

So pure,—so fall'n! How dare to think
Of the first common kindred link?
Yet, Jenny, till the world shall burn
210   It seems that all things take their turn;
And who shall say but this fair tree
May need, in changes that may be,
Your children's children's charity?
Scorned then, no doubt, as you are scorn'd!
215   Shall no man hold his pride forewarn'd
Till in the end, the Day of Days,
At Judgment, one of his own race,
As frail and lost as you, shall rise,—
His daughter, with his mother's eyes?

220   How Jenny's clock ticks on the shelf!
Might not the dial scorn itself
That has such hours to register?
Yet as to me, even so to her
Are golden sun and silver moon,
225   In daily largesse of earth's boon,
Counted for life-coins to one tune.
And if, as blindfold fates are toss'd,
Through some one man this life be lost,
Shall soul not somehow pay for soul?

230   Fair shines the gilded aureole
In which our highest painters place
Some living woman's simple face.
And the stilled features thus descried
As Jenny's long throat droops aside,—
235   The shadows where the cheeks are thin,
And pure wide curve from ear to chin,—
With Raffael's, Leonardo's hand
To show them to men's souls, might stand,
Whole ages long, the whole world through,
240   For preachings of what God can do.
What has man done here? How atone,
Great God, for this which man has done?
And for the body and soul which by
Man's pitiless doom must now comply
245   With lifelong hell, what lullaby

Of sweet forgetful second birth
Remains? All dark. No sign on earth
What measure of God's rest endows
The many mansions of his house.

250   If but a woman's heart might see
Such erring heart unerringly
For once! But that can never be.

Like a rose shut in a book
In which pure women may not look,
255   For its base pages claim control
To crush the flower within the soul;
Where through each dead rose-leaf that clings,
Pale as transparent Psyche-wings,
To the vile text, are traced such things
260   As might make lady's cheek indeed
More than a living rose to read;
So nought save foolish foulness may
Watch with hard eyes the sure decay;
And so the life-blood of this rose,
265   Puddled with shameful knowledge, flows
Through leaves no chaste hand may unclose:
Yet still it keeps such faded show
Of when 'twas gathered long ago,
That the crushed petals' lovely grain,
270   The sweetness of the sanguine stain,
Seen of a woman's eyes, must make
Her pitiful heart, so prone to ache,
Love roses better for its sake:—
Only that this can never be:—
275   Even so unto her sex is she.

Yet, Jenny, looking long at you,
The woman almost fades from view.
A cipher of man's changeless sum
Of lust, past, present, and to come,
280   Is left. A riddle that one shrinks
To challenge from the scornful sphinx.

Like a toad within a stone
Seated while Time crumbles on;
Which sits there since the earth was curs'd
285   For Man's transgression at the first;
Which, living through all centuries,
Not once has seen the sun arise;
Whose life, to its cold circle charmed,
The earth's whole summers have not warmed;

290   Which always—whitherso the stone
Be flung—sits there, deaf, blind, alone;—
Aye, and shall not be driven out
Till that which shuts him round about
Break at the very Master's stroke,
295   And the dust thereof vanish as smoke,
And the seed of Man vanish as dust:—
Even so within this world is Lust.

Come, come, what use in thoughts like this?
Poor little Jenny, good to kiss,—
300   You'd not believe by what strange roads
Thought travels, when your beauty goads
A man to-night to think of toads!
Jenny, wake up . . . Why, there's the dawn!

And there's an early waggon drawn
305   To market, and some sheep that jog
Bleating before a barking dog;
And the old streets come peering through
Another night that London knew;
And all as ghostlike as the lamps.

310   So on the wings of day decamps
My last night's frolic. Glooms begin
To shiver off as lights creep in
Past the gauze curtains half drawn-to,
And the lamp's doubled shade grows blue,—
315   Your lamp, my Jenny, kept alight,
Like a wise virgin's, all one night!
And in the alcove coolly spread
Glimmers with dawn your empty bed;
And yonder your fair face I see
320   Reflected lying on my knee,
Where teems with first foreshadowings
Your pier-glass scrawled with diamond rings
And on your bosom all night worn
Yesterday's rose now droops forlorn,
325   But dies not yet this summer morn.

And now without, as if some word
Had called upon them that they heard,
The London sparrows far and nigh
Clamour together suddenly;
330   And Jenny's cage-bird grown awake
Here in their song his part must take,
Because here too the day doth break.

And somehow in myself the dawn
Among stirred clouds and veils withdrawn
335 Strikes greyly on her. Let her sleep.
But will it wake her if I heap
These cushions thus beneath her head
Where my knee was? No,—there's your bed,
My Jenny, while you dream. And there
340 I lay among your golden hair
Perhaps the subject of your dreams,
These golden coins.
                                   For still one deems
That Jenny's flattering sleep confers
New magic on the magic purse,—
345 Grim web, how clogged with shrivelled flies!
Between the threads fine fumes arise
And shape their pictures in the brain.
There roll no streets in glare and rain,
Nor flagrant man-swine whets his tusk;
350 But delicately sighs in musk
The homage of the dim boudoir;
Or like a palpitating star
Thrilled into song, the opera-night
Breathes faint in the quick pulse of light;
355 Or at the carriage-window shine
Rich wares for choice; or, free to dine,
Whirls through its hour of health (divine
For her) the concourse of the Park.
And though in the discounted dark
360 Her functions there and here are one,
Beneath the lamps and in the sun
There reigns at least the acknowledged belle
Apparelled beyond parallel.
Ah Jenny, yes, we know your dreams.

365 For even the Paphian Venus seems
A goddess o'er the realms of love,
When silver-shrined in shadowy grove:
Aye, or let offerings nicely plac'd
But hide Priapus to the waist,
370 And whoso looks on him shall see
An eligible deity.

Why, Jenny, waking here alone
May help you to remember one,
Though all the memory's long outworn
375 Of many a double-pillowed morn.
I think I see you when you wake,
And rub your eyes for me, and shake

My gold, in rising, from your hair,
A Danaë for a moment there.

380   Jenny, my love rang true! for still
Love at first sight is vague, until
That tinkling makes him audible.

And must I mock you to the last,
Ashamed of my own shame,—aghast
385   Because some thoughts not born amiss
Rose at a poor fair face like this?
Well, of such thoughts so much I know:
In my life, as in hers, they show,
By a far gleam which I may near,
390   A dark path I can strive to clear.

Only one kiss. Good-bye, my dear.

THE PARIS RAILWAY-STATION

In France, (to baffle thieves and murderers)
A journey takes two days of passport work
At least. The plan's sometimes a tedious one,
But bears its fruit. Because, the other day,
5   In passing by the Morgue, we saw a man
(The thing is common, and we never should
Have known of it, only we passed that way)
Who had been stabbed and tumbled in the Seine,
Where he had stayed some days. The face was black,
10   And, like a negro's, swollen; all the flesh
Had furred, and broken into a green mould.

Now, very likely, he who did the job
Was standing among those who stood with us,
To look upon the corpse. You fancy him—
15   Smoking an early pipe, and watching, as
An artist, the effect of his last work.
This always if it had not struck him that
'Twere best to leave while yet the body took
Its crust of rot beneath the Seine. It may:
20   But, if it did not, he can now remain
Without much fear. *Only*, if he should want
To travel, and have not his passport yet,
(Deep dogs these French police!) he may be caught.

Therefore you see (lest, being murderers,
25 We should not have the sense to go before
The thing were known, or to stay afterwards)
There is good reason why—having resolved
To start for Belgium—we were kept three days
To learn about the passports first, then do
30 As we had learned. This notwithstanding, in
The fulness of the time 'tis come to pass.

SUDDEN LIGHT

I have been here before,
But when or how I cannot tell:
I know the grass beyond the door,
The sweet keen smell,
5 The sighing sound, the lights around the shore.

You have been mine before,—
How long ago I may not know:
But just when at that swallow's soar
Your neck turned so,
10 Some veil did fall,—I knew it all of yore.

Has this been thus before?
And shall not thus time's eddying flight
Still with our lives our love restore
In death's despite,
15 And day and night yield one delight once more?

ALAS, SO LONG!

Ah! dear one, we were young so long,
It seemed that youth would never go,
For skies and trees were ever in song
And water in singing flow
5 In the days we never again shall know.
Alas, so long!
Ah! then was it all Spring weather?
Nay but we were young and together.

Ah! dear one, I've been old so long,
10 It seems that age is loth to part,
Though days and years have never a song,
And oh! have they still the art

That warmed the pulses of heart to heart?
　　　Alas, so long!
15　　　Ah! then was it all Spring weather?
　　　Nay, but we were young and together.

Ah! dear one, you've been dead so long,—
　　　How long until we meet again,
Where hours may never lose their song
20　　　Nor flowers forget the rain
In glad noonlight that never shall wane?
　　　Alas, so long!
　　　Ah! shall it be then Spring weather,
　　　And ah! shall we be young together?

THE WOODSPURGE

The wind flapped loose, the wind was still,
Shaken out dead from tree and hill:
I had walked on at the wind's will,—
I sat now, for the wind was still.

5　　Between my knees my forehead was,—
My lips, drawn in, said not Alas!
My hair was over in the grass,
My naked ears heard the day pass.

My eyes, wide open, had the run
10　　Of some ten weeds to fix upon;
Among those few, out of the sun,
The woodspurge flowered, three cups in one.

From perfect grief there need not be
Wisdom or even memory:
15　　One thing then learnt remains to me,—
The woodspurge has a cup of three.

AN OLD SONG ENDED

'*How should I your true love know*
　　From another one?'
'*By his cockle-hat and staff*
　　And his sandal-shoon.'

5   'And what signs have told you now
      That he hastens home?'
    'Lo! the spring is nearly gone,
      He is nearly come.'

    'For a token is there nought,
10   Say, that he should bring?'
    'He will bear a ring I gave
      And another ring.'

    'How may I, when he shall ask,
      Tell him who lies there?'
15   'Nay, but leave my face unveiled
      And unbound my hair.'

    'Can you say to me some word
      I shall say to him?'
    'Say I'm looking in his eyes
20   Though my eyes are dim.'

From THE HOUSE OF LIFE

Sonnet XXXIV

THE DARK GLASS

Not I myself know all my love for thee:
  How should I reach so far, who cannot weigh
  To-morrow's dower by gage of yesterday?
Shall birth and death, and all dark names that be
5 As doors and windows bared to some loud sea,
  Lash deaf mine ears and blind my face with spray;
  And shall my sense pierce love,—the last relay
And ultimate outpost of eternity?

Lo! what am I to Love, the lord of all?
10 One murmuring shell he gathers from the sand,—
  One little heart-flame sheltered in his hand.
Yet through thine eyes he grants me clearest call
And veriest touch of powers primordial
  That any hour-girt life may understand.

Sonnet XL

SEVERED SELVES

Two separate divided silences,
    Which, brought together, would find loving voice;
    Two glances which together would rejoice
In love, now lost like stars beyond dark trees;
5 Two hands apart whose touch alone gives ease;
    Two bosoms which, heart-shrined with mutual flame,
    Would, meeting in one clasp, be made the same;
Two souls, the shores wave-mocked of sundering seas:—

Such are we now. Ah! may our hope forecast
10   Indeed one hour again, when on this stream
    Of darkened love once more the light shall gleam?—
An hour how slow to come, how quickly past,—
Which blooms and fades, and only leaves at last,
    Faint as shed flowers, the attenuated dream.

Sonnet LXXXIII

BARREN SPRING

Once more the changed year's turning wheel returns:
    And as a girl sails balanced in the wind,
    And now before and now again behind
Stoops as it swoops, with cheek that laughs and burns,—
5 So Spring comes merry towards me here, but earns
    No answering smile from me, whose life is twin'd
    With the dead boughs that winter still must bind,
And whom to-day the Spring no more concerns.

Behold, this crocus is a withering flame;
10   This snowdrop, snow; this apple-blossom's part
    To breed the fruit that breeds the serpent's art.
Nay, for these Spring-flowers, turn thy face from them,
Nor stay till on the year's last lily-stem
    The white cup shrivels round the golden heart.

Sonnet XCVII

A SUPERSCRIPTION

Look in my face; my name is Might-have-been;
    I am also called No-more, Too-late, Farewell;
    Unto thine ear I hold the dead-sea shell
Cast up thy Life's foam-fretted feet between;
5 Unto thine eyes the glass where that is seen
    Which had Life's form and Love's, but by my spell
    Is now a shaken shadow intolerable,
Of ultimate things unuttered the frail screen.

Mark me, how still I am! But should there dart
10 One moment through thy soul the soft surprise
    Of that winged Peace which lulls the breath of sighs,—
Then shalt thou see me smile, and turn apart
Thy visage to mine ambush at thy heart
    Sleepless with cold commemorative eyes.

Christina Rossetti

Christina Rossetti (1830–94), the sister of Dante Gabriel, led an uneventful life. She never married, although she was at one time engaged to James Collinson, one of the Pre-Raphaelite Brotherhood. Christina was a devout Anglican, and this prevented her from accepting Collinson, who was a Roman Catholic: he decided to become an Anglican and was accepted, but then turned back to Roman Catholicism, and the engagement was broken off for good. Later C. B. Cayley, another suitor, was rejected because he was an agnostic. In later years Christina became increasingly devout and increasingly eccentric. Her poetry is dominated by her religion, particularly in the later years; at its best it possesses a delicacy of feeling and a fineness of touch which are admirable.

GOBLIN MARKET

Morning and evening
Maids heard the goblins cry:
'Come buy our orchard fruits,
Come buy, come buy:
5 Apples and quinces,
Lemons and oranges,
Plump unpecked cherries,
Melons and raspberries,
Bloom-down-cheeked peaches,
10 Swart-headed mulberries,
Wild free-born cranberries,
Crab-apples, dewberries,
Pine-apples, blackberries,
Apricots, strawberries;—
15 All ripe together
In summer weather,—
Morns that pass by,
Fair eves that fly;
Come buy, come buy:
20 Our grapes fresh from the vine,
Pomegranates full and fine,
Dates and sharp bullaces,
Rare pears and greengages,

Damsons and bilberries,
25 Taste them and try:
Currants and gooseberries,
Bright-fire-like barberries,
Figs to fill your mouth,
Citrons from the South,
30 Sweet to tongue and sound to eye;
Come buy, come buy.'

Evening by evening
Among the brookside rushes,
Laura bowed her head to hear,
35 Lizzie veiled her blushes:
Crouching close together
In the cooling weather,
With clasping arms and cautioning lips,
With tingling cheeks and finger tips.
40 'Lie close,' Laura said,
Pricking up her golden head:
'We must not look at goblin men,
We must not buy their fruits:
Who knows upon what soil they fed
45 Their hungry thirsty roots?'
'Come buy,' call the goblins
Hobbling down the glen.
'Oh,' cried Lizzie, 'Laura, Laura,
You should not peep at goblin men.'
50 Lizzie covered up her eyes,
Covered close lest they should look;
Laura reared her glossy head,
And whispered like the restless brook:
'Look, Lizzie, look, Lizzie,
55 Down the glen tramp little men.
One hauls a basket,
One bears a plate,
One lugs a golden dish
Of many pounds weight.
60 How fair the vine must grow
Whose grapes are so luscious;
How warm the wind must blow
Through those fruit bushes.'
'No,' said Lizzie: 'No, no, no;
65 Their offers should not charm us,
Their evil gifts would harm us.'
She thrust a dimpled finger
In each ear, shut eyes and ran:
Curious Laura chose to linger
70 Wondering at each merchant man.

One had a cat's face,
One whisked a tail,
One tramped at a rat's pace,
One crawled like a snail,
75 One like a wombat prowled obtuse and furry,
One like a ratel tumbled hurry skurry.
She heard a voice like voice of doves
Cooing all together:
They sounded kind and full of loves
80 In the pleasant weather.

Laura stretched her gleaming neck
Like a rush-imbedded swan,
Like a lily from the beck,
Like a moonlit poplar branch,
85 Like a vessel at the launch
When its last restraint is gone.

Backwards up the mossy glen
Turned and trooped the goblin men,
With their shrill repeated cry,
90 'Come buy, come buy.'
When they reached where Laura was
They stood stock still upon the moss,
Leering at each other,
Brother with queer brother;
95 Signalling each other,
Brother with sly brother.
One set his basket down,
One reared his plate;
One began to weave a crown
100 Of tendrils, leaves, and rough nuts brown
(Men sell not such in any town);
One heaved the golden weight
Of dish and fruit to offer her:
'Come buy, come buy,' was still their cry.
105 Laura stared but did not stir,
Longed but had no money:
The whisk-tailed merchant bade her taste
In tones as smooth as honey,
The cat-faced purr'd,
110 The rat-paced spoke a word
Of welcome, and the snail-paced even was heard;
One parrot-voiced and jolly
Cried 'Pretty Goblin' still for 'Pretty Polly;'—
One whistled like a bird.

115 But sweet-tooth Laura spoke in haste:

116

'Good Folk, I have no coin;
To take were to purloin:
I have no copper in my purse,
I have no silver either,
120 And all my gold is on the furze
That shakes in windy weather
Above the rusty heather.'
'You have much gold upon your head,'
They answered all together:
125 'Buy from us with a golden curl.'
She clipped a precious golden lock,
She dropped a tear more rare than pearl,
Then sucked their fruit globes fair or red:
Sweeter than honey from the rock,
130 Stronger than man-rejoicing wine,
Clearer than water flowed that juice;
She never tasted such before.
How should it cloy with length of use?
She sucked and sucked and sucked the more
135 Fruits which that unknown orchard bore;
She sucked until her lips were sore;
Then flung the emptied rinds away
But gathered up one kernel stone,
And knew not was it night or day
140 As she turned home alone.

Lizzie met her at the gate
Full of wise upbraidings:
'Dear, you should not stay so late,
Twilight is not good for maidens;
145 Should not loiter in the glen
In the haunts of goblin men.
Do you not remember Jeanie,
How she met them in the moonlight,
Took their gifts both choice and many,
150 Ate their fruits and wore their flowers
Plucked from bowers
Where summer ripens at all hours?
But ever in the noonlight
She pined and pined away;
155 Sought them by night and day,
Found them no more, but dwindled and grew grey;
Then fell with the first snow,
While to this day no grass will grow
Where she lies low:
160 I planted daisies there a year ago
That never blow.
You should not loiter so.'

'Nay, hush,' said Laura:
'Nay, hush, my sister:
165   I ate and ate my fill,
Yet my mouth waters still;
To-morrow night I will
Buy more;' and kissed her:
'Have done with sorrow;
170   I'll bring you plums to-morrow
Fresh on their mother twigs,
Cherries worth getting;
You cannot think what figs
My teeth have met in,
175   What melons icy-cold
Piled on a dish of gold
Too huge for me to hold,
What peaches with a velvet nap,
Pellucid grapes without one seed:
180   Odorous indeed must be the mead
Whereon they grow, and pure the wave they drink
With lilies at the brink,
And sugar-sweet their sap.'

Golden head by golden head,
185   Like two pigeons in one nest
Folded in each other's wings,
They lay down in their curtained bed:
Like two blossoms on one stem,
Like two flakes of new-fall'n snow,
190   Like two wands of ivory
Tipped with gold for awful kings.
Moon and stars gazed in at them,
Wind sang to them lullaby,
Lumbering owls forebore to fly,
195   Not a bat flapped to and fro
Round their rest:
Cheek to cheek and breast to breast
Locked together in one nest.

Early in the morning
200   When the first cock crowed his warning,
Neat like bees, as sweet and busy,
Laura rose with Lizzie:
Fetched in honey, milked the cows,
Aired and set to rights the house,
205   Kneaded cakes of whitest wheat,
Cakes for dainty mouths to eat,
Next churned butter, whipped up cream,
Fed their poultry, sat and sewed;

Talked as modest maidens should:
210 Lizzie with an open heart,
Laura in an absent dream,
One content, one sick in part;
One warbling for the mere bright day's delight,
One longing for the night.

215 At length slow evening came:
They went with pitchers to the reedy brook;
Lizzie most placid in her look,
Laura most like a leaping flame.
They drew the gurgling water from its deep;
220 Lizzie plucked purple and rich golden flags,
Then turning homeward said: 'The sunset flushes
Those furthest loftiest crags;
Come, Laura, not another maiden lags.
No wilful squirrel wags,
225 The beasts and birds are fast asleep.'
But Laura loitered still among the rushes
And said the bank was steep.

And said the hour was early still,
The dew not fall'n, the wind not chill;
230 Listening ever, but not catching
The customary cry,
'Come buy, come buy,'
With its iterated jingle
Of sugar-baited words:
235 Not for all her watching
Once discerning even one goblin
Racing, whisking, tumbling, hobbling;
Let alone the herds
That used to tramp along the glen,
240 In groups or single,
Of brisk fruit-merchant men.

Till Lizzie urged, 'O Laura, come;
I hear the fruit-call, but I dare not look:
You should not loiter longer at this brook:
245 Come with me home.
The stars rise, the moon bends her arc,
Each glowworm winks her spark,
Let us get home before the night grows dark:
For clouds may gather
250 Though this is summer weather.
Put out the lights and drench us through;
Then if we lost our way what should we do?'

Laura turned cold as stone
To find her sister heard that cry alone,
255   That goblin cry,
'Come buy our fruits, come buy.'
Must she then buy no more such dainty fruit?
Must she no more such succous pasture find,
Gone deaf and blind?
260   Her tree of life drooped from the root:
She said not one word in her heart's sore ache;
But peering thro' the dimness, nought discerning,
Trudged home, her pitcher dripping all the way;
So crept to bed, and lay
265   Silent till Lizzie slept;
Then sat up in a passionate yearning,
And gnashed her teeth for baulked desire, and wept
As if her heart would break.

Day after day, night after night,
270   Laura kept watch in vain
In sullen silence of exceeding pain.
She never caught again the goblin cry:
'Come buy, come buy;'—
She never spied the goblin men
275   Hawking their fruits along the glen:
But when the noon waxed bright
Her hair grew thin and grey;
She dwindled, as the fair full moon doth turn
To swift decay and burn
280   Her fire away.

One day remembering her kernel-stone
She set it by a wall that faced the south;
Dewed it with tears, hoped for a root,
Watched for a waxing shoot,
285   But there came none;
It never saw the sun,
It never felt the trickling moisture run:
While with sunk eyes and faded mouth
She dreamed of melons, as a traveller sees
290   False waves in desert drouth
With shade of leaf-crowned trees,
And burns the thirstier in the sandful breeze.

She no more swept the house,
Tended the fowls or cows,
295   Fetched honey, kneaded cakes of wheat,
Brought water from the brook:
But sat down listless in the chimney-nook
And would not eat.

Tender Lizzie could not bear
300   To watch her sister's cankerous care
Yet not to share.
She night and morning
Caught the goblins' cry:
'Come buy our orchard fruits,
305   Come buy, come buy:'—
Beside the brook, along the glen,
She heard the tramp of goblin men,
The voice and stir
Poor Laura could not hear;
310   Longed to buy fruit to comfort her,
But feared to pay too dear.
She thought of Jeanie in her grave,
Who should have been a bride;
But who for joys brides hope to have
315   Fell sick and died
In her gay prime,
In earliest Winter time,
With the first glazing rime,
With the first snow-fall of crisp Winter time.

320   Till Laura dwindling
Seemed knocking at Death's door:
Then Lizzie weighed no more
Better and worse;
But put a silver penny in her purse,
325   Kissed Laura, crossed the heath with clumps of furze
At twilight, halted by the brook:
And for the first time in her life
Began to listen and look.

Laughed every goblin
330   When they spied her peeping:
Came towards her hobbling,
Flying, running, leaping,
Puffing and blowing,
Chuckling, clapping, crowing,
335   Clucking and gobbling,
Mopping and mowing,
Full of airs and graces,
Pulling wry faces,
Demure grimaces,
340   Cat-like and rat-like,
Ratel- and wombat-like,
Snail-paced in a hurry,
Parrot-voiced and whistler,
Helter skelter, hurry skurry,

345   Chattering like magpies,
                  Fluttering like pigeons,
                  Gliding like fishes,—
                  Hugged her and kissed her:
                  Squeezed and caressed her:
350   Stretched up their dishes,
                  Panniers, and plates:
                  'Look at our apples
                  Russet and dun,
                  Bob at our cherries,
355   Bite at our peaches,
                  Citrons and dates,
                  Grapes for the asking,
                  Pears red with basking
                  Out in the sun,
360   Plums on their twigs;
                  Pluck them and suck them,
                  Pomegranates, figs.'—

                  'Good folk,' said Lizzie,
                  Mindful of Jeanie:
365   'Give me much and many:'—

                  Held out her apron,
                  Tossed them her penny.
                  'Nay, take a seat with us,
                  Honour and eat with us,'
370   They answered grinning:
                  'Our feast is but beginning.
                  Night yet is early,
                  Warm and dew-pearly,
                  Wakeful and starry:
375   Such fruits as these
                  No man can carry;
                  Half their bloom would fly,
                  Half their dew would dry,
                  Half their flavour would pass by.
380   Sit down and feast with us,
                  Be welcome guest with us,
                  Cheer you and rest with us.'—
                  'Thank you,' said Lizzie: 'But one waits
                  At home alone for me:
385   So without further parleying,
                  If you will not sell me any
                  Of your fruits though much and many,
                  Give me back my silver penny
                  I tossed you for a fee.'—
390   They began to scratch their pates,

No longer wagging, purring,
But visibly demurring,
Grunting and snarling.
One called her proud,
395   Cross-grained, uncivil;
Their tones waxed loud,
Their looks were evil.
Lashing their tails
They trod and hustled her,
400   Elbowed and jostled her,
Clawed with their nails,
Barking, mewing, hissing, mocking,
Tore her gown and soiled her stocking,
Twitched her hair out by the roots,
405   Stamped upon her tender feet,
Held her hands and squeezed their fruits
Against her mouth to make her eat.

White and golden Lizzie stood,
Like a lily in a flood,—
410   Like a rock of blue-veined stone
Lashed by tides obstreperously,—
Like a beacon left alone
In a hoary roaring sea.
Sending up a golden fire,—
415   Like a fruit-crowned orange-tree
White with blossoms honey-sweet
Sore beset by wasp and bee,—
Like a royal virgin town
Topped with gilded dome and spire
420   Close beleaguered by a fleet
Mad to tug her standard down.

One may lead a horse to water,
Twenty cannot make him drink.
Though the goblins cuffed and caught her,
425   Coaxed and fought her,
Bullied and besought her,
Scratched her, pinched her black as ink,
Kicked and knocked her,
Mauled and mocked her,
430   Lizzie uttered not a word;
Would not open lip from lip
Lest they should cram a mouthful in:
But laughed in heart to feel the drip
Of juice that syrupped all her face,
435   And lodged in dimples of her chin,
And streaked her neck which quaked like curd.

At last the evil people,
Worn out by her resistance,
Flung back her penny, kicked their fruit
440　Along whichever road they took,
Not leaving root or stone or shoot;
Some writhed into the ground,
Some dived into the brook
With ring and ripple,
445　Some scudded on the gale without a sound,
Some vanished in the distance.

In a smart, ache, tingle,
Lizzie went her way;
Knew not was it night or day;
450　Sprang up the bank, tore thro' the furze,
Threaded copse and dingle,
And heard her penny jingle
Bouncing in her purse,—
Its bounce was music to her ear.
455　She ran and ran
As if she feared some goblin man
Dogged her with gibe or curse
Or something worse:
But not one goblin skurried after,
460　Nor was she pricked by fear;
The kind heart made her windy-paced
That urged her home quite out of breath with haste
And inward laughter.

She cried, 'Laura,' up the garden,
465　'Did you miss me?
Come and kiss me.
Never mind my bruises,
Hug me, kiss me, suck my juices
Squeezed from goblin fruits for you,
470　Goblin pulp and goblin dew.
Eat me, drink me, love me;
Laura, make much of me;
For your sake I have braved the glen
And had to do with goblin merchant men.'

475　Laura started from her chair,
Flung her arms up in the air,
Clutched her hair:
'Lizzie, Lizzie, have you tasted
For my sake the fruit forbidden?
480　Must your light like mine be hidden,

Your young life like mine be wasted,
Undone in mine undoing,
And ruined in my ruin,
Thirsty, cankered, goblin-ridden?'—
485   She clung about her sister,
Kissed and kissed and kissed her:
Tears once again
Refreshed her shrunken eyes,
Dropping like rain
490   After long sultry drouth;
Shaking with aguish fear, and pain,
She kissed and kissed her with a hungry mouth.

Her lips began to scorch,
That juice was wormwood to her tongue,
495   She loathed the feast:
Writhing as one possessed she leaped and sung,
Rent all her robe, and wrung
Her hands in lamentable haste,
And beat her breast.
500   Her locks streamed like the torch
Borne by a racer at full speed,
Or like the mane of horses in their flight,
Or like an eagle when she stems the light
Straight toward the sun,
505   Or like a caged thing freed,
Or like a flying flag when armies run.

Swift fire spread through her veins, knocked at her heart,
Met the fire smouldering there
And overbore its lesser flame;
510   She gorged on bitterness without a name:
Ah! fool, to choose such part
Of soul-consuming care!
Sense failed in the mortal strife:
Like the watch-tower of a town
515   Which an earthquake shatters down,
Like a lightning-stricken mast,
Like a wind-uprooted tree
Spun about,
Like a foam-topped waterspout
520   Cast down headlong in the sea,
She fell at last;
Pleasure past and anguish past,
Is it death or is it life?

Life out of death.
525   That night long Lizzie watched by her,

Counted her pulse's flagging stir,
Felt for her breath,
Held water to her lips, and cooled her face
With tears and fanning leaves:
530 But when the first birds chirped about their eaves,
And early reapers plodded to the place
Of golden sheaves,
And dew-wet grass
Bowed in the morning winds so brisk to pass,
535 And new buds with new day
Opened of cup-like lilies on the stream,
Laura awoke as from a dream,
Laughed in the innocent old way,
Hugged Lizzie but not twice or thrice;
540 Her gleaming locks showed not one thread of grey,
Her breath was sweet as May
And light danced in her eyes.

Days, weeks, months, years
Afterwards, when both were wives
545 With children of their own;
Their mother-hearts beset with fears,
Their lives bound up in tender lives;
Laura would call the little ones
And tell them of her early prime,
550 Those pleasant days long gone
Of not-returning time:
Would talk about the haunted glen,
The wicked, quaint fruit-merchant men,
Their fruits like honey to the throat
555 But poison in the blood;
(Men sell not such in any town):
Would tell them how her sister stood
In deadly peril to do her good,
And win the fiery antidote:
560 Then joining hands to little hands
Would bid them cling together,
'For there is no friend like a sister
In calm or stormy weather;
To cheer one on the tedious way,
565 To fetch one if one goes astray,
To lift one if one totters down,
To strengthen whilst one stands.'

REMEMBER

Remember me when I am gone away,
    Gone far away into the silent land;
    When you can no more hold me by the hand,
Nor I half turn to go yet turning stay.
5 Remember me when no more day by day
    You tell me of our future that you plann'd:
    Only remember me; you understand
It will be late to counsel then or pray.
Yet if you should forget me for a while
10   And afterwards remember, do not grieve:
    For if the darkness and corruption leave
    A vestige of the thoughts that once I had,
Better by far you should forget and smile
    Than that you should remember and be sad.

A BIRTHDAY

My heart is like a singing bird
    Whose nest is in a watered shoot:
My heart is like an apple-tree
    Whose boughs are bent with thickset fruit;
5 My heart is like a rainbow shell
    That paddles in a halcyon sea;
My heart is gladder than all these
    Because my love is come to me.

Raise me a dais of silk and down;
10   Hang it with vair and purple dyes;
Carve it in doves and pomegranates,
    And peacocks with a hundred eyes;
Work it in gold and silver grapes,
    In leaves and silver fleurs-de-lys;
15 Because the birthday of my life
    Is come, my love is come to me.

MAUDE CLARE

Out of the church she followed them
    With a lofty step and mien:
His bride was like a village maid,
    Maude Clare was like a queen.

127

5   'Son Thomas,' his lady mother said,
           With smiles, almost with tears:
        'May Nell and you but live as true
           As we have done for years;

        'Your father thirty years ago
10   Had just your tale to tell;
        But he was not so pale as you,
           Nor I so pale as Nell.'

        My lord was pale with inward strife,
           And Nell was pale with pride;
15   My lord gazed long on pale Maude Clare
           Or ever he kissed the bride.

        'Lo, I have brought my gift, my lord,
           Have brought my gift,' she said:
        'To bless the hearth, to bless the board,
20   To bless the marriage-bed.

        'Here's my half of the golden chain
           You wore about your neck,
        That day we waded ankle-deep
           For lilies in the beck.

25   'Here's my half of the faded leaves
           We plucked from budding bough,
        With feet amongst the lily leaves,—
           The lilies are budding now.'

        He strove to match her scorn with scorn,
30   He faltered in his place:
        'Lady,' he said,—'Maude Clare,' he said,—
           'Maude Clare':—and hid his face.

        She turned to Nell: 'My Lady Nell,
           I have a gift for you;
35   Though, were it fruit, the bloom were gone,
           Or, were it flowers, the dew.

        'Take my share of a fickle heart,
           Mine of a paltry love:
        Take it or leave it as you will,
40   I wash my hands thereof.'

        'And what you leave,' said Nell, 'I'll take,
           And what you spurn I'll wear;
        For he's my lord for better and worse,
           And him I love, Maude Clare.

45   'Yea though you're taller by the head,
           More wise, and much more fair,
       I'll love him till he loves me best—
           Me best of all, Maude Clare.'

ECHO

Come to me in the silence of the night;
      Come in the speaking silence of a dream:
Come with soft rounded cheeks and eyes as bright
        As sunlight on a stream;
5   Come back in tears,
O memory, hope, love of finished years.

Oh dream how sweet, too sweet, too bitter sweet,
      Whose wakening should have been in Paradise,
Where souls brimfull of love abide and meet;
10   Where thirsting longing eyes
          Watch the slow door
That opening, letting in, lets out no more.

Yet come to me in dreams, that I may live
      My very life again though cold in death:
15 Come back to me in dreams, that I may give
        Pulse for pulse, breath for breath:
          Speak low, lean low,
As long ago, my love, how long ago!

A DIRGE

Why were you born when the snow was falling?
You should have come to the cuckoo's calling,
Or when grapes are green in the cluster,
Or at least when lithe swallows muster
5   For their far off flying
        From summer dying.

Why did you die when the lambs were cropping?
You should have died at the apples' dropping,
When the grasshopper comes to trouble,
10 And the wheat-fields are sodden stubble,
        And all winds go sighing
        For sweet things dying.

CHRISTINA ROSSETTI

A FROG'S FATE

Contemptuous of his home beyond
The village and the village-pond,
A large-souled Frog who spurned each byeway
Hopped along the imperial highway.

5   Nor grunting pig nor barking dog
Could disconcert so great a Frog.
The morning dew was lingering yet,
His sides to cool, his tongue to wet:
The night-dew, when the night should come,
10   A travelled Frog would send him home.

Not so, alas! The wayside grass
Sees him no more: not so, alas!
A broad-wheeled waggon unawares
Ran him down, his joys, his cares.
15   From dying choke one feeble croak
The Frog's perpetual silence broke:—
'Ye buoyant Frogs, ye great and small,
Even I am mortal after all!
My road to fame turns out a wry way;
20   I perish on the hideous highway;
Oh for my old familiar byeway!'

The choking Frog sobbed and was gone;
The Waggoner strode whistling on.
Unconscious of the carnage done,
25   Whistling that Waggoner strode on—
Whistling (it may have happened so)
'A froggy would a-wooing go.'
A hypothetic frog trolled he,
Obtuse to a reality.

30   O rich and poor, O great and small,
Such oversights beset us all.
The mangled Frog abides incog,
The uninteresting actual frog:
The hypothetic frog alone
35   Is the one frog we dwell upon.

UP-HILL

Does the road wind up-hill all the way?
    Yes, to the very end.
Will the day's journey take the whole long day?
    From morn to night, my friend.

5   But is there for the night a resting-place?
    A roof for when the slow dark hours begin.
May not the darkness hide it from my face?
    You cannot miss that inn.

Shall I meet other wayfarers at night?
10   Those who have gone before.
Then must I knock, or call when just in sight?
    They will not keep you standing at that door.

Shall I find comfort, travel-sore and weak?
    Of labour you shall find the sum.
15   Will there be beds for me and all who seek?
    Yea, beds for all who come.

Alexander Smith

Of poor Scots parentage, Alexander Smith (1830–67) was a member of the 'Spasmodic' school of poets, who enjoyed a vogue in the 1840s and 1850s but are now largely forgotten. They wrote highly-coloured closet dramas, excessive in sentiment and free in metre, in which idealistic Hamlet-like heroes declared themselves at odds with a hostile and materialistic society. Tennyson's *Maud*, Clough's 'Dipsychus' and Meredith's *Modern Love* all show traces of their influence.

In his review 'Recent English Poetry' (1853), Clough singled out Smith's *Life Drama* (1853) for favourable comparison with Arnold's poetry, but 'Glasgow' is taken from Smith's best volume, *City Poems* (1857). Clough wrote approvingly of Smith's use of images 'drawn from the busy seat of industry' and Smith's poem successfully adapts traditional poetic language to express his awe at the fearful splendour and extent of the new industrial landscape.

GLASGOW

Sing, Poet, 'tis a merry world;
That cottage smoke is rolled and curled
    In sport, that every moss
Is happy, every inch of soil;—
5   Before *me* runs a road of toil
      With my grave cut across.
Sing, trailing showers and breezy downs—
I know the tragic hearts of towns.

City! I am true son of thine;
10   Ne'er dwelt I where great mornings shine
    Around the bleating pens;
Ne'er by the rivulets I strayed,
And ne'er upon my childhood weighed
    The silence of the glens.
15   Instead of shores where ocean beats,
I hear the ebb and flow of streets.

Black Labour draws his weary waves,
Into their secret-moaning caves;
 But with the morning light,
That sea again will overflow
With a long weary sound of woe,
 Again to faint in night.
Wave am I in that sea of woes,
Which, night and morning, ebbs and flows.

I dwelt within a gloomy court,
Wherein did never sunbeam sport;
 Yet there my heart was stirr'd.
My very blood did dance and thrill,
When on my narrow window-sill,
 Spring lighted like a bird.
Poor flowers—I watched them pine for weeks,
With leaves as pale as human cheeks.

Afar, one summer, I was borne;
Through golden vapours of the morn,
 I heard the hills of sheep:
I trod with a wild ecstasy
The bright fringe of the living sea:
 And on a ruined keep
I sat, and watched an endless plain
Blacken beneath the gloom of rain.

O fair the lightly sprinkled waste,
O'er which a laughing shower has raced!
 O fair the April shoots!
O fair the woods on summer days,
While a blue hyacinthine haze
 Is dreaming round the roots!
In thee, O City! I discern
Another beauty, sad and stern.

Draw thy fierce streams of blinding ore,
Smite on a thousand anvils, roar
 Down to the harbour-bars;
Smoulder in smoky sunsets, flare
On rainy nights, when street and square
 Lie empty to the stars.
From terrace proud to alley base
I know thee as my mother's face.

When sunset bathes thee in his gold,
In wreaths of bronze thy sides are rolled,

Thy smoke is dusky fire;
60 And, from the glory round thee poured,
A sunbeam like an angel's sword
Shivers upon a spire.
Thus have I watched thee, Terror! Dream!
While the blue Night crept up the stream.

65 The wild Train plunges in the hills,
He shrieks across the midnight rills;
Streams through the shifting glare,
The roar and flap of foundry fires,
That shake with light the sleeping shires;
70 And on the moorlands bare,
He sees afar a crown of light
Hang o'er thee in the hollow night.

At midnight, when thy suburbs lie
As silent as a noonday sky,
75 When larks with heat are mute,
I love to linger on thy bridge,
All lonely as a mountain ridge,
Disturbed but by my foot;
While the black lazy stream beneath,
80 Steals from its far-off wilds of heath.

And through thy heart, as through a dream,
Flows on that black disdainful stream;
All scornfully it flows,
Between the huddled gloom of masts,
85 Silent as pines unvexed by blasts—
'Tween lamps in streaming rows.
O wondrous sight! O stream of dread!
O long dark river of the dead!

Afar, the banner of the year
90 Unfurls: but dimly prisoned here,
'Tis only when I greet
A dropt rose lying in my way,
A butterfly that flutters gay
Athwart the noisy street,
95 I know the happy Summer smiles
Around thy suburbs, miles on miles.

'T were neither pæan now, nor dirge,
The flash and thunder of the surge

134

On flat sands wide and bare;
100   No haunting joy or anguish dwells
In the green light of sunny dells,
   Or in the starry air.
Alike to me the desert flower,
The rainbow laughing o'er the shower.

105   While o'er thy walls the darkness sails,
I lean against the churchyard rails;
   Up in the midnight towers
The belfried spire, the street is dead,
I hear in silence overhead
110   The clang of iron hours:
It moves me not—I know her tomb
Is yonder in the shapeless gloom.

All raptures of this mortal breath,
Solemnities of life and death,
115   Dwell in thy noise alone:
Of me thou hast become a part—
Some kindred with my human heart
      Lives in thy streets of stone;
For we have been familiar more
120   Than galley-slave and weary oar.

The beech is dipped in wine; the shower
Is burnished; on the swinging flower
      The latest bee doth sit.
The low sun stares through dust of gold,
125   And o'er the darkening heath and wold
      The large ghost-moth doth flit.
In every orchard Autumn stands,
With apples in his golden hands.

But all these sights and sounds are strange;
130   Then wherefore from thee should I range?
      Thou hast my kith and kin:
My childhood, youth, and manhood brave;
Thou hast that unforgotten grave
      Within thy central din.
135   A sacredness of love and death
Dwells in thy noise and smoky breath.

James Thomson

The son of a sailor, James Thomson (1834–82) was born at Port Glasgow but spent most of his childhood in a London orphanage. A career as an army schoolmaster was cut short in 1862, and for the rest of his life he led a precarious, bohemian existence as a clerk and journalist. His friendship with Charles Bradlaugh, the militant atheist, gave him the support of secularist circles in London, and it was in Bradlaugh's journal, the *National Reformer*, that 'The City of Dreadful Night' first appeared from March to May 1874. Two volumes of poetry were published in 1880 through the efforts of another friend, Bertram Dobell, the scholar and bookseller; but Thomson never became successful, and was never adopted by the Victorian literary establishment. Chronic alcoholism led finally to destitution and a wretched premature death in University College Hospital.

Thomson is often known as 'James Thomson ("B.V.")' to distinguish him from the eighteenth-century James Thomson, author of *The Seasons*. The initials 'B.V.' are taken from Thomson's pseudonym, Bysshe Vanolis, which is itself a tribute to two poets he admired, Shelley and Novalis.

'The City of Dreadful Night' occupies a unique position in Victorian poetry. Its value as a cultural document is uncontested, both as a statement of atheistic despair in a godless mechanistic universe, and (at a time when poets were conspicuously failing to meet the challenge of a mass industrial society) as a criticism of the anonymity of modern urban life. Its status as a poem is more precarious: critics have found its rhetoric crude, its generic and latinized diction ponderous, and its metrics monotonous. Nevertheless, it is a remarkable and individual work, which needs to be judged entire, rather than in the snippets which are usually anthologized.

THE CITY OF DREADFUL NIGHT

Per me si va nella città dolente.

DANTE

Poi di tanto adoprar, di tanti moti
D'ogni celeste, ogni terrena cosa,
Girando senza posa,
Per tornar sempre là donde son mosse;
Uso alcuno, alcun frutto
Indovinar non so.

136

Sola nel mondo eterna, a cui si volve
Ogni creata cosa,
In te, morte, si posa
Nostra ignuda natura;
Lieta no, ma sicura
Dell' antico dolor . . .
Però ch' esser beato
Nega ai mortali e nega a' morti il fato.

LEOPARDI

PROEM

Lo, thus, as prostrate, 'In the dust I write
    My heart's deep languor and my soul's sad tears.'
Yet why evoke the spectres of black night
    To blot the sunshine of exultant years?
5 Why disinter dead faith from mouldering hidden?
Why break the seals of mute despair unbidden,
    And wail life's discords into careless ears?

Because a cold rage seizes one at whiles
    To show the bitter old and wrinkled truth
10 Stripped naked of all vesture that beguiles,
    False dreams, false hopes, false masks and modes of youth;
Because it gives some sense of power and passion
In helpless impotence to try to fashion
    Our woe in living words howe'er uncouth.

15 Surely I write not for the hopeful young,
    Or those who deem their happiness of worth,
Or such as pasture and grow fat among
    The shows of life and feel nor doubt nor dearth,
Or pious spirits with a God above them
20 To sanctify and glorify and love them,
    Or sages who foresee a heaven on earth.

For none of these I write, and none of these
    Could read the writing if they deigned to try:
So may they flourish, in their due degrees,
25   On our sweet earth and in their unplaced sky.
If any cares for the weak words here written,
It must be some one desolate, Fate-smitten,
    Whose faith and hope are dead, and who would die.

Yes, here and there some weary wanderer
30   In that same city of tremendous night,
Will understand the speech, and feel a stir

Of fellowship in all-disastrous fight;
'I suffer mute and lonely, yet another
Uplifts his voice to let me know a brother
35   Travels the same wild paths though out of sight.'

O sad Fraternity, do I unfold
      Your dolorous mysteries shrouded from of yore?
Nay, be assured; no secret can be told
      To any who divined it not before:
40 None uninitiate by many a presage
Will comprehend the language of the message,
      Although proclaimed aloud for evermore.

I

The City is of Night; perchance of Death,
      But certainly of Night; for never there
Can come the lucid morning's fragrant breath
      After the dewy dawning's cold grey air;
5 The moon and stars may shine with scorn or pity;
The sun has never visited that city,
      For it dissolveth in the daylight fair.

Dissolveth like a dream of night away;
      Though present in distempered gloom of thought
10 And deadly weariness of heart all day.
      But when a dream night after night is brought
Throughout a week, and such weeks few or many
Recur each year for several years, can any
      Discern that dream from real life in aught?

15 For life is but a dream whose shapes return,
      Some frequently, some seldom, some by night
And some by day, some night and day: we learn,
      The while all change and many vanish quite,
In their recurrence with recurrent changes
20 A certain seeming order; where this ranges
      We count things real; such is memory's might.

A river girds the city west and south,
      The main north channel of a broad lagoon,
Regurging with the salt tides from the mouth;
25   Waste marshes shine and glister to the moon
For leagues, then moorland black, then stony ridges;
Great piers and causeways, many noble bridges,
      Connect the town and islet suburbs strewn.

138

Upon an easy slope it lies at large,
30   And scarcely overlaps the long curved crest
Which swells out two leagues from the river marge.
      A trackless wilderness rolls north and west,
Savannahs, savage woods, enormous mountains,
Bleak uplands, black ravines with torrent fountains;
35   And eastwards rolls the shipless sea's unrest.

The city is not ruinous, although
      Great ruins of an unremembered past,
With others of a few short years ago
      More sad, are found within its precincts vast.
40 The street-lamps always burn; but scarce a casement
In house or palace front from roof to basement
      Doth glow or gleam athwart the mirk air cast.

The street-lamps burn amidst the baleful glooms,
      Amidst the soundless solitudes immense
45 Of rangèd mansions dark and still as tombs.
      The silence which benumbs or strains the sense
Fulfils with awe the soul's despair unweeping:
Myriads of habitants are ever sleeping,
      Or dead, or fled from nameless pestilence!

50 Yet as in some necropolis you find
      Perchance one mourner to a thousand dead,
So there; worn faces that look deaf and blind
      Like tragic masks of stone. With weary tread,
Each wrapt in his own doom, they wander, wander,
55 Or sit foredone and desolately ponder
      Through sleepless hours with heavy drooping head.

Mature men chiefly, few in age or youth,
      A woman rarely, now and then a child:
A child! If here the heart turns sick with ruth
60   To see a little one from birth defiled,
Or lame or blind, as preordained to languish
Through youthless life, think how it bleeds with anguish
      To meet one erring in that homeless wild.

They often murmur to themselves, they speak
65   To one another seldom, for their woe
Broods maddening inwardly and scorns to wreak
      Itself abroad; and if at whiles it grow
To frenzy which must rave, none heeds the clamour,
Unless there waits some victim of like glamour,
70   To rave in turn, who lends attentive show.

The City is of Night, but not of Sleep;
　　There sweet sleep is not for the weary brain;
The pitiless hours like years and ages creep,
　　A night seems termless hell. This dreadful strain
75　Of thought and consciousness which never ceases,
　　Or which some moments' stupor but increases,
　　　　This, worse than woe, makes wretches there insane.

They leave all hope behind who enter there:
　　One certitude while sane they cannot leave,
80　One anodyne for torture and despair;
　　The certitude of Death, which no reprieve
Can put off long; and which, divinely tender,
But waits the outstretched hand to promptly render
　　　　That draught whose slumber nothing can bereave.

II

Because he seemed to walk with an intent
　　I followed him; who, shadowlike and frail,
Unswervingly though slowly onward went,
　　Regardless, wrapt in thought as in a veil:
5　Thus step for step with lonely sounding feet
We travelled many a long dim silent street.

At length he paused: a black mass in the gloom,
　　A tower that merged into the heavy sky;
Around, the huddled stones of grave and tomb:
10　Some old God's-acre now corruption's sty:
He murmured to himself with dull despair,
　　Here Faith died, poisoned by this charnel air.

Then turning to the right went on once more,
　　And travelled weary roads without suspense;
15　And reached at last a low wall's open door,
　　Whose villa gleamed beyond the foliage dense:
He gazed, and muttered with a hard despair,
Here Love died, stabbed by its own worshipped pair.

Then turning to the right resumed his march,
20　And travelled streets and lanes with wondrous strength,
Until on stooping through a narrow arch
　　We stood before a squalid house at length:
He gazed, and whispered with a cold despair,
Here Hope died, starved out in its utmost lair.

25　When he had spoken thus, before he stirred,
　　I spoke, perplexed by something in the signs
Of desolation I had seen and heard
　　In this drear pilgrimage to ruined shrines:

140

When Faith and Love and Hope are dead indeed,
30   Can Life still live? By what doth it proceed?

As whom his one intense thought overpowers,
    He answered coldly, Take a watch, erase
The signs and figures of the circling hours,
    Detach the hands, remove the dial-face;
35 The works proceed until run down; although
Bereft of purpose, void of use, still go.

Then turning to the right paced on again,
    And traversed squares and travelled streets whose glooms
Seemed more and more familiar to my ken;
40   And reached that sullen temple of the tombs;
And paused to murmur with the old despair,
Here Faith died, poisoned by this charnel air.

I ceased to follow, for the knot of doubt
    Was severed sharply with a cruel knife:
45 He circled thus for ever tracing out
    The series of the fraction left of Life;
Perpetual recurrence in the scope
Of but three terms, dead Faith, dead Love, dead Hope.

III

Although lamps burn along the silent streets,
    Even when moonlight silvers empty squares
The dark holds countless lanes and close retreats;
    But when the night its sphereless mantle wears
5 The open spaces yawn with gloom abysmal,
The sombre mansions loom immense and dismal,
    The lanes are black as subterranean lairs.

And soon the eye a strange new vision learns:
    The night remains for it as dark and dense,
10 Yet clearly in this darkness it discerns
    As in the daylight with its natural sense;
Perceives a shade in shadow not obscurely,
Pursues a stir of black in blackness surely,
    Sees spectres also in the gloom intense.

15 The ear, too, with the silence vast and deep
    Becomes familiar though unreconciled;
Hears breathings as of hidden life asleep,
    And muffled throbs as of pent passions wild,
Far murmurs, speech of pity or derision;
20 But all more dubious than the things of vision,
    So that it knows not when it is beguiled.

No time abates the first despair and awe,
　　But wonder ceases soon; the weirdest thing
Is felt least strange beneath the lawless law
25　　　Where Death-in-Life is the eternal king;
Crushed impotent beneath this reign of terror,
Dazed with such mysteries of woe and error,
　　The soul is too outworn for wondering.

IV

He stood alone within the spacious square
　　Declaiming from the central grassy mound,
With head uncovered and with streaming hair,
　　As if large multitudes were gathered round:
5　A stalwart shape, the gestures full of might,
The glances burning with unnatural light:—

As I came through the desert thus it was,
As I came through the desert: All was black,
In heaven no single star, on earth no track;
10　A brooding hush without a stir or note,
The air so thick it clotted in my throat;
And thus for hours; then some enormous things
Swooped past with savage cries and clanking wings:
　　But I strode on austere;
15　　　No hope could have no fear.

As I came through the desert thus it was,
As I came through the desert: Eyes of fire
Glared at me throbbing with a starved desire;
The hoarse and heavy and carnivorous breath
20　Was hot upon me from deep jaws of death;
Sharp claws, swift talons, fleshless fingers cold
Plucked at me from the bushes, tried to hold:
　　But I strode on austere;
　　　No hope could have no fear.

25　As I came through the desert thus it was,
As I came through the desert: Lo you, there,
That hillock burning with a brazen glare;
Those myriad dusky flames with points a-glow
Which writhed and hissed and darted to and fro;
30　A Sabbath of the Serpents, heaped pell-mell
For Devil's roll-call and some *fête* of Hell:
　　Yet I strode on austere;
　　　No hope could have no fear.

As I came through the desert thus it was,
35　As I came through the desert: Meteors ran
And crossed their javelins on the black sky-span;

142

The zenith opened to a gulf of flame,
The dreadful thunderbolts jarred earth's fixed frame;
The ground all heaved in waves of fire that surged
40 And weltered round me sole there unsubmerged:
Yet I strode on austere;
No hope could have no fear.

As I came through the desert thus it was,
As I came through the desert: Air once more,
45 And I was close upon a wild sea-shore;
Enormous cliffs arose on either hand,
The deep tide thundered up a league-broad strand;
White foambelts seethed there, wan spray swept and flew;
The sky broke, moon and stars and clouds and blue:
50 And I strode on austere;
No hope could have no fear.

As I came through the desert thus it was,
As I came through the desert: On the left
The sun arose and crowned a broad crag-cleft;
55 There stopped and burned out black, except a rim,
A bleeding eyeless socket, red and dim;
Whereon the moon fell suddenly south-west,
And stood above the right-hand cliffs at rest:
Still I strode on austere;
60 No hope could have no fear.

As I came through the desert thus it was,
As I came through the desert: From the right
A shape came slowly with a ruddy light;
A woman with a red lamp in her hand,
65 Bareheaded and barefooted on that strand;
O desolation moving with such grace!
O anguish with such beauty in thy face!
I fell as on my bier,
Hope travailed with such fear.

70 As I came through the desert thus it was,
As I came through the desert: I was twain,
Two selves distinct that cannot join again;
One stood apart and knew but could not stir,
And watched the other stark in swoon and her;
75 And she came on, and never turned aside,
Between such sun and moon and roaring tide:
And as she came more near
My soul grew mad with fear.

As I came through the desert thus it was,
80   As I came through the desert: Hell is mild
And piteous matched with that accursèd wild;
A large black sign was on her breast that bowed,
A broad black band ran down her snow-white shroud;
That lamp she held was her own burning heart,
85   Whose blood-drops trickled step by step apart:
      The mystery was clear;
      Mad rage had swallowed fear.

As I came through the desert thus it was,
As I came through the desert: By the sea
90   She knelt and bent above that senseless me;
Those lamp-drops fell upon my white brow there,
She tried to cleanse them with her tears and hair;
She murmured words of pity, love, and woe,
She heeded not the level rushing flow:
95   And mad with rage and fear,
      I stood stonebound so near.

As I came through the desert thus it was,
As I came through the desert: When the tide
Swept up to her there kneeling by my side,
100   She clasped that corpse-like me, and they were borne
Away, and this vile me was left forlorn;
I know the whole sea cannot quench that heart,
Or cleanse that brow, or wash those two apart:
      They love; their doom is drear,
105   Yet they nor hope nor fear;
      But I, what do I here?

V

How he arrives there none can clearly know;
    Athwart the mountains and immense wild tracts,
Or flung a waif upon that vast sea-flow,
    Or down the river's boiling cataracts:
5   To reach it is as dying fever-stricken;
To leave it, slow faint birth intense pangs quicken;
    And memory swoons in both the tragic acts.

But being there one feels a citizen;
    Escape seems hopeless to the heart forlorn:
10   Can Death-in-Life be brought to life again?
    And yet release does come; there comes a morn
When he awakes from slumbering so sweetly
That all the world is changed for him completely,
    And he is verily as if new-born.

15 He scarcely can believe the blissful change,
        He weeps perchance who wept not while accurst;
    Never again will he approach the range
        Infected by that evil spell now burst:
    Poor wretch! who once hath paced that dolent city
20 Shall pace it often, doomed beyond all pity,
        With horror ever deepening from the first.

    Though he possess sweet babes and loving wife,
        A home of peace by loyal friendships cheered,
    And love them more than death or happy life,
25   They shall avail not; he must dree his weird;
    Renounce all blessings for that imprecation,
    Steal forth and haunt that builded desolation,
        Of woe and terrors and thick darkness reared.

VI

    I sat forlornly by the river-side,
        And watched the bridge-lamps glow like golden stars
    Above the blackness of the swelling tide,
        Down which they struck rough gold in ruddier bars;
5   And heard the heave and plashing of the flow
    Against the wall a dozen feet below.

    Large elm-trees stood along that river-walk;
        And under one, a few steps from my seat,
    I heard strange voices join in stranger talk,
10   Although I had not heard approaching feet:
    These bodiless voices in my waking dream
    Flowed dark words blending with the sombre stream:—

    And you have after all come back; come back.
    I was about to follow on your track.
15 And you have failed: our spark of hope is black.

    That I have failed is proved by my return:
    The spark is quenched, nor ever more will burn,
    But listen; and the story you shall learn.

    I reached the portal common spirits fear,
20 And read the words above it, dark yet clear,
    'Leave hope behind, all ye who enter here':

    And would have passed in, gratified to gain
    That positive eternity of pain,
    Instead of this insufferable inane.

25   A demon warder clutched me, Not so fast;
First leave your hopes behind!—But years have passed
Since I left all behind me, to the last:

You cannot count for hope, with all your wit,
This bleak despair that drives me to the Pit:
30   How could I seek to enter void of it?

He snarled, What thing is this which apes a soul,
And would find entrance to our gulf of dole
Without the payment of the settled toll?

Outside the gate he showed an open chest:
35   Here pay their entrance fees the souls unblest;
Cast in some hope, you enter with the rest.

This is Pandora's box; whose lid shall shut,
And Hell-gate too, when hopes have filled it; but
They are so thin that it will never glut.

40   I stood a few steps backwards, desolate;
And watched the spirits pass me to their fate,
And fling off hope, and enter at the gate.

When one casts off a load he springs upright,
Squares back his shoulders, breathes with all his might,
45   And briskly paces forward strong and light:

But these, as if they took some burden, bowed;
The whole frame sank; however strong and proud
Before, they crept in quite infirm and cowed.

And as they passed me, earnestly from each
50   A morsel of his hope I did beseech,
To pay my entrance; but all mocked my speech.

Not one would cede a tittle of his store,
Though knowing that in instants three or four
He must resign the whole for evermore.

55   So I returned. Our destiny is fell;
For in this Limbo we must ever dwell,
Shut out alike from Heaven and Earth and Hell.

The other sighed back, Yea; but if we grope
With care through all this Limbo's dreary scope,
60   We yet may pick up some minute lost hope;

And, sharing it between us, entrance win,
In spite of fiends so jealous for gross sin:
Let us without delay our search begin.

VII

Some say that phantoms haunt those shadowy streets,
    And mingle freely there with sparse mankind;
And tell of ancient woes and black defeats,
    And murmur mysteries in the grave enshrined:
5   But others think them visions of illusion,
Or even men gone far in self-confusion;
    No man there being wholly sane in mind.

And yet a man who raves, however mad,
    Who bares his heart and tells of his own fall,
10 Reserves some inmost secret good or bad:
    The phantoms have no reticence at all:
The nudity of flesh will blush though tameless,
The extreme nudity of bone grins shameless,
    The unsexed skeleton mocks shroud and pall.

15 I have seen phantoms there that were as men
    And men that were as phantoms flit and roam;
Marked shapes that were not living to my ken,
    Caught breathings acrid as with Dead Sea foam:
The City rests for man so weird and awful,
20 That his intrusion there might seem unlawful,
    And phantoms there may have their proper home.

VIII

While I still lingered on that river-walk,
    And watched the tide as black as our black doom,
I heard another couple join in talk,
    And saw them to the left hand in the gloom
5 Seated against an elm bole on the ground,
Their eyes intent upon the stream profound.

'I never knew another man on earth
    But had some joy and solace in his life,
    Some chance of triumph in the dreadful strife:
10 My doom has been unmitigated dearth.'

'We gaze upon the river, and we note
The various vessels large and small that float,
Ignoring every wrecked and sunken boat.'

147

'And yet I asked no splendid dower, no spoil
15   Of sway or fame or rank or even wealth;
        But homely love with common food and health,
And nightly sleep to balance daily toil.'

'This all-too humble soul would arrogate
Unto itself some signalising hate
20   From the supreme indifference of Fate!'

'Who is most wretched in this dolorous place?
        I think myself; yet I would rather be
        My miserable self than He, than He
Who formed such creatures to His own disgrace.

25   'The vilest thing must be less vile than Thou
        From whom it had its being, God and Lord!
        Creator of all woe and sin! abhorred,
Malignant and implacable! I vow

'That not for all Thy power furled and unfurled,
30   For all the temples to Thy glory built,
        Would I assume the ignominious guilt
Of having made such men in such a world.'

'As if a Being, God or Fiend, could reign,
At once so wicked, foolish, and insane,
35   As to produce men when He might refrain!

'The world rolls round for ever like a mill;
It grinds out death and life and good and ill;
It has no purpose, heart or mind or will.

'While air of Space and Time's full river flow
40   The mill must blindly whirl unresting so:
It may be wearing out, but who can know?

'Man might know one thing were his sight less dim;
That it whirls not to suit his petty whim,
That it is quite indifferent to him.

45   'Nay, does it treat him harshly as he saith?
It grinds him some slow years of bitter breath,
Then grinds him back into eternal death.'

IX

It is full strange to him who hears and feels,
        When wandering there in some deserted street,
The booming and the jar of ponderous wheels,
        The trampling clash of heavy ironshod feet:

5 Who in this Venice of the Black Sea rideth?
Who in this city of the stars abideth
  To buy or sell as those in daylight sweet?

The rolling thunder seems to fill the sky
  As it comes on; the horses snort and strain,
10 The harness jingles, as it passes by;
  The hugeness of an overburthened wain:
A man sits nodding on the shaft or trudges
Three parts asleep beside his fellow-drudges:
  And so it rolls into the night again.

15 What merchandise? whence, whither, and for whom?
  Perchance it is a Fate-appointed hearse,
Bearing away to some mysterious tomb
  Or Limbo of the scornful universe
The joy, the peace, the life-hope, the abortions
20 Of all things good which should have been our portions,
  But have been strangled by that City's curse.

X

The mansion stood apart in its own ground;
In front thereof a fragrant garden-lawn,
High trees about it, and the whole walled round:
  The massy iron gates were both withdrawn;
5 And every window of its front shed light,
Portentous in that City of the Night.

But though thus lighted it was deadly still
  As all the countless bulks of solid gloom;
Perchance a congregation to fulfil
10 Solemnities of silence in this doom,
Mysterious rites of dolour and despair
Permitting not a breath of chant or prayer?

Broad steps ascended to a terrace broad
  Whereon lay still light from the open door;
15 The hall was noble, and its aspect awed,
  Hung round with heavy black from dome to floor;
And ample stairways rose to left and right
Whose balustrades were also draped with night.

I paced from room to room, from hall to hall,
20 Nor any life throughout the maze discerned;
But each was hung with its funereal pall,
  And held a shrine, around which tapers burned,
With picture or with statue or with bust,
All copied from the same fair form of dust:

149

25   A woman very young and very fair;
            Beloved by bounteous life and joy and youth,
      And loving these sweet lovers, so that care
            And age and death seemed not for her in sooth:
      Alike as stars, all beautiful and bright,
30   These shapes lit up that mausoléan night.

      At length I heard a murmur as of lips,
            And reached an open oratory hung
      With heaviest blackness of the whole eclipse;
            Beneath the dome a fuming censer swung;
35   And one lay there upon a low white bed,
      With tapers burning at the foot and head:

      The Lady of the images: supine,
            Deathstill, lifesweet, with folded palms she lay:
      And kneeling there as at a sacred shrine
40   A young man wan and worn who seemed to pray:
      A crucifix of dim and ghostly white
      Surmounted the large altar left in night:—

      The chambers of the mansion of my heart,
      In every one whereof thine image dwells,
45   Are black with grief eternal for thy sake.

      The inmost oratory of my soul,
      Wherein thou ever dwellest quick or dead,
      Is black with grief eternal for thy sake.

      I kneel beside thee and I clasp the cross,
50   With eyes for ever fixed upon that face,
      So beautiful and dreadful in its calm.

      I kneel here patient as thou liest there;
      As patient as a statue carved in stone,
      Of adoration and eternal grief.

55   While thou dost not awake I cannot move;
      And something tells me thou wilt never wake,
      And I alive feel turning into stone.

      Most beautiful were Death to end my grief,
      Most hateful to destroy the sight of thee,
60   Dear vision better than all death or life.

      But I renounce all choice of life or death,
      For either shall be ever at thy side,
      And thus in bliss or woe be ever well.—

He murmured thus and thus in monotone,
    Intent upon that uncorrupted face,
65 Entranced except his moving lips alone:
    I glided with hushed footsteps from the place.
This was the festival that filled with light
That palace in the City of the Night.

XI

What men are they who haunt these fatal glooms,
    And fill their living mouths with dust of death,
And make their habitations in the tombs,
    And breathe eternal sighs with mortal breath,
5 And pierce life's pleasant veil of various error
To reach that void of darkness and old terror
    Wherein expire the lamps of hope and faith?

They have much wisdom yet they are not wise,
    They have much goodness yet they do not well,
10 (The fools we know have their own Paradise,
    The wicked also have their proper Hell);
They have much strength but still their doom is stronger,
Much patience but their time endureth longer,
    Much valour but life mocks it with some spell.

15 They are most rational and yet insane:
    An outward madness not to be controlled;
A perfect reason in the central brain,
    Which has no power, but sitteth wan and cold,
And sees the madness, and foresees as plainly
20 The ruin in its path, and trieth vainly
    To cheat itself refusing to behold.

And some are great in rank and wealth and power,
    And some renowned for genius and for worth;
And some are poor and mean, who brood and cower
    And shrink from notice, and accept all dearth
25 Of body, heart and soul, and leave to others
All boons of life: yet these and those are brothers,
    The saddest and the weariest men on earth.

XII

Our isolated units could be brought
    To act together for some common end?
For one by one, each silent with his thought,
    I marked a long loose line approach and wend
5 Athwart the great cathedral's cloistered square,
And slowly vanish from the moonlit air.

151

Then I would follow in among the last:
　　And in the porch a shrouded figure stood,
Who challenged each one pausing ere he passed,
10　　　With deep eyes burning through a blank white hood:
Whence come you in the world of life and light
To this our City of Tremendous Night?—

From pleading in a senate of rich lords
For some scant justice to our countless hordes
15　Who toil half-starved with scarce a human right:
I wake from daydreams to this real night.

From wandering through many a solemn scene
Of opium visions, with a heart serene
And intellect miraculously bright:
20　I wake from daydreams to this real night.

From making hundreds laugh and roar with glee
By my transcendent feats of mimicry,
And humour wanton as an elfish sprite:
I wake from daydreams to this real night.

25　From prayer and fasting in a lonely cell,
Which brought an ecstasy ineffable
Of love and adoration and delight:
I wake from daydreams to this real night.

From ruling on a splendid kingly throne
30　A nation which beneath my rule has grown
Year after year in wealth and arts and might:
I wake from daydreams to this real night.

From preaching to an audience fired with faith
The Lamb who died to save our souls from death,
35　Whose blood hath washed our scarlet sins wool-white:
I wake from daydreams to this real night.

From drinking fiery poison in a den
Crowded with tawdry girls and squalid men,
Who hoarsely laugh and curse and brawl and fight:
40　I wake from daydreams to this real night.

From picturing with all beauty and all grace
First Eden and the parents of our race,
A luminous rapture unto all men's sight:
I wake from daydreams to this real night.

45 From writing a great work with patient plan
To justify the ways of God to man,
And show how ill must fade and perish quite:
I wake from daydreams to this real night.

From desperate fighting with a little band
50 Against the powerful tyrants of our land,
To free our brethren in their own despite:
I wake from daydreams to this real night.

Thus, challenged by that warder sad and stern,
Each one responded with his countersign,
55 Then entered the cathedral; and in turn
I entered also, having given mine;
But lingered near until I heard no more,
And marked the closing of the massive door.

XIII

Of all things human which are strange and wild
This is perchance the wildest and most strange,
And showeth man most utterly beguiled,
To those who haunt that sunless City's range;
5 That he bemoans himself for aye, repeating
How Time is deadly swift, how life is fleeting,
How naught is constant on the earth but change.

The hours are heavy on him and the days;
The burden of the months he scarce can bear;
10 And often in his secret soul he prays
To sleep through barren periods unaware,
Arousing at some longed-for date of pleasure;
Which having passed and yielded him small treasure,
He would outsleep another term of care.

15 Yet in his marvellous fancy he must make
Quick wings for Time, and see it fly from us;
This Time which crawleth like a monstrous snake,
Wounded and slow and very venomous;
Which creeps blindwormlike round the earth and ocean,
20 Distilling poison at each painful motion,
And seems condemned to circle ever thus.

And since he cannot spend and use aright
The little time here given him in trust,
But wasteth it in weary undelight
25 Of foolish toil and trouble, strife and lust,

He naturally claimeth to inherit
The everlasting Future, that his merit
　　May have full scope; as surely is most just.

O length of the intolerable hours,
30　　O nights that are as æons of slow pain,
O Time, too ample for our vital powers,
　　O Life, whose woeful vanities remain
Immutable for all of all our legions
Through all the centuries and in all the regions,
35　　Not of your speed and variance *we* complain.

We do not ask a longer term of strife,
　　Weakness and weariness and nameless woes;
We do not claim renewed and endless life
　　When this which is our torment here shall close,
40　An everlasting conscious inanition!
We yearn for speedy death in full fruition,
　　Dateless oblivion and divine repose.

XIV
Large glooms were gathered in the mighty fane,
　　With tinted moongleams slanting here and there;
And all was hush: no swelling organ-strain,
　　No chant, no voice or murmuring of prayer;
5　No priests came forth, no tinkling censers fumed,
And the high altar space was unillumed.

Around the pillars and against the walls
　　Leaned men and shadows; others seemed to brood
Bent or recumbent in secluded stalls.
10　　Perchance they were not a great multitude
Save in that city of so lonely streets
Where one may count up every face he meets.

All patiently awaited the event
　　Without a stir or sound, as if no less
15　Self-occupied, doomstricken while attent.
　　And then we heard a voice of solemn stress
From the dark pulpit, and our gaze there met
Two eyes which burned as never eyes burned yet:

Two steadfast and intolerable eyes
20　　Burning beneath a broad and rugged brow;
The head behind it of enormous size.
　　And as black fir-groves in a large wind bow,
Our rooted congregation, gloom-arrayed,
By that great sad voice deep and full were swayed:—

154

25 O melancholy Brothers, dark, dark, dark!
O battling in black floods without an ark!
  O spectral wanderers of unholy Night!
My soul hath bled for you these sunless years,
With bitter blood-drops running down like tears:
30   Oh, dark, dark, dark, withdrawn from joy and light!

My heart is sick with anguish for your bale;
Your woe hath been my anguish; yea, I quail
  And perish in your perishing unblest.
And I have searched the heights and depths, the scope
35 Of all our universe, with desperate hope
  To find some solace for your wild unrest.

And now at last authentic word I bring,
Witnessed by every dead and living thing;
  Good tidings of great joy for you, for all:
40 There is no God; no Fiend with names divine
Made us and tortures us; if we must pine,
  It is to satiate no Being's gall.

It was the dark delusion of a dream,
That living Person conscious and supreme,
45 Whom we must curse for cursing us with life;
Whom we must curse because the life He gave
Could not be buried in the quiet grave,
  Could not be killed by poison or by knife.

This little life is all we must endure,
50 The grave's most holy peace is ever sure,
  We fall asleep and never wake again;
Nothing is of us but the mouldering flesh,
Whose elements dissolve and merge afresh
  In earth, air, water, plants, and other men.

55 We finish thus; and all our wretched race
Shall finish with its cycle, and give place
  To other beings, with their own time-doom:
Infinite æons ere our kind began;
Infinite æons after the last man
60 Has joined the mammoth in earth's tomb and womb.

We bow down to the universal laws,
Which never had for man a special clause
  Of cruelty or kindness, love or hate:
If toads and vultures are obscene to sight,
65 If tigers burn with beauty and with might,
  Is it by favour or by wrath of Fate?

155

All substance lives and struggles evermore
Through countless shapes continually at war,
By countless interactions interknit:
70   If one is born a certain day on earth,
All times and forces tended to that birth,
      Not all the world could change or hinder it.

I find no hint throughout the Universe
Of good or ill, of blessing or of curse;
75   I find alone Necessity Supreme;
With infinite Mystery, abysmal, dark,
Unlighted ever by the faintest spark
      For us the flitting shadows of a dream.

O Brothers of sad lives! they are so brief;
80   A few short years must bring us all relief:
      Can we not bear these years of labouring breath?
But if you would not this poor life fulfil,
Lo, you are free to end it when you will,
      Without the fear of waking after death.—

85   The organ-like vibrations of his voice
      Thrilled through the vaulted aisles and died away;
The yearning of the tones which bade rejoice
      Was sad and tender as a requiem lay:
Our shadowy congregation rested still
90   As brooding on that 'End it when you will.'

XV

Wherever men are gathered, all the air
      Is charged with human feeling, human thought;
Each shout and cry and laugh, each curse and prayer,
      Are into its vibrations surely wrought;
5   Unspoken passion, wordless meditation,
Are breathed into it with our respiration;
      It is with our life fraught and overfraught.

So that no man there breathes earth's simple breath,
      As if alone on mountains or wide seas;
10   But nourishes warm life or hastens death
      With joys and sorrows, health and foul disease,
Wisdom and folly, good and evil labours,
Incessant of his multitudinous neighbours;
      He in his turn affecting all of these.

15   That City's atmosphere is dark and dense,
      Although not many exiles wander there,
With many a potent evil influence,
      Each adding poison to the poisoned air;

Infections of unutterable sadness,
20   Infections of incalculable madness,
        Infections of incurable despair.

XVI

Our shadowy congregation rested still,
    As musing on that message we had heard
And brooding on that 'End it when you will;'
    Perchance awaiting yet some other word;
5   When keen as lightning through a muffled sky
Sprang forth a shrill and lamentable cry:—

The man speaks sooth, alas! the man speaks sooth:
    We have no personal life beyond the grave;
There is no God; Fate knows nor wrath nor ruth:
10   Can I find here the comfort which I crave?

In all eternity I had one chance,
    One few years' term of gracious human life:
The splendours of the intellect's advance,
    The sweetness of the home with babes and wife;

15 The social pleasures with their genial wit;
    The fascination of the worlds of art,
The glories of the worlds of nature, lit
    By large imagination's glowing heart;

The rapture of mere being, full of health;
20 The careless childhood and the ardent youth,
The strenuous manhood winning various wealth,
    The reverend age serene with life's long truth:

All the sublime prerogatives of Man:
    The storied memories of the times of old,
25 The patient tracking of the world's great plan
    Through sequences and changes myriadfold.

This chance was never offered me before;
    For me the infinite Past is blank and dumb:
This chance recurreth never, nevermore;
30   Blank, blank for me the infinite To-come.

And this sole chance was frustrate from my birth;
    A mockery, a delusion; and my breath
Of noble human life upon this earth
    So racks me that I sigh for senseless death.

35 My wine of life is poison mixed with gall,
        My noonday passes in a nightmare dream,
    I worse than lose the years which are my all:
        What can console me for the loss supreme?

    Speak not of comfort where no comfort is,
40   Speak not at all: can words make foul things fair?
    Our life's a cheat, our death a black abyss:
        Hush and be mute envisaging despair.—

    This vehement voice came from the northern aisle
        Rapid and shrill to its abrupt harsh close;
45 And none gave answer for a certain while,
        For words must shrink from these most wordless woes;
    At last the pulpit speaker simply said,
    With humid eyes and thoughtful drooping head:—

    My Brother, my poor Brothers, it is thus;
50 This life itself holds nothing good for us,
        But it ends soon and nevermore can be;
    And we knew nothing of it ere our birth,
    And shall know nothing when consigned to earth:
        I ponder these thoughts and they comfort me.

                    XVII
    How the moon triumphs through the endless nights!
        How the stars throb and glitter as they wheel
    Their thick processions of supernal lights
        Around the blue vault obdurate as steel!
5   And men regard with passionate awe and yearning
    The mighty marching and the golden burning,
        And think the heavens respond to what they feel.

    Boats gliding like dark shadows of a dream,
        Are glorified from vision as they pass
10 The quivering moonbridge on the deep black stream;
    Cold windows kindle their dead glooms of glass
    To restless crystals; cornice, dome, and column
    Emerge from chaos in the splendour solemn;
        Like faëry lakes gleam lawns of dewy grass.

15 With such a living light these dead eyes shine,
        These eyes of sightless heaven, that as we gaze
    We read a pity, tremulous, divine,
        Or cold majestic scorn in their pure rays:

                    158

Fond man! they are not haughty, are not tender;
20   There is no heart or mind in all their splendour,
        They thread mere puppets all their marvellous maze.

If we could near them with the flight unflown,
        We should but find them worlds as sad as this,
Or suns all self-consuming like our own
25   Enringed by planet worlds as much amiss:
They wax and wane through fusion and confusion;
The spheres eternal are a grand illusion,
        The empyréan is a void abyss.

XVIII

I wandered in a suburb of the north,
        And reached a spot whence three close lanes led down,
Beneath thick trees and hedgerows winding forth
        Like deep brook channels, deep and dark and lown:
5   The air above was wan with misty light,
The dull grey south showed one vague blur of white.

I took the left-hand lane and slowly trod
        Its earthen footpath, brushing as I went
The humid leafage; and my feet were shod
10   With heavy languor, and my frame downbent,
With infinite sleepless weariness outworn,
So many nights I thus had paced forlorn.

After a hundred steps I grew aware
        Of something crawling in the lane below;
15   It seemed a wounded creature prostrate there
        That sobbed with pangs in making progress slow,
The hind limbs stretched to push, the fore limbs then
To drag; for it would die in its own den.

But coming level with it I discerned
20   That it had been a man; for at my tread
It stopped in its sore travail and half-turned,
        Leaning upon its right, and raised its head,
And with the left hand twitched back as in ire
Long grey unreverend locks befouled with mire.

25   A haggard filthy face with bloodshot eyes,
        An infamy for manhood to behold.
He gasped all trembling. What, you want my prize?
        You leave, to rob me, wine and lust and gold
And all that men go mad upon, since you
30   Have traced my sacred secret of the clue?

You think that I am weak and must submit;
    Yet I but scratch you with this poisoned blade,
And you are dead as if I clove with it
    That false fierce greedy heart. Betrayed! betrayed!
35   I fling this phial if you seek to pass,
And you are forthwith shrivelled up like grass.

And then with sudden change, Take thought! take thought!
    Have pity on me! it is mine alone.
If you could find, it would avail you naught;
40   Seek elsewhere on the pathway of your own:
For who of mortal or immortal race
The lifetrack of another can retrace?

Did you but know my agony and toil!
    Two lanes diverge up yonder from this lane;
45   My thin blood marks the long length of their soil;
    Such clue I left, who sought my clue in vain:
My hands and knees are worn both flesh and bone;
I cannot move but with continual moan.

But I am in the very way at last
50   To find the long-lost broken golden thread
Which reunites my present with my past,
    If you but go your own way. And I said,
I will retire as soon as you have told
Whereunto leadeth this lost thread of gold.

And so you know it not! he hissed with scorn;
55   I feared you, imbecile! It leads me back
From this accursed night without a morn,
    And through the deserts which have else no track,
And through vast wastes of horror-haunted time,
60   To Eden innocence in Eden's clime:

And I become a nursling soft and pure,
    An infant cradled on its mother's knee,
Without a past, love-cherished and secure;
    Which if it saw this loathsome present Me,
65   Would plunge its face into the pillowing breast,
And scream abhorrence hard to lull to rest.

He turned to grope; and I retiring brushed
    Thin shreds of gossamer from off my face,
And mused, His life would grow, the germ uncrushed;
70   He should to antenatal night retrace,
And hide his elements in that large womb
Beyond the reach of man-evolving Doom.

And even thus, what weary way were planned,
        To seek oblivion through the far-off gate
75 Of birth, when that of death is close at hand!
        For this is law, if law there be in Fate:
What never has been, yet may have its when;
The thing which has been, never is again.

XIX

The mighty river flowing dark and deep,
        With ebb and flood from the remote sea-tides
Vague-sounding through the City's sleepless sleep,
        Is named the River of the Suicides;
5   For night by night some lorn wretch overweary,
And shuddering from the future yet more dreary,
        Within its cold secure oblivion hides.

One plunges from a bridge's parapet,
        As by some blind and sudden frenzy hurled;
10 Another wades in slow with purpose set
        Until the waters are above him furled;
Another in a boat with dreamlike motion
Glides drifting down into the desert ocean,
        To starve or sink from out the desert world.

15 They perish from their suffering surely thus,
        For none beholding them attempts to save,
The while each thinks how soon, solicitous,
        He may seek refuge in the self-same wave;
Some hour when tired of ever-vain endurance
20 Impatience will forerun the sweet assurance
        Of perfect peace eventual in the grave.

When this poor tragic-farce has palled us long,
        Why actors and spectators do we stay?—
To fill our so-short *rôles* out right or wrong;
25   To see what shifts are yet in the dull play
For our illusion; to refrain from grieving
Dear foolish friends by our untimely leaving:
        But those asleep at home, how blest are they!

Yet it is but for one night after all:
30   What matters one brief night of dreary pain?
When after it the weary eyelids fall
        Upon the weary eyes and wasted brain;
And all sad scenes and thoughts and feelings vanish
In that sweet sleep no power can ever banish,
        That one best sleep which never wakes again.

XX

I sat me weary on a pillar's base,
  And leaned against the shaft; for broad moonlight
O'erflowed the peacefulness of cloistered space,
  A shore of shadow slanting from the right:
5 The great cathedral's western front stood there,
A wave-worn rock in that calm sea of air.

Before it, opposite my place of rest,
  Two figures faced each other, large, austere;
A couchant sphinx in shadow to the breast,
10 An angel standing in the moonlight clear;
So mighty by magnificence of form,
They were not dwarfed beneath that mass enorm.

Upon the cross-hilt of a naked sword
  The angel's hands, as prompt to smite, were held;
15 His vigilant intense regard was poured
  Upon the creature placidly unquelled,
Whose front was set at level gaze which took
No heed of aught, a solemn trance-like look.

And as I pondered these opposèd shapes
20 My eyelids sank in stupor, that dull swoon
Which drugs and with a leaden mantle drapes
  The outworn to worse weariness. But soon
A sharp and clashing noise the stillness broke,
And from the evil lethargy I woke.

25 The angel's wings had fallen, stone on stone,
  And lay there shattered; hence the sudden sound:
A warrior leaning on his sword alone
  Now watched the sphinx with that regard profound;
The sphinx unchanged looked forthright, as aware
30 Of nothing in the vast abyss of air.

Again I sank in that repose unsweet,
  Again a clashing noise my slumber rent;
The warrior's sword lay broken at his feet:
  An unarmed man with raised hands impotent
35 Now stood before the sphinx, which ever kept
Such mien as if with open eyes it slept.

My eyelids sank in spite of wonder grown;
  A louder crash upstartled me in dread:
The man had fallen forward, stone on stone,
40 And lay there shattered, with his trunkless head
Between the monster's large quiescent paws,
Beneath its grand front changeless as life's laws,

The moon had circled westward full and bright,
    And made the temple-front a mystic dream,
45 And bathed the whole enclosure with its light,
    The sworded angel's wrecks, the sphinx supreme:
I pondered long that cold majestic face
Whose vision seemed of infinite void space.

XXI

Anear the centre of that northern crest
    Stands out a level upland bleak and bare,
From which the city east and south and west
5   Sinks gently in long waves; and thronèd there
An Image sits, stupendous, superhuman,
The bronze colossus of a wingèd Woman,
    Upon a graded granite base foursquare.

Low-seated she leans forward massively,
    With cheek on clenched left hand, the forearm's might
10 Erect, its elbow on her rounded knee;
    Across a clasped book in her lap the right
Upholds a pair of compasses; she gazes
With full set eyes, but wandering in thick mazes
    Of sombre thought beholds no outward sight.

15 Words cannot picture her; but all men know
    That solemn sketch the pure sad artist wrought
Three centuries and threescore years ago,
    With phantasies of his peculiar thought:
The instruments of carpentry and science
20 Scattered about her feet, in strange alliance
    With the keen wolf-hound sleeping undistraught;

Scales, hour-glass, bell, and magic-square above;
    The grave and solid infant perched beside,
With open winglets that might bear a dove,
25   Intent upon its tablets, heavy-eyed;
Her folded wings as of a mighty eagle,
But all too impotent to lift the regal
    Robustness of her earth-born strength and pride;

And with those wings, and that light wreath which seems
30   To mock her grand head and the knotted frown
Of forehead charged with baleful thoughts and dreams,
    The household bunch of keys, the housewife's gown
Voluminous, indented, and yet rigid
As if a shell of burnished metal frigid,
35   The feet thick-shod to tread all weakness down;

The comet hanging o'er the waste dark seas,
    The massy rainbow curved in front of it
Beyond the village with the masts and trees;
    The snaky imp, dog-headed, from the Pit,
40 Bearing upon its batlike leathern pinions
Her name unfolded in the sun's dominions,
    The 'MELENCOLIA' that transcends all wit.

Thus has the artist copied her, and thus
    Surrounded to expound her form sublime,
45 Her fate heroic and calamitous;
    Fronting the dreadful mysteries of Time,
Unvanquished in defeat and desolation,
Undaunted in the hopeless conflagration
    Of the day setting on her baffled prime.

50 Baffled and beaten back she works on still,
    Weary and sick of soul she works the more,
Sustained by her indomitable will:
    The hands shall fashion and the brain shall pore,
And all her sorrow shall be turned to labour,
55 Till Death the friend-foe piercing with his sabre
    That mighty heart of hearts ends bitter war.

But as if blacker night could dawn on night,
    With tenfold gloom on moonless night unstarred,
A sense more tragic than defeat and blight,
60   More desperate than strife with hope debarred,
More fatal than the adamantine Never
Encompassing her passionate endeavour,
    Dawns glooming in her tenebrous regard:

The sense that every struggle brings defeat
65   Because Fate holds no prize to crown success;
That all the oracles are dumb or cheat
    Because they have no secret to express;
That none can pierce the vast black veil uncertain
Because there is no light beyond the curtain;
70   That all is vanity and nothingness.

Titanic from her high throne in the north,
    That City's sombre Patroness and Queen,
In bronze sublimity she gazes forth
    Over her Capital of teen and threne,
75 Over the river with its isles and bridges,
The marsh and moorland, to the stern rock-ridges,
    Confronting them with a coëval mien

164

The moving moon and stars from east to west
   Circle before her in the sea of air;
Shadows and gleams glide round her solemn rest.
   Her subjects often gaze up to her there:
The strong to drink new strength of iron endurance,
The weak new terrors; all, renewed assurance
   And confirmation of the old despair.

80

William Morris

William Morris (1834–96) was a man of extraordinary energy and versatility. He was a prolific writer, a painter, a decorator and designer, a printer, a manufacturer and an active socialist. In 1856 he came under the influence of Rossetti, and participated in what became a second phase of the Pre-Raphaelite movement, including the decoration of the Oxford Union building with fresco in 1857. His first volume of poetry, *The Defence of Guenevere*, was published in 1858. In 1861 he founded the firm of Morris, Marshall, Faulkner & Co., manufacturers and decorators, which provided furnishings and decorations for houses and churches. In the middle of a busy and active career he found time to write, from 1866 onwards, *The Earthly Paradise*, a poem of immense length published from 1868 to 1870. He then became interested in Icelandic, published translations, and composed *The Story of Sigurd the Volsung* (published 1876). In later years he became increasingly involved in political matters, and in 1884 became the leader of the Socialist League. He withdrew from this in 1890, and in the same year founded the Kelmscott Press (named after his house near Lechlade on the upper Thames). His life is notable, not only for its indefatigable industry, but for his continuous attempts to relate art to the ordinary concerns of life, and his striving to combat the mechanical and dehumanizing influences which he saw around him. His poetry of the Middle Ages is remarkable for its combination of beauty and violence, and his refusal to avoid the brutality of the age. His other poetry may be seen as one side of his attempt to surround men's lives with beauty, not the beauty of art for art's sake, but a beauty which penetrated the patterns of daily living.

THE DEFENCE OF GUENEVERE

But, knowing now that they would have her speak,
She threw her wet hair backward from her brow,
Her hand close to her mouth touching her cheek,

As though she had had there a shameful blow,
5   And feeling it shameful to feel ought but shame
All through her heart, yet felt her cheek burned so,

She must a little touch it; like one lame
She walked away from Gauwaine, with her head
Still lifted up; and on her cheek of flame

10 The tears dried quick; she stopped at last and said:
'O knights and lords, it seems but little skill
To talk of well-known things past now and dead.

'God wot I ought to say, I have done ill,
And pray you all forgiveness heartily!
15 Because you must be right such great lords—still

'Listen, suppose your time were come to die,
And you were quite alone and very weak;
Yea, laid a dying while very mightily

'The wind was ruffling up the narrow streak
20 Of river through your broad lands running well:
Suppose a hush should come, then some one speak:

' "One of these cloths is heaven, and one is hell,
Now choose one cloth for ever, which they be,
I will not tell you, you must somehow tell

25 ' "Of your own strength and mightiness; here, see!"
Yea, yea, my lord, and you to ope your eyes,
At foot of your familiar bed to see

'A great God's angel standing, with such dyes,
Not known on earth, on his great wings, and hands,
30 Held out two ways, light from the inner skies

'Showing him well, and making his commands
Seem to be God's commands, moreover, too,
Holding within his hands the cloths on wands;

'And one of these strange choosing cloths was blue,
35 Wavy and long, and one cut short and red;
No man could tell the better of the two.

'After a shivering half-hour you said,
"God help! heaven's colour, the blue;" and he said, "hell."
Perhaps you then would roll upon your bed,

40 'And cry to all good men that loved you well,
"Ah Christ! if only I had known, known, known;"
Launcelot went away, then I could tell,

'Like wisest man how all things would be, moan,
And roll and hurt myself, and long to die,
45   And yet fear much to die for what was sown.

'Nevertheless you, O Sir Gauwaine, lie,
Whatever may have happened through these years,
God knows I speak truth, saying that you lie.'

Her voice was low at first, being full of tears,
50   But as it cleared, it grew full loud and shrill,
Growing a windy shriek in all men's ears,

A ringing in their startled brains, until
She said that Gauwaine lied, then her voice sunk,
And her great eyes began again to fill,

55   Though still she stood right up, and never shrunk,
But spoke on bravely, glorious lady fair!
Whatever tears her full lips may have drunk,

She stood, and seemed to think, and wrung her hair,
Spoke out at last with no more trace of shame,
60   With passionate twisting of her body there:

'It chanced upon a day that Launcelot came
To dwell at Arthur's court: at Christmas-time
This happened; when the heralds sung his name,

' "Son of King Ban of Benwick," seemed to chime
65   Along with all the bells that rang that day,
O'er the white roofs, with little change of rhyme.

'Christmas and whitened winter passed away,
And over me the April sunshine came,
Made very awful with black hail-clouds, yea

70   'And in the Summer I grew white with flame,
And bowed my head down—Autumn, and the sick
Sure knowledge things would never be the same,

'However often Spring might be most thick
Of blossoms and buds, smote on me, and I grew
75   Careless of most things, let the clock tick, tick,

'To my unhappy pulse, that beat right through
My eager body; while I laughed out loud,
And let my lips curl up at false or true,

'Seemed cold and shallow without any cloud.
80 Behold my judges, then the cloths were brought:
While I was dizzied thus, old thoughts would crowd,

'Belonging to the time ere I was bought
By Arthur's great name and his little love,
Must I give up for ever then, I thought,

85 'That which I deemed would ever round me move
Glorifying all things; for a little word,
Scarce ever meant at all, must I now prove

'Stone-cold for ever? Pray you, does the Lord
Will that all folks should be quite happy and good?
90 I love God now a little, if this cord

'Were broken, once for all what striving could
Make me love anything in earth or heaven.
So day by day it grew, as if one should

'Slip slowly down some path worn smooth and even,
95 Down to a cool sea on a summer day;
Yet still in slipping was there some small leaven

'Of stretched hands catching small stones by the way,
Until one surely reached the sea at last,
And felt strange new joy as the worn head lay

100 'Back, with the hair like sea-weed; yea all past
Sweat of the forehead, dryness of the lips,
Washed utterly out by the dear waves o'ercast

'In the lone sea, far off from any ships!
Do I not know now of a day in Spring?
105 No minute of that wild day ever slips

'From out my memory; I hear thrushes sing,
And wheresoever I may be, straightway
Thoughts of it all come up with most fresh sting;

'I was half mad with beauty on that day,
110 And went without my ladies all alone,
In a quiet garden walled round every way;

'I was right joyful of that wall of stone,
That shut the flowers and trees up with the sky,
And trebled all the beauty: to the bone,

115 'Yea right through to my heart, grown very shy
     With weary thoughts, it pierced, and made me glad;
     Exceedingly glad, and I knew verily,

     'A little thing just then had made me mad;
     I dared not think, as I was wont to do,
120 Sometimes, upon my beauty; if I had

     'Held out my long hand up against the blue,
     And, looking on the tenderly darken'd fingers,
     Thought that by rights one ought to see quite through,

     'There, see you, where the soft still light yet lingers,
125 Round by the edges; what should I have done,
     If this had joined with yellow spotted singers,

     'And startling green drawn upward by the sun?
     But shouting, loosed out, see now! all my hair,
     And trancedly stood watching the west wind run

130 'With faintest half-heard breathing sound—why there
     I lose my head e'en now in doing this;
     But shortly listen—In that garden fair

     'Came Launcelot walking; this is true, the kiss
     Wherewith we kissed in meeting that spring day,
135 I scarce dare talk of the remember'd bliss,

     'When both our mouths went wandering in one way,
     And aching sorely, met among the leaves;
     Our hands being left behind strained far away.

     'Never within a yard of my bright sleeves
140 Had Launcelot come before—and now, so nigh!
     After that day why is it Guenevere grieves?

     'Nevertheless you, O Sir Gauwaine, lie,
     Whatever happened on through all those years,
     God knows I speak truth, saying that you lie.

145 'Being such a lady could I weep these tears
     If this were true? A great queen such as I
     Having sinn'd this way, straight her conscience sears;

     'And afterwards she liveth hatefully,
     Slaying and poisoning, certes never weeps,—
150 Gauwaine be friends now, speak me lovingly.

'Do I not see how God's dear pity creeps
All through your frame, and trembles in your mouth?
Remember in what grave your mother sleeps,

155   'Buried in some place far down in the south,
Men are forgetting as I speak to you;
By her head sever'd in that awful drouth

'Of pity that drew Agravaine's fell blow,
I pray your pity! Let me not scream out
For ever after, when the shrill winds blow

160   'Through half your castle-locks! let me not shout
For ever after in the winter night
When you ride out alone! in battle-rout

'Let not my rusting tears make your sword light!
Ah! God of mercy how he turns away!
165   So, ever must I dress me to the fight,

'So—let God's justice work! Gauwaine, I say,
See me hew down your proofs: yea all men know
Even as you said how Mellyagraunce one day,

'One bitter day in *la Fausse Garde*, for so
170   All good knights held it after, saw—
Yea, sirs, by cursed unknightly outrage; though

'You, Gauwaine, held his word without a flaw,
This Mellyagraunce saw blood upon my bed—
Whose blood then pray you? is there any law

175   'To make a queen say why some spots of red
Lie on her coverlet? or will you say,
"Your hands are white, lady, as when you wed,

' "Where did you bleed?" and must I stammer out—"Nay,
I blush indeed, fair lord, only to rend
180   My sleeve up to my shoulder, where there lay

' "A knife-point last night:" so must I defend
The honour of the Lady Guenevere?
Not so, fair lords, even if the world should end

'This very day, and you were judges here
185   Instead of God. Did you see Mellyagraunce
When Launcelot stood by him? what white fear

'Curdled his blood, and how his teeth did dance,
His side sink in? as my knight cried and said,
"Slayer of unarm'd men, here is a chance!

190 ' "Setter of traps, I pray you guard your head,
By God I am so glad to fight with you,
Stripper of ladies, that my hand feels lead

' "For driving weight; hurrah now! draw and do,
For all my wounds are moving in my breast,
195 And I am getting mad with waiting so."

'He struck his hands together o'er the beast,
Who fell down flat, and grovell'd at his feet,
And groan'd at being slain so young—"at least."

'My knight said, "Rise you, sir, who are so fleet
200 At catching ladies, half-arm'd will I fight,
My left side all uncovered!" then I weet,

'Up sprang Sir Mellyagraunce with great delight
Upon his knave's face; not until just then
Did I quite hate him, as I saw my knight

205 'Along the lists look to my stake and pen
With such a joyous smile, it made me sigh
From agony beneath my waist-chain, when

'The fight began, and to me they drew nigh;
Ever Sir Launcelot kept him on the right,
210 And traversed warily, and ever high

'And fast leapt caitiff's sword, until my knight
Sudden threw up his sword to his left hand,
Caught it, and swung it; that was all the fight.

'Except a spout of blood on the hot land;
215 For it was hottest summer; and I know
I wonder'd how the fire, while I should stand,

'And burn, against the heat, would quiver so,
Yards above my head; thus these matters went;
Which things were only warnings of the woe

220 'That fell on me. Yet Mellyagraunce was shent,
For Mellyagraunce had fought against the Lord;
Therefore, my lords, take heed lest you be blent

'With all this wickedness; say no rash word
Against me, being so beautiful; my eyes,
225 Wept all away to grey, may bring some sword

'To drown you in your blood; see my breast rise,
Like waves of purple sea, as here I stand;
And how my arms are moved in wonderful wise,

'Yea also at my full heart's strong command,
230 See through my long throat how the words go up
In ripples to my mouth; how in my hand

'The shadow lies like wine within a cup
Of marvellously colour'd gold; yea now
This little wind is rising, look you up,

235 'And wonder how the light is falling so
Within my moving tresses: will you dare,
When you have looked a little on my brow,

'To say this thing is vile? or will you care
For any plausible lies of cunning woof,
240 When you can see my face with no lie there

'For ever? am I not a gracious proof—
"But in your chamber Launcelot was found"—
Is there a good knight then would stand aloof,

'When a queen says with gentle queenly sound:
245 "O true as steel come now and talk with me,
I love to see your step upon the ground

' "Unwavering, also well I love to see
That gracious smile light up your face, and hear
Your wonderful words, that all mean verily

250 ' "The thing they seem to mean: good friend, so dear
To me in everything, come here to-night,
Or else the hours will pass most dull and drear;

' "If you come not, I fear this time I might
Get thinking over much of times gone by,
255 When I was young, and green hope was in sight;

' "For no man cares now to know why I sigh;
And no man comes to sing me pleasant songs,
Nor any brings me the sweet flowers that lie

173

' "So thick in the gardens; therefore one so longs
260   To see you, Launcelot; that we may be
Like children once again, free from all wrongs

' "Just for one night." Did he not come to me?
What thing could keep true Launcelot away
If I said "come"? there was one less than three

265   'In my quiet room that night, and we were gay;
Till sudden I rose up, weak, pale, and sick,
Because a bawling broke our dream up, yea

'I looked at Launcelot's face and could not speak,
For he looked helpless too, for a little while;
270   Then I remember how I tried to shriek,

'And could not, but fell down; from tile to tile
The stones they threw up rattled o'er my head,
And made me dizzier; till within a while

'My maids were all about me, and my head
275   On Launcelot's breast was being soothed away
From its white chattering, until Launcelot said—

'By God! I will not tell you more to-day,
Judge any way you will—what matters it?
You know quite well the story of that fray,

280   'How Launcelot still'd their bawling, the mad fit
That caught up Gauwaine—all, all, verily,
But just that which would save me; these things flit.

'Nevertheless you, O Sir Gauwaine, lie,
Whatever may have happen'd these long years,
285   God knows I speak truth, saying that you lie!

'All I have said is truth, by Christ's dear tears.'
She would not speak another word, but stood
Turn'd sideways; listening, like a man who hears

His brother's trumpet sounding through the wood
290   Of his foes' lances. She lean'd eagerly,
And gave a slight spring sometimes, as she could

At last hear something really; joyfully
Her cheek grew crimson, as the headlong speed
Of the roan charger drew all men to see,
295   The knight who came was Launcelot at good need.

From THE EARTHLY PARADISE

AN APOLOGY

Of Heaven or Hell I have no power to sing,
I cannot ease the burden of your fears,
Or make quick-coming death a little thing,
Or bring again the pleasure of past years,
5   Nor for my words shall ye forget your tears,
Or hope again for aught that I can say,
The idle singer of an empty day.

But rather, when aweary of your mirth,
From full hearts still unsatisfied ye sigh,
10   And, feeling kindly unto all the earth,
Grudge every minute as it passes by,
Made the more mindful that the sweet days die—
—Remember me a little then I pray,
The idle singer of an empty day.

15   The heavy trouble, the bewildering care
That weighs us down who live and earn our bread,
These idle verses have no power to bear;
So let me sing of names remembered,
Because they, living not, can ne'er be dead,
20   Or long time take their memory quite away
From us poor singers of an empty day.

Dreamer of dreams, born out of my due time,
Why should I strive to set the crooked straight?
Let it suffice me that my murmuring rhyme
25   Beats with light wing against the ivory gate,
Telling a tale not too importunate
To those who in the sleepy region stay,
Lulled by the singer of an empty day.

Folk say, a wizard to a northern king
30   At Christmas-tide such wondrous things did show,
That through one window men beheld the spring,
And through another saw the summer glow,
And through a third the fruited vines a-row,
While still, unheard, but in its wonted way,
35   Piped the drear wind of that December day.

So with this Earthly Paradise it is,
If ye will read aright, and pardon me,
Who strive to build a shadowy isle of bliss
Midmost the beating of the steely sea,
40 Where tossed about all hearts of men must be;
Whose ravening monsters mighty men shall slay,
Not the poor singer of an empty day.

From PROLOGUE: THE WANDERERS

Forget six counties overhung with smoke,
Forget the snorting steam and piston stroke,
Forget the spreading of the hideous town;
Think rather of the pack-horse on the down,
5 And dream of London, small, and white, and clean,
The clear Thames bordered by its gardens green;
Think, that below bridge the green lapping waves
Smite some few keels that bear Levantine staves,
Cut from the yew wood on the burnt-up hill,
10 And pointed jars that Greek hands toiled to fill,
And treasured scanty spice from some far sea,
Florence gold cloth, and Ypres napery,
And cloth of Bruges, and hogsheads of Guienne;
While nigh the thronged wharf Geoffrey Chaucer's pen
15 Moves over bills of lading—mid such times
Shall dwell the hollow puppets of my rhymes.

THE OUTLANDERS

Outlanders, whence come ye last?
 The snow in the street and the wind on the door.
Through what green seas and great have ye passed?
 Minstrels and maids, stand forth on the floor.

5 From far away, O masters mine,
 The snow in the street and the wind on the door.
We come to bear you goodly wine,
 Minstrels and maids, stand forth on the floor.

From far away we come to you,
10 *The snow in the street and the wind on the door.*
To tell of great tidings strange and true.
 Minstrels and maids, stand forth on the floor.

News, news of the Trinity,
The snow in the street and the wind on the door.
15 And Mary and Joseph from over the sea!
Minstrels and maids, stand forth on the floor.

For as we wandered far and wide,
The snow in the street and the wind on the door.
What hap do ye deem there should us betide!
20 *Minstrels and maids, stand forth on the floor.*

Under a bent when the night was deep,
The snow in the street and the wind on the door.
There lay three shepherds tending their sheep.
Minstrels and maids, stand forth on the floor.

25 'O ye shepherds, what have ye seen,
The snow in the street and the wind on the door.
To slay your sorrow, and heal your teen?'
Minstrels and maids, stand forth on the floor.

'In an ox-stall this night we saw,
30 *The snow in the street and the wind on the door.*
A babe and a maid without a flaw.
Minstrels and maids, stand forth on the floor.

'There was an old man there beside,
The snow in the street and the wind on the door.
35 His hair was white and his hood was wide.
Minstrels and maids, stand forth on the floor.

'And as we gazed this thing upon,
The snow in the street and the wind on the door.
Those twain knelt down to the Little One.
40 *Minstrels and maids, stand forth on the floor.*

'And a marvellous song we straight did hear,
The snow in the street and the wind on the door.
That slew our sorrow and healed our care.'
Minstrels and maids, stand forth on the floor.

45 News of a fair and a marvellous thing,
The snow in the street and the wind on the door.
Nowell, nowell, nowell, we sing!
Minstrels and maids, stand forth on the floor.

177

AUGUST

Across the gap made by our English hinds,
Amidst the Roman's handiwork, behold
Far off the long-roofed church; the shepherd binds
The withy round the hurdles of his fold,
5   Down in the foss the river fed of old,
That through long lapse of time has grown to be
The little grassy valley that you see.

Rest here awhile, not yet the eve is still,
The bees are wandering yet, and you may hear
10   The barley mowers on the trenchéd hill,
The sheep-bells, and the restless changing weir,
All little sounds made musical and clear
Beneath the sky that burning August gives,
While yet the thought of glorious Summer lives.

15   Ah, love! such happy days, such days as these,
Must we still waste them, craving for the best,
Like lovers o'er the painted images
Of those who once their yearning hearts have blessed?
Have we been happy on our day of rest?
20   Thine eyes say 'yes,'—but if it came again,
Perchance its ending would not seem so vain.

Now came fulfilment of the year's desire,
The tall wheat, coloured by the August fire
Grew heavy-headed, dreading its decay,
25   And blacker grew the elm-trees day by day.
About the edges of the yellow corn,
And o'er the gardens grown somewhat outworn
The bees went hurrying to fill up their store;
The apple-boughs bent over more and more;
30   With peach and apricot the garden wall
Was odorous, and the pears began to fall
From off the high tree with each freshening breeze.
So in a house bordered about with trees,
A little raised above the waving gold
35   The Wanderers heard this marvellous story told,
While 'twixt the gleaming flasks of ancient wine,
They watched the reapers' slow advancing line.

OCTOBER

O love, turn from the unchanging sea, and gaze
Down these grey slopes upon the year grown old,
A-dying mid the autumn-scented haze,
That hangeth o'er the hollow in the wold,
5   Where the wind-bitten ancient elms enfold
Grey church, long barn, orchard, and red-roofed stead,
Wrought in dead days for men a long while dead.

Come down, O love; may not our hands still meet,
Since still we live to-day, forgetting June,
10   Forgetting May, deeming October sweet—
—O hearken, hearken! through the afternoon,
The grey tower sings a strange old tinkling tune!
Sweet, sweet, and sad, the toiling year's last breath,
Too satiate of life to strive with death.

15   And we too—will it not be soft and kind,
That rest from life, from patience and from pain;
That rest from bliss we know not when we find;
That rest from Love which ne'er the end can gain?—
—Hark, how the tune swells, that erewhile did wane!
20   Look up, love!—ah, cling close and never move!
How can I have enough of life and love?

FEBRUARY

Noon—and the north-west sweeps the empty road,
The rain-washed fields from hedge to hedge are bare;
Beneath the leafless elms some hind's abode
Looks small and void, and no smoke meets the air
5   From its poor hearth: one lonely rook doth dare
The gale, and beats above the unseen corn,
Then turns, and whirling down the wind is borne.

Shall it not hap that on some dawn of May
Thou shalt awake, and, thinking of days dead,
10   See nothing clear but this same dreary day,
Of all the days that have passed o'er thine head?
Shalt thou not wonder, looking from thy bed,
Through green leaves on the windless east a-fire,
That this day too thine heart doth still desire?

15   Shalt thou not wonder that it liveth yet,
        The useless hope, the useless craving pain,
        That made thy face, that lonely noontide, wet
        With more than beating of the chilly rain?
        Shalt thou not hope for joy new born again,
20   Since no grief ever born can ever die
        Through changeless change of seasons passing by?

L'ENVOI

    Here are we for the last time face to face,
    Thou and I, Book, before I bid thee speed
    Upon thy perilous journey to that place
    For which I have done on thee pilgrim's weed,
5   Striving to get thee all things for thy need—
    —I love thee, whatso time or men may say
    Of the poor singer of an empty day.

    Good reason why I love thee, e'en if thou
    Be mocked or clean forgot as time wears on;
10   For ever as thy fashioning did grow,
    Kind word and praise because of thee I won
    From those without whom were my world all gone.
    My hope fallen dead, my singing cast away,
    And I set soothly in an empty day.

15   I love thee; yet this last time must it be
    That thou must hold thy peace and I must speak,
    Lest if thou babble I begin to see
    Thy gear too thin, thy limbs and heart too weak,
    To find the land thou goest forth to seek—
20   —Though what harm if thou die upon the way,
    Thou idle singer of an empty day?

    But though this land desired thou never reach,
    Yet folk who know it mayst thou meet or death;
    Therefore a word unto thee would I teach
25   To answer these, who, noting thy weak breath,
    Thy wandering eyes, thy heart of little faith,
    May make thy fond desire a sport and play,
    Mocking the singer of an empty day.

That land's name, say'st thou? and the road thereto?
30 Nay, Book, thou mockest, saying thou know'st it not;
Surely no book of verse I ever knew
But ever was the heart within him hot
To gain the Land of Matters Unforgot—
—There, now we both laugh—as the whole world may,
35 At us poor singers of an empty day.

Nay, let it pass, and hearken! Hast thou heard
That therein I believe I have a friend,
Of whom for love I may not be afeard?
It is to him indeed I bid thee wend;
40 Yea, he perchance may meet thee ere thou end,
Dying so far off from the hedge of bay,
Thou idle singer of an empty day!

Well, think of him, I bid thee, on the road,
And if it hap that midst of thy defeat,
45 Fainting beneath thy follies' heavy load,
My Master, GEOFFRY CHAUCER, thou do meet,
Then shalt thou win a space of rest full sweet;
Then be thou bold, and speak the words I say,
The idle singer of an empty day!

50 'O Master, O thou great of heart and tongue,
Thou well mayst ask me why I wander here,
In raiment rent of stories oft besung!
But of thy gentleness draw thou anear,
And then the heart of one who held thee dear
55 Mayst thou behold! So near as that I lay
Unto the singer of an empty day.

'For this he ever said, who sent me forth
To seek a place amid thy company;
That howsoever little was my worth,
60 Yet was he worth e'en just so much as I;
He said that rhyme hath little skill to lie;
Nor feigned to cast his worser part away;
In idle singing for an empty day.

'I have beheld him tremble oft enough
65 At things he could not choose but trust to me,
Although he knew the world was wise and rough:
And never did he fail to let me see
His love,—his folly and faithlessness, maybe;
And still in turn I gave him voice to pray
70 Such prayers as cling about an empty day.

'Thou, keen-eyed, reading me, mayst read him through,
For surely little is there left behind;
No power great deeds unnameable to do;
No knowledge for which words he may not find,
75   No love of things as vague as autumn wind—
  —Earth of the earth lies hidden by my clay,
The idle singer of an empty day!

'Children we twain are, saith he, late made wise
In love, but in all else most childish still,
80   And seeking still the pleasure of our eyes,
And what our ears with sweetest sound may fill;
Not fearing Love, lest these things he should kill;
Howe'er his pain by pleasure doth he lay,
Making a strange tale of an empty day.

85   'Death have we hated, knowing not what it meant;
Life have we loved, through green leaf and through sere,
Though still the less we knew of its intent:
The Earth and Heaven through countless year on year,
Slow changing, were to us but curtains fair,
90   Hung round about a little room, where play
Weeping and laughter of man's empty day.

'O Master, if thine heart could love us yet,
Spite of things left undone, and wrongly done,
Some place in loving hearts then should we get,
95   For thou, sweet-souled, didst never stand alone,
But knew'st the joy and woe of many an one—
  —By lovers dead, who live through thee, we pray,
Help thou us singers of an empty day!'

Fearest thou, Book, what answer thou mayst gain
100   Lest he should scorn thee, and thereof thou die?
Nay, it shall not be.—Thou mayst toil in vain,
And never draw the House of Fame anigh;
Yet he and his shall know whereof we cry,
Shall call it not ill done to strive to lay
105   The ghosts that crowd about life's empty day.

Then let the others go! and if indeed
In some old garden thou and I have wrought,
And made fresh flowers spring up from hoarded seed,
And fragrance of old days and deeds have brought
110   Back to folk weary; all was not for nought.
  —No little part it was for me to play—
The idle singer of an empty day.

Algernon Charles Swinburne

Algernon Charles Swinburne (1837–1909) was the son of a naval officer, and was educated at Eton and Oxford. In 1857 he first met Rossetti, Burne-Jones and Morris, and became associated with the second wave of the Pre-Raphaelite movement. His friendship with Rossetti, which lasted from 1861 to the early 1870s, was a great influence upon his work: it encouraged his independent, original and daring approach to the writing of poetry. Many of his poems, particularly those published in *Poems and Ballads* (1866), shocked the Victorian reading public; they would have doubtless been more shocked if they had known of Swinburne's sexual deviations and his bouts of drunkenness. In 1879, alarmed for his health, Theodore Watts-Dunton took him to his house, No. 2, The Pines, Putney, where he lived pleasantly and harmlessly, writing a good deal, for the last thirty years of his life.

For the young man in the 1860s, seeking to rebel against the conventions and morals of his parents but not quite sure how to do it, Swinburne's poetry came as a release and a revelation. It was erotic, pagan and sensuous, with an imagery that was full of colour and life, and rhythms that were powerful and compelling. As late as the turn of the century, according to Leonard Woolf (*Sowing*, pp. 167–71), Swinburne had this power to fascinate the young and rebellious.

For the older generation, of course, it was a different matter; and much contemporary criticism of Swinburne was violent in the extreme. A more serious criticism asserts that his poetry is short of ideas; but at its best, it is capable of possessing an exquisite beauty and a passionate energy, with a moving awareness of passing time and the beauty of sexual love.

From ATALANTA IN CALYDON

CHORUS

When the hounds of spring are on winter's traces,
    The mother of months in meadow or plain
Fills the shadows and windy places
    With lisp of leaves and ripple of rain;

5   And the brown bright nightingale amorous
      Is half assuaged for Itylus,
For the Thracian ships and the foreign faces,
      The tongueless vigil, and all the pain.

Come with bows bent and with emptying of quivers,
10   Maiden most perfect, lady of light,
With a noise of winds and many rivers,
      With a clamour of waters, and with might;
Bind on thy sandals, O thou most fleet,
Over the splendour and speed of thy feet;
15   For the faint east quickens, the wan west shivers,
      Round the feet of the day and the feet of the night.

Where shall we find her, how shall we sing to her,
      Fold our hands round her knees, and cling?
O that man's heart were as fire and could spring to her,
20   Fire, or the strength of the streams that spring!
For the stars and the winds are unto her
As raiment, as songs of the harp-player;
For the risen stars and the fallen cling to her,
      And the southwest-wind and the west-wind sing.

25   For winter's rains and ruins are over,
      And all the seasons of snows and sins;
The days dividing lover and lover,
      The light that loses, the night that wins;
And time remembered is grief forgotten,
30   And frosts are slain and flowers begotten,
And in green underwood and cover
      Blossom by blossom the spring begins.

The full streams feed on flower of rushes,
      Ripe grasses trammel a travelling foot,
35   The faint fresh flame of the young year flushes
      From leaf to flower and flower to fruit;
And fruit and leaf are as gold and fire,
And the oat is heard above the lyre,
And the hoofèd heel of a satyr crushes
40   The chestnut-husk at the chestnut-root.

And Pan by noon and Bacchus by night,
      Fleeter of foot than the fleet-foot kid,
Follows with dancing and fills with delight
      The Mænad and the Bassarid;
45   And soft as lips that laugh and hide
The laughing leaves of the trees divide,
And screen from seeing and leave in sight
      The god pursuing, the maiden hid.

The ivy falls with the Bacchanal's hair
50   Over her eyebrows hiding her eyes;
The wild vine slipping down leaves bare
    Her bright breast shortening into sighs;
The wild vine slips with the weight of its leaves,
But the berried ivy catches and cleaves
55 To the limbs that glitter, the feet that scare
    The wolf that follows, the fawn that flies.

THE TRIUMPH OF TIME

Before our lives divide for ever,
    While time is with us and hands are free,
(Time, swift to fasten and swift to sever
    Hand from hand, as we stand by the sea)
5 I will say no word that a man might say
Whose whole life's love goes down in a day;
For this could never have been; and never,
    Though the gods and the years relent, shall be.

Is it worth a tear, is it worth an hour,
10   To think of things that are well outworn?
Of fruitless husk and fugitive flower,
    The dream foregone and the deed forborne?
Though joy be done with and grief be vain,
Time shall not sever us wholly in twain;
15 Earth is not spoilt for a single shower;
    But the rain has ruined the ungrown corn.

It will grow not again, this fruit of my heart,
    Smitten with sunbeams, ruined with rain.
The singing seasons divide and depart,
20   Winter and summer depart in twain.
It will grow not again, it is ruined at root,
The bloodlike blossom, the dull red fruit;
Though the heart yet sickens, the lips yet smart,
    With sullen savour of poisonous pain.

25 I have given no man of my fruit to eat;
    I trod the grapes, I have drunken the wine.
Had you eaten and drunken and found it sweet,
    This wild new growth of the corn and vine,
This wine and bread without lees or leaven,
30 We had grown as gods, as the gods in heaven,
Souls fair to look upon, goodly to greet,
    One splendid spirit, your soul and mine.

In the change of years, in the coil of things,
    In the clamour and rumour of life to be,
35   We, drinking love at the furthest springs,
    Covered with love as a covering tree,
We had grown as gods, as the gods above,
Filled from the heart to the lips with love,
Held fast in his hands, clothed warm with his wings,
40   O love, my love, had you loved but me!

We had stood as the sure stars stand, and moved
    As the moon moves, loving the world; and seen
Grief collapse as a thing disproved,
    Death consume as a thing unclean.
45   Twain halves of a perfect heart, made fast
Soul to soul while the years fell past;
Had you loved me once, as you have not loved;
    Had the chance been with us that has not been.

I have put my days and dreams out of mind,
50   Days that are over, dreams that are done.
Though we seek life through, we shall surely find
    There is none of them clear to us now, not one.
But clear are these things; the grass and the sand,
Where, sure as the eyes reach, ever at hand,
55   With lips wide open and face burnt blind,
    The strong sea-daisies feast on the sun.

The low downs lean to the sea; the stream,
    One loose thin pulseless tremulous vein,
Rapid and vivid and dumb as a dream,
60   Works downward, sick of the sun and the rain;
No wind is rough with the rank rare flowers;
The sweet sea, mother of loves and hours,
Shudders and shines as the grey winds gleam,
    Turning her smile to a fugitive pain.

65   Mother of loves that are swift to fade,
    Mother of mutable winds and hours.
A barren mother, a mother-maid,
    Cold and clean as her faint salt flowers.
I would we twain were even as she,
70   Lost in the night and the light of the sea,
Where faint sounds falter and wan beams wade,
    Break, and are broken, and shed into showers.

The loves and hours of the life of a man,
    They are swift and sad, being born of the sea.
75   Hours that rejoice and regret for a span,
    Born with a man's breath, mortal as he;

Loves that are lost ere they come to birth,
Weeds of the wave, without fruit upon earth.
I lose what I long for, save what I can,
80   My love, my love, and no love for me!

It is not much that a man can save
    On the sands of life, in the straits of time,
Who swims in sight of the great third wave
    That never a swimmer shall cross or climb.
85 Some waif washed up with the strays and spars
That ebb-tide shows to the shore and the stars;
Weed from the water, grass from a grave,
    A broken blossom, a ruined rhyme.

There will no man do for your sake, I think,
90   What I would have done for the least word said.
I had wrung life dry for your lips to drink,
    Broken it up for your daily bread:
Body for body and blood for blood,
As the flow of the full sea risen to flood
95 That yearns and trembles before it sink,
    I had given, and lain down for you, glad and dead.

Yea, hope at highest and all her fruit,
    And time at fullest and all his dower,
I had given you surely, and life to boot,
100   Were we once made one for a single hour.
But now, you are twain, you are cloven apart,
Flesh of his flesh, but heart of my heart;
And deep in one is the bitter root,
    And sweet for one is the lifelong flower.

105 To have died if you cared I should die for you, clung
    To my life if you bade me, played my part
As it pleased you—these were the thoughts that stung,
    The dreams that smote with a keener dart
Than shafts of love or arrows of death;
110 These were but as fire is, dust, or breath,
Or poisonous foam on the tender tongue
    Of the little snakes that eat my heart.

I wish we were dead together to-day,
    Lost sight of, hidden away out of sight,
115 Clasped and clothed in the cloven clay,
    Out of the world's way, out of the light,
Out of the ages of worldly weather,
Forgotten of all men altogether.
As the world's first dead, taken wholly away,
120   Made one with death, filled full of the night.

How we should slumber, how we should sleep,
    Far in the dark with the dreams and the dews!
And dreaming, grow to each other, and weep,
    Laugh low, live softly, murmur and muse;
125   Yea, and it may be, struck through by the dream,
Feel the dust quicken and quiver, and seem
Alive as of old to the lips, and leap
    Spirit to spirit as lovers use.

Sick dreams and sad of a dull delight;
130   For what shall it profit when men are dead
To have dreamed, to have loved with the whole soul's might,
    To have looked for day when the day was fled?
Let come what will, there is one thing worth,
To have had fair love in the life upon earth:
135   To have held love safe till the day grew night,
    While skies had colour and lips were red.

Would I lose you now? would I take you then,
    If I lose you now that my heart has need?
And come what may after death to men,
140   What thing worth this will the dead years breed?
Lose life, lose all; but at least I know,
O sweet life's love, having loved you so,
Had I reached you on earth, I should lose not again,
    In death nor life, nor in dream or deed.

145   Yea, I know this well: were you once sealed mine,
    Mine in the blood's beat, mine in the breath,
Mixed into me as honey in wine,
    Not time, that sayeth and gainsayeth,
Nor all strong things had severed us then;
150   Not wrath of gods, nor wisdom of men,
Nor all things earthly, nor all divine,
    Nor joy nor sorrow, nor life nor death.

I had grown pure as the dawn and the dew,
    You had grown strong as the sun or the sea.
155   But none shall triumph a whole life through:
    For death is one, and the fates are three.
At the door of life, by the gate of breath,
There are worse things waiting for men than death;
Death could not sever my soul and you,
160   As these have severed your soul from me.

You have chosen and clung to the chance they sent you,
    Life sweet as perfume and pure as prayer.
But will it not one day in heaven repent you?
    Will they solace you wholly, the days that were?

165 Will you lift up your eyes between sadness and bliss,
Meet mine, and see where the great love is,
And tremble and turn and be changed? Content you;
 The gate is strait; I shall not be there.

But you, had you chosen, had you stretched hand,
170 Had you seen good such a thing were done,
I too might have stood with the souls that stand
 In the sun's sight, clothed with the light of the sun;
But who now on earth need care how I live?
Have the high gods anything left to give,
175 Save dust and laurels and gold and sand?
 Which gifts are goodly; but I will none.

O all fair lovers about the world,
 There is none of you, none, that shall comfort me.
My thoughts are as dead things, wrecked and whirled
180 Round and round in a gulf of the sea;
And still, through the sound and the straining stream,
Through the coil and chafe, they gleam in a dream,
The bright fine lips so cruelly curled,
 And strange swift eyes where the soul sits free.

185 Free, without pity, withheld from woe,
 Ignorant; fair as the eyes are fair.
Would I have you change now, change at a blow,
 Startled and stricken, awake and aware?
Yea, if I could, would I have you see
190 My very love of you filling me,
And know my soul to the quick, as I know
 The likeness and look of your throat and hair?

I shall not change you. Nay, though I might,
 Would I change my sweet one love with a word?
195 I had rather your hair should change in a night,
 Clear now as the plume of a black bright bird;
Your face fail suddenly, cease, turn grey,
Die as a leaf that dies in a day.
I will keep my soul in a place out of sight,
200 Far off, where the pulse of it is not heard.

Far off it walks, in a bleak blown space,
 Full of the sound of the sorrow of years.
I have woven a veil for the weeping face,
 Whose lips have drunken the wine of tears;
205 I have found a way for the failing feet,
A place for slumber and sorrow to meet;
There is no rumour about the place,
 Nor light, nor any that sees or hears.

I have hidden my soul out of sight, and said
210   'Let none take pity upon thee, none
Comfort thy crying: for lo, thou art dead,
       Lie still now, safe out of sight of the sun.
Have I not built thee a grave, and wrought
Thy grave-clothes on thee of grievous thought,
215   With soft spun verses and tears unshed,
       And sweet light visions of things undone?

'I have given thee garments and balm and myrrh,
       And gold, and beautiful burial things.
But thou, be at peace now, make no stir;
220   Is not thy grave as a royal king's?
Fret not thyself though the end were sore;
Sleep, be patient, vex me no more.
Sleep; what hast thou to do with her?
       The eyes that weep, with the mouth that sings?'

225   Where the dead red leaves of the years lie rotten,
       The cold old crimes and the deeds thrown by,
The misconceived and the misbegotten,
       I would find a sin to do ere I die,
Sure to dissolve and destroy me all through,
230   That would set you higher in heaven, serve you
And leave you happy, when clean forgotten,
       As a dead man out of mind, am I.

Your lithe hands draw me, your face burns through me,
       I am swift to follow you, keen to see;
235   But love lacks might to redeem or undo me;
       As I have been, I know I shall surely be;
'What should such fellows as I do?' Nay,
My part were worse if I chose to play;
For the worst is this after all; if they knew me,
240   Not a soul upon earth would pity me.

And I play not for pity of these; but you,
       If you saw with your soul what man am I,
You would praise me at least that my soul all through
       Clove to you, loathing the lives that lie;
245   The souls and lips that are bought and sold,
The smiles of silver and kisses of gold,
The lapdog loves that whine as they chew,
       The little lovers that curse and cry.

There are fairer women, I hear; that may be;
250   But I, that I love you and find you fair,
Who are more than fair in my eyes if they be,
       Do the high gods know or the great gods care?

Though the swords in my heart for one were seven,
Should the iron hollow of doubtful heaven,
That knows not itself whether night-time or day be,
    Reverberate words and a foolish prayer?

I will go back to the great sweet mother,
    Mother and lover of men, the sea.
I will go down to her, I and none other,
    Close with her, kiss her and mix her with me;
Cling to her, strive with her, hold her fast:
O fair white mother, in days long past
Born without sister, born without brother,
    Set free my soul as thy soul is free.

O fair green-girdled mother of mine,
    Sea, that art clothed with the sun and the rain,
Thy sweet hard kisses are strong like wine,
    Thy large embraces are keen like pain.
Save me and hide me with all thy waves,
Find me one grave of thy thousand graves,
Those pure cold populous graves of thine
    Wrought without hand in a world without stain.

I shall sleep, and move with the moving ships,
    Change as the winds change, veer in the tide;
My lips will feast on the foam of thy lips,
    I shall rise with thy rising, with thee subside;
Sleep, and not know if she be, if she were,
Filled full with life to the eyes and hair,
As a rose is fulfilled to the roseleaf tips
    With splendid summer and perfume and pride.

This woven raiment of nights and days,
    Were it once cast off and unwound from me,
Naked and glad would I walk in thy ways,
    Alive and aware of thy ways and thee;
Clear of the whole world, hidden at home,
Clothed with the green and crowned with the foam,
A pulse of the life of thy straits and bays,
    A vein in the heart of the streams of the sea.

Fair mother, fed with the lives of men,
    Thou art subtle and cruel of heart, men say.
Thou hast taken, and shalt not render again;
    Thou art full of thy dead, and cold as they.
But death is the worst that comes of thee;
Thou art fed with our dead, O mother, O sea,
But when hast thou fed on our hearts? or when,
    Having given us love, hast thou taken away?

O tender-hearted, O perfect lover,
 Thy lips are bitter, and sweet thine heart.
The hopes that hurt and the dreams that hover,
300 Shall they not vanish away and apart?
But thou, thou art sure, thou art older than earth;
Thou art strong for death and fruitful of birth;
Thy depths conceal and thy gulfs discover;
 From the first thou wert; in the end thou art.

305 And grief shall endure not for ever, I know.
  As things that are not shall these things be;
We shall live through seasons of sun and of snow,
 And none be grievous as this to me.
We shall hear, as one in a trance that hears,
310 The sound of time, the rhyme of the years;
Wrecked hope and passionate pain will grow
  As tender things of a spring-tide sea.

Sea-fruit that swings in the waves that hiss,
 Drowned gold and purple and royal rings.
315 And all time past, was it all for this?
  Times unforgotten, and treasures of things?
Swift years of liking and sweet long laughter,
That wist not well of the years thereafter
Till love woke, smitten at heart by a kiss,
320 With lips that trembled and trailing wings?

There lived a singer in France of old
 By the tideless dolorous midland sea.
In a land of sand and ruin and gold
 There shone one woman, and none but she.
325 And finding life for her love's sake fail,
Being fain to see her, he bade set sail,
Touched land, and saw her as life grew cold,
 And praised God, seeing; and so died he.

Died, praising God for his gift and grace:
330 For she bowed down to him weeping, and said
'Live;' and her tears were shed on his face
 Or ever the life in his face was shed.
The sharp tears fell through her hair, and stung
Once, and her close lips touched him and clung
335 Once, and grew one with his lips for a space;
  And so drew back, and the man was dead.

O brother, the gods were good to you.
 Sleep, and be glad while the world endures.
Be well content as the years wear through;
340 Give thanks for life, and the loves and lures;

Give thanks for life, O brother, and death,
For the sweet last sound of her feet, her breath,
For gifts she gave you, gracious and few,
   Tears and kisses, that lady of yours.

345   Rest, and be glad of the gods; but I,
   How shall I praise them, or how take rest?
There is not room under all the sky
   For me that know not of worst or best,
Dream or desire of the days before,
350   Sweet things or bitterness, any more.
Love will not come to me now though I die,
   As love came close to you, breast to breast.

I shall never be friends again with roses;
   I shall loathe sweet tunes, where a note grown strong
355   Relents and recoils, and climbs and closes,
   As a wave of the sea turned back by song.
There are sounds where the soul's delight takes fire,
Face to face with its own desire;
A delight that rebels, a desire that reposes;
360   I shall hate sweet music my whole life long.

The pulse of war and passion of wonder,
   The heavens that murmur, the sounds that shine,
The stars that sing and the loves that thunder,
   The music burning at heart like wine,
365   An armed archangel whose hands raise up
All senses mixed in the spirit's cup
Till flesh and spirit are molten in sunder—
   These things are over, and no more mine.

These were a part of the playing I heard
370   Once, ere my love and my heart were at strife;
Love that sings and hath wings as a bird,
   Balm of the wound and heft of the knife.
Fairer than earth is the sea, and sleep
Than overwatching of eyes that weep,
375   Now time has done with his one sweet word,
   The wine and leaven of lovely life.

I shall go my ways, tread out my measure,
   Fill the days of my daily breath
With fugitive things not good to treasure,
380   Do as the world doth, say as it saith;
But if we had loved each other—O sweet,
Had you felt, lying under the palms of your feet,
The heart of my heart, beating harder with pleasure
   To feel you tread it to dust and death—

385 Ah, had I not taken my life up and given
   All that life gives and the years let go,
 The wine and honey, the balm and leaven,
   The dreams reared high and the hopes brought low?
 Come life, come death, not a word be said;
390 Should I lose you living, and vex you dead?
 I never shall tell you on earth; and in heaven,
   If I cry to you then, will you hear or know?

HYMN TO PROSERPINE

(AFTER THE PROCLAMATION IN ROME OF THE CHRISTIAN FAITH)

Vicisti, Galilæe

I have lived long enough, having seen one thing, that love
  hath an end;
Goddess and maiden and queen, be near me now and
  befriend.
Thou art more than the day or the morrow, the seasons that
  laugh or that weep;
For these give joy and sorrow; but thou, Proserpina, sleep.
5 Sweet is the treading of wine, and sweet the feet of the dove;
But a goodlier gift is thine than foam of the grapes or love.
Yea, is not even Apollo, with hair and harpstring of gold,
A bitter God to follow, a beautiful God to behold?
I am sick of singing: the bays burn deep and chafe: I am fain
10 To rest a little from praise and grievous pleasure and pain.
For the Gods we know not of, who give us our daily breath,
We know they are cruel as love or life, and lovely as death.
O Gods dethroned and deceased, cast forth, wiped out in a
  day!
From your wrath is the world released, redeemed from your
  chains, men say.
15 New Gods are crowned in the city; their flowers have broken
  your rods;
They are merciful, clothed with pity, the young compassionate
  Gods.
But for me their new device is barren, the days are bare;
Things long past over suffice, and men forgotten that were.
Time and the Gods are at strife; ye dwell in the midst
  thereof,
20 Draining a little life from the barren breasts of love.
I say to you, cease, take rest; yea, I say to you all, be at
  peace,

Till the bitter milk of her breast and the barren bosom shall
cease.
Wilt thou yet take all, Galilean? but these thou shalt not
take,
The laurel, the palms and the pæan, the breasts of the
nymphs in the brake;

25 Breasts more soft than a dove's, that tremble with tenderer
breath;
And all the wings of the Loves, and all the joy before death;
All the feet of the hours that sound as a single lyre,
Dropped and deep in the flowers, with strings that flicker
like fire.
More than these wilt thou give, things fairer than all these
things?

30 Nay, for a little we live, and life hath mutable wings.
A little while and we die; shall life not thrive as it may?
For no man under the sky lives twice, outliving his day.
And grief is a grievous thing, and a man hath enough of his
tears:
Why should he labour, and bring fresh grief to blacken his
years?

35 Thou hast conquered, O pale Galilean; the world has grown
grey from thy breath;
We have drunken of things Lethean, and fed on the fullness
of death.
Laurel is green for a season, and love is sweet for a day;
But love grows bitter with treason, and laurel outlives not
May.
Sleep, shall we sleep after all? for the world is not sweet in
the end;

40 For the old faiths loosen and fall, the new years ruin and
rend.
Fate is a sea without shore, and the soul is a rock that
abides;
But her ears are vexed with the roar and her face with the
foam of the tides.
O lips that the live blood faints in, the leavings of racks and
rods!
O ghastly glories of saints, dead limbs of gibbeted Gods!

45 Though all men abase them before you in spirit, and all
knees bend,
I kneel not neither adore you, but standing, look to the end.
All delicate days and pleasant, all spirits and sorrows are
cast
Far out with the foam of the present that sweeps to the
surf of the past:
Where beyond the extreme sea-wall, and between the remote
sea-gates,

50 Waste water washes, and tall ships founder, and deep death
        waits:
    Where, mighty with deepening sides, clad about with the
        seas as with wings,
    And impelled of invisible tides, and fulfilled of unspeakable
        things,
    White-eyed and poisonous-finned, shark-toothed and
        serpentine-curled,
    Rolls, under the whitening wind of the future, the wave of
        the world.
55 The depths stand naked in sunder behind it, the storms flee
        away;
    In the hollow before it the thunder is taken and snared as a
        prey;
    In its sides is the north-wind bound; and its salt is of all
        men's tears;
    With light of ruin, and sound of changes, and pulse of
        years:
    With travail of day after day, and with trouble of hour upon
        hour;
60 And bitter as blood is the spray; and the crests are as fangs
        that devour:
    And its vapour and storm of its steam as the sighing of
        spirits to be;
    And its noise as the noise in a dream; and its depth as the
        roots of the sea:
    And the height of its heads as the height of the utmost stars
        of the air:
    And the ends of the earth at the might thereof tremble, and
        time is made bare.
65 Will ye bridle the deep sea with reins, will ye chasten the
        high sea with rods?
    Will ye take her to chain her with chains, who is older than
        all ye Gods?
    All ye as a wind shall go by, as a fire shall ye pass and be
        past;
    Ye are Gods, and behold, ye shall die, and the waves be
        upon you at last.
    In the darkness of time, in the deeps of the years, in the
        changes of things,
70 Ye shall sleep as a slain man sleeps, and the world shall
        forget you for kings.
    Though the feet of thine high priests tread where thy lords
        and our forefathers trod,
    Though these that were Gods are dead, and thou being
        dead art a God,
    Though before thee the throned Cytherean be fallen, and
        hidden her head,

Yet thy kingdom shall pass, Galilean, thy dead shall go
    down to thee dead.
75   Of the maiden thy mother men sing as a goddess with grace
    clad around;
Thou art throned where another was king; where another
    was queen she is crowned.
Yea, once we had sight of another: but now she is queen,
    say these.
Not as thine, not as thine was our mother, a blossom of
    flowering seas,
Clothed round with the world's desire as with raiment, and
    fair as the foam,
80   And fleeter than kindled fire, and a goddess, and mother of
    Rome.
For thine came pale and a maiden, and sister to sorrow; but
    ours,
Her deep hair heavily laden with odour and colour of
    flowers,
White rose of the rose-white water, a silver splendour, a flame,
Bent down unto us that besought her, and earth grew sweet
    with her name.
85   For thine came weeping, a slave among slaves, and rejected;
    but she
Came flushed from the full-flushed wave, and imperial, her
    foot on the sea.
And the wonderful waters knew her, the winds and the
    viewless ways,
And the roses grew rosier, and bluer the sea-blue stream of
    the bays.
Ye are fallen, our lords, by what token? we wist that ye
    should not fall.
90   Ye were all so fair that are broken; and one more fair than
    ye all.
But I turn to her still, having seen she shall surely abide in
    the end;
Goddess and maiden and queen, be near me now and
    befriend.
O daughter of earth, of my mother, her crown and blossom
    of birth,
I am also, I also, thy brother; I go as I came unto earth.
95   In the night where thine eyes are as moons are in heaven,
    the night where thou art,
Where the silence is more than all tunes, where sleep overflows
    from the heart,
Where the poppies are sweet as the rose in our world, and
    the red rose is white,
And the wind falls faint as it blows with the fume of the
    flowers of the night,

And the murmur of spirits that sleep in the shadow of Gods
    from afar
100   Grows dim in thine ears and deep as the deep dim soul of a
    star,
In the sweet low light of thy face, under heavens untrod by
    the sun,
Let my soul with their souls find place, and forget what is done
    and undone.
Thou art more than the Gods who number the days of our
    temporal breath;
For these give labour and slumber; but thou, Proserpina,
    death.
105   Therefore now at thy feet I abide for a season in silence. I
    know
I shall die as my fathers died, and sleep as they sleep; even so.
For the glass of the years is brittle wherein we gaze for a
    span;
A little soul for a little bears up this corpse which is man.[1]
So long I endure, no longer; and laugh not again, neither
    weep.
110   For there is no God found stronger than death; and death
    is a sleep.

[1] ψυχάριον εἶ βαστάζον νεκρόν.

EPICTETUS

THE LAKE OF GAUBE

The sun is lord and god, sublime, serene,
    And sovereign on the mountains: earth and air
Lie prone in passion, blind with bliss unseen
    By force of sight and might of rapture, fair
5   As dreams that die and know not what they were.
The lawns, the gorges, and the peaks, are one
Glad glory, thrilled with sense of unison
In strong compulsive silence of the sun.

Flowers dense and keen as midnight stars aflame
10   And living things of light like flames in flower
That glance and flash as though no hand might tame
    Lightnings whose life outshone their stormlit hour
    And played and laughed on earth, with all their power
Gone, and with all their joy of life made long
15   And harmless as the lightning life of song,
Shine sweet like stars when darkness feels them strong.

198

The deep mild purple flaked with moonbright gold
    That makes the scales seem flowers of hardened light,
The flamelike tongue, the feet that noon leaves cold,
20   The kindly trust in man, when once the sight
    Grew less than strange, and faith bade fear take flight,
Outlive the little harmless life that shone
And gladdened eyes that loved it, and was gone
Ere love might fear that fear had looked thereon.

25 Fear held the bright thing hateful, even as fear,
      Whose name is one with hate and horror, saith
That heaven, the dark deep heaven of water near,
      Is deadly deep as hell and dark as death.
      The rapturous plunge that quickens blood and breath
30 With pause more sweet than passion, ere they strive
To raise again the limbs that yet would dive
Deeper, should there have slain the soul alive.

As the bright salamander in fire of the noonshine exults and
      is glad of his day,
The spirit that quickens my body rejoices to pass from the
      sunlight away,
35 To pass from the glow of the mountainous flowerage, the
      high multitudinous bloom,
Far down through the fathomless night of the water, the
      gladness of silence and gloom.
Death-dark and delicious as death in the dream of a lover
      and dreamer may be,
It clasps and encompasses body and soul with delight to be
      living and free:
Free utterly now, though the freedom endure but the space
      of a perilous breath,
40 And living, though girdled about with the darkness and
      coldness and strangeness of death:
Each limb and each pulse of the body rejoicing, each nerve
      of the spirit at rest,
All sense of the soul's life rapture, a passionate peace in its
      blindness blest.
So plunges the downward swimmer, embraced of the water
      unfathomed of man,
The darkness unplummeted, icier than seas in midwinter,
      for blessing or ban:
45 And swiftly and sweetly, when strength and breath fall short,
      and the dive is done,
Shoots up as a shaft from the dark depth shot, sped straight
      into sight of the sun;
And sheer through the snow-soft water, more dark than the
      roof of the pines above,

Strikes forth, and is glad as a bird whose flight is impelled
    and sustained of love.
As a sea-mew's love of the sea-wind breasted and ridden for
    rapture's sake
50 Is the love of his body and soul for the darkling delight of
    the soundless lake:
As the silent speed of a dream too living to live for a
    thought's space more
Is the flight of his limbs through the still strong chill of the
    darkness from shore to shore.
Might life be as this is and death be as life that casts off time
    as a robe,
The likeness of infinite heaven were a symbol revealed of the
    lake of Gaube.

55 Whose thought has fathomed and measured
    The darkness of life and of death,
The secret within them treasured,
    The spirit that is not breath?
Whose vision has yet beholden
60   The splendour of death and of life?
Though sunset as dawn be golden,
    Is the word of them peace, not strife?
Deep silence answers: the glory
    We dream of may be but a dream,
65 And the sun of the soul wax hoary
    As ashes that show not a gleam.
But well shall it be with us ever
    Who drive through the darkness here,
If the soul that we live by never,
70   For aught that a lie saith, fear.

W. E. Henley

William Ernest Henley (1849–1903) was the son of a Gloucester book-seller. Crippled from childhood by tubercular arthritis, he had already lost one foot when he travelled to Edinburgh in 1873 to place himself under Joseph Lister, who was then fighting to prove the value of antiseptic surgery. 'In Hospital' is the record of his suffering, endurance and eventual discharge after twenty months; its dingy, scrupulous realism, and free metres that mimic the stress of an actual experience were a marked departure from prevailing canons of taste. Later Henley became an influential editor, and his *National Observer* became the rallying point for opposition to the aestheticism of the *Yellow Book* in the nineties.

IN HOSPITAL

On ne saurait dire à quel point un homme, seul dans son lit et malade, devient personnel.—

BALZAC

I
ENTER PATIENT

The morning mists still haunt the stony street;
The northern summer air is shrill and cold;
And lo, the Hospital, gray, quiet, old,
Where Life and Death like friendly chafferers meet.
5   Thro' the loud spaciousness and draughty gloom
A small, strange child—so agèd yet so young!—
Her little arm besplinted and beslung,
Precedes me gravely to the waiting-room.
I limp behind, my confidence all gone.
10 The gray-haired soldier-porter waves me on,
And on I crawl, and still my spirits fail:
A tragic meanness seems so to environ
These corridors and stairs of stone and iron,
Cold, naked, clean—half-workhouse and half-jail.

II
WAITING

A square, squat room (a cellar on promotion),
    Drab to the soul, drab to the very daylight;
    Plasters astray in unnatural-looking tinware;
    Scissors and lint and apothecary's jars.

5   Here, on a bench a skeleton would writhe from,
    Angry and sore, I wait to be admitted:
    Wait till my heart is lead upon my stomach,
    While at their ease two dressers do their chores.

One has a probe—it feels to me a crowbar.
10   A small boy sniffs and shudders after bluestone.
    A poor old tramp explains his poor old ulcers.
    Life is (I think) a blunder and a shame.

III
INTERIOR

    The gaunt brown walls
Look infinite in their decent meanness.
There is nothing of home in the noisy kettle,
    The fulsome fire.

5   The atmosphere
Suggests the trail of a ghostly druggist.
Dressings and lint on the long, lean table—
    Whom are they for?

    The patients yawn,
10   Or lie as in training for shroud and coffin.
A nurse in the corridor scolds and wrangles.
    It's grim and strange.

    Far footfalls clank.
The bad burn waits with his head unbandaged.
15   My neighbour chokes in the clutch of chloral ...
    O, a gruesome world!

IV
BEFORE

Behold me waiting—waiting for the knife.
A little while, and at a leap I storm
The thick, sweet mystery of chloroform,
The drunken dark, the little death-in-life.

5   The gods are good to me: I have no wife,
     No innocent child, to think of as I near
     The fateful minute; nothing all-too dear
     Unmans me for my bout of passive strife.
     Yet am I tremulous and a trifle sick,
10   And, face to face with chance, I shrink a little:
     My hopes are strong, my will is something weak.
     Here comes the basket? Thank you. I am ready.
     But, gentlemen my porters, life is brittle:
     You carry Cæsar and his fortunes—steady!

V

OPERATION

You are carried in a basket,
     Like a carcase from the shambles,
     To the theatre, a cockpit
     Where they stretch you on a table.

5   Then they bid you close your eyelids,
     And they mask you with a napkin,
     And the anæsthetic reaches
     Hot and subtle through your being.

And you gasp and reel and shudder
10   In a rushing, swaying rapture,
     While the voices at your elbow
     Fade—receding—fainter—farther.

Lights about you shower and tumble,
     And your blood seems crystallising—
15   Edged and vibrant, yet within you
     Racked and hurried back and forward.

Then the lights grow fast and furious,
     And you hear a noise of waters,
     And you wrestle, blind and dizzy,
20   In an agony of effort,

Till a sudden lull accepts you,
     And you sound an utter darkness ...
     And awaken ... with a struggle ...
     On a hushed, attentive audience.

203

VI
AFTER

Like as a flamelet blanketed in smoke,
So through the anæsthetic shows my life;
So flashes and so fades my thought, at strife
With the strong stupor that I heave and choke
5   And sicken at, it is so foully sweet.
Faces look strange from space—and disappear.
Far voices, sudden loud, offend my ear—
And hush as sudden. Then my senses fleet:
All were a blank, save for this dull, new pain
10 That grinds my leg and foot; and brokenly
Time and the place glimpse on to me again;
And, unsurprised, out of uncertainty,
I awake—relapsing—somewhat faint and fain,
To an immense, complacent dreamery.

VII
VIGIL

Lived on one's back,
In the long hours of repose,
Life is a practical nightmare—
Hideous asleep or awake.

5   Shoulders and loins
Ache - - -!
Ache, and the mattress,
Run into boulders and hummocks,
Glows like a kiln, while the bed-clothes—
10 Tumbling, importunate, daft—
Ramble and roll, and the gas,
Screwed to its lowermost,
An inevitable atom of light,
Haunts, and a stertorous sleeper
15 Snores me to hate and despair.

All the old time
   Surges malignant before me;
Old voices, old kisses, old songs
Blossom derisive about me;
20 While the new days
Pass me in endless procession;
A pageant of shadows
Silently, leeringly wending
On ... and still on ... still on!

25   Far in the stillness a cat
Languishes loudly. A cinder
Falls, and the shadows
Lurch to the leap of the flame. The next man to me
Turns with a moan; and the snorer,
30   The drug like a rope at his throat,
Gasps, gurgles, snorts himself free, as the night-nurse,
Noiseless and strange,
Her bull's eye half-lanterned in apron
(Whispering me, 'Are ye no' sleepin' yet?'),
35   Passes, list-slippered and peering,
Round ... and is gone.

Sleep comes at last—
Sleep full of dreams and misgivings—
Broken with brutal and sordid
40   Voices and sounds that impose on me,
Ere I can wake to it,
The unnatural, intolerable day.

VIII
STAFF-NURSE: OLD STYLE

The greater masters of the commonplace,
REMBRANDT and good SIR WALTER—only these
Could paint her all to you: experienced ease
And antique liveliness and ponderous grace;
5   The sweet old roses of her sunken face;
The depth and malice of her sly, gray eyes;
The broad Scots tongue that flatters, scolds, defies;
The thick Scots wit that fells you like a mace.
These thirty years has she been nursing here,
10   Some of them under SYME, her hero still.
Much is she worth, and even more is made of her.
Patients and students hold her very dear.
The doctors love her, tease her, use her skill.
They say 'The Chief' himself is half-afraid of her.

IX
LADY-PROBATIONER

Some three, or five, or seven, and thirty years;
A Roman nose; a dimpling double-chin;
Dark eyes and shy that, ignorant of sin,
Are yet acquainted, it would seem, with tears;

5   A comely shape; a slim, high-coloured hand,
    Graced, rather oddly, with a signet ring;
    A bashful air, becoming everything;
    A well-bred silence always at command.
    Her plain print gown, prim cap, and bright steel chain
10 Look out of place on her, and I remain
    Absorbed in her, as in a pleasant mystery.
    Quick, skilful, quiet, soft in speech and touch ...
    'Do you like nursing?' 'Yes, Sir, very much.'
    Somehow, I rather think she has a history.

X

STAFF-NURSE: NEW STYLE

    Blue-eyed and bright of face but waning fast
    Into the sere of virginal decay,
    I view her as she enters, day by day,
    As a sweet sunset almost overpast.
5   Kindly and calm, patrician to the last,
    Superbly falls her gown of sober gray,
    And on her chignon's elegant array
    The plainest cap is somehow touched with caste.
    She talks BEETHOVEN; frowns disapprobation
10 At BALZAC's name, sighs it at 'poor GEORGE SAND's;
    Knows that she has exceeding pretty hands;
    Speaks Latin with a right accentuation;
    And gives at need (as one who understands)
    Draught, counsel, diagnosis, exhortation.

XI

CLINICAL

    Hist? ...
    Through the corridor's echoes
    Louder and nearer
    Comes a great shuffling of feet.
5   Quick, every one of you,
    Straight your quilts, and be decent!
    Here's the Professor.

    In he comes first
    With the bright look we know,
10 From the broad, white brows the kind eyes
    Soothing yet nerving you. Here at his elbow,
    White-capped, white-aproned, the Nurse,
    Towel on arm and her inkstand
    Fretful with quills.
15 Here in the ruck, anyhow,

206

Surging along,
Louts, duffers, exquisites, students, and prigs—
Whiskers and foreheads, scarf-pins and spectacles—
Hustles the Class! And they ring themselves
20 Round the first bed, where the Chief
(His dressers and clerks at attention),
Bends in inspection already.

So shows the ring
Seen from behind round a conjurer
25 Doing his pitch in the street.
High shoulders, low shoulders, broad shoulders, narrow ones,
Round, square, and angular, serry and shove;
While from within a voice,
Gravely and weightily fluent,
30 Sounds; and then ceases; and suddenly
(Look at the stress of the shoulders!)
Out of a quiver of silence,
Over the hiss of the spray,
Comes a low cry, and the sound
35 Of breath quick intaken through teeth
Clenched in resolve. And the Master
Breaks from the crowd, and goes,
Wiping his hands,
To the next bed, with his pupils
40 Flocking and whispering behind him.

Now one can see.
Case Number One
Sits (rather pale) with his bedclothes
Stripped up, and showing his foot
45 (Alas for God's Image!)
Swaddled in wet, white lint
Brilliantly hideous with red.

XII
ETCHING

Two and thirty is the ploughman.
He's a man of gallant inches,
And his hair is close and curly,
    And his beard;
5 But his face is wan and sunken,
And his eyes are large and brilliant,
And his shoulder-blades are sharp,
    And his knees.

He is weak of wits, religious,
10   Full of sentiment and yearning,
    Gentle, faded—with a cough
        And a snore.
    When his wife (who was a widow,
    And is many years his elder)
15   Fails to write, and that is always,
        He desponds.

Let his melancholy wander,
And he'll tell you pretty stories
Of the women that have wooed him
20   Long ago;
Or he'll sing of bonnie lasses
Keeping sheep among the heather,
With a crackling, hackling click
    In his voice.

XIII
CASUALTY

As with varnish red and glistening
    Dripped his hair; his feet looked rigid;
    Raised, he settled stiffly sideways:
    You could see his hurts were spinal.

5 He had fallen from an engine,
    And been dragged along the metals.
    It was hopeless, and they knew it;
    So they covered him, and left him.

As he lay, by fits half sentient,
10   Inarticulately moaning,
    With his stockinged soles protruded
    Stark and awkward from the blankets,

To his bed there came a woman,
    Stood and looked and sighed a little,
15   And departed without speaking,
    As himself a few hours after.

I was told it was his sweetheart.
    They were on the eve of marriage.
    She was quiet as a statue,
20   But her lip was gray and writhen.

XIV
AVE, CAESAR!

From the winter's gray despair,
From the summer's golden languor,
Death, the lover of Life,
Frees us for ever.

5   Inevitable, silent, unseen,
Everywhere always,
Shadow by night and as light in the day,
Signs she at last to her chosen;
And, as she waves them forth,
10   Sorrow and Joy
Lay by their looks and their voices,
Set down their hopes, and are made
One in the dim Forever.

Into the winter's gray delight,
15   Into the summer's golden dream,
Holy and high and impartial,
Death, the mother of Life,
Mingles all men for ever.

XV
'THE CHIEF'

His brow spreads large and placid, and his eye
Is deep and bright, with steady looks that still.
Soft lines of tranquil thought his face fulfill—
His face at once benign and proud and shy.
5   If envy scout, if ignorance deny,
His faultless patience, his unyielding will,
Beautiful gentleness and splendid skill,
Innumerable gratitudes reply.
His wise, rare smile is sweet with certainties,
10   And seems in all his patients to compel
Such love and faith as failure cannot quell.
We hold him for another Herakles,
Battling with custom, prejudice, disease,
As once the son of Zeus with Death and Hell.

XVI
HOUSE-SURGEON

Exceeding tall, but built so well his height
Half-disappears in flow of chest and limb;

Moustache and whisker trooper-like in trim;
Frank-faced, frank-eyed, frank-hearted; always bright
And always punctual—morning, noon, and night;
Bland as a Jesuit, sober as a hymn;
Humorous, and yet without a touch of whim;
Gentle and amiable, yet full of fight.
His piety, though fresh and true in strain,
Has not yet whitewashed up his common mood
To the dead blank of his particular Schism.
Sweet, unaggressive, tolerant, most humane,
Wild artists like his kindly elderhood,
And cultivate his mild Philistinism.

5

10

XVII

INTERLUDE

O, the fun, the fun and frolic
    That *The Wind that Shakes the Barley*
    Scatters through a penny-whistle
    Tickled with artistic fingers!

Kate the scrubber (forty summers,
    Stout but sportive) treads a measure,
    Grinning, in herself a ballet,
    Fixed as fate upon her audience.

Stumps are shaking, crutch-supported;
    Splinted fingers tap the rhythm;
    And a head all helmed with plasters
    Wags a measured approbation.

Of their mattress-life oblivious,
    All the patients, brisk and cheerful,
    Are encouraging the dancer,
    And applauding the musician.

Dim the gas-lights in the output
    Of so many ardent smokers,
    Full of shadow lurch the corners,
    And the doctor peeps and passes.

There are, maybe, some suspicions
    Of an alcoholic presence . . .
    'Tak' a sup of this, my wumman!' . . .
    New Year comes but once a twelve-month.

5

10

15

20

XVIII
CHILDREN: PRIVATE WARD

Here in this dim, dull, double-bedded room,
I play the father to a brace of boys,
Ailing but apt for every sort of noise,
Bedfast but brilliant yet with health and bloom.
5   Roden, the Irishman, is 'sieven past',
Blue-eyed, snub-nosed, chubby, and fair of face.
Willie's but six, and seems to like the place,
A cheerful little collier to the last.
They eat, and laugh, and sing, and fight, all day;
10 All night they sleep like dormice. See them play
At Operations:—Roden, the Professor,
Saws, lectures, takes the artery up, and ties;
Willie, self-chloroformed, with half-shut eyes,
Holding the limb and moaning—Case and Dresser.

XIX
SCRUBBER

She's tall and gaunt, and in her hard, sad face
With flashes of the old fun's animation
There lowers the fixed and peevish resignation
Bred of a past where troubles came apace.
5   She tells me that her husband, ere he died,
Saw seven of their children pass away,
And never knew the little lass at play
Out on the green, in whom he's deified.
Her kin dispersed, her friends forgot and gone,
10 All simple faith her honest Irish mind,
Scolding her spoiled young saint, she labours on:
Telling her dreams, taking her patients' part,
Trailing her coat sometimes: and you shall find
No rougher, quainter speech, nor kinder heart.

XX
VISITOR

Her little face is like a walnut shell
With wrinkling lines; her soft, white hair adorns
Her withered brows in quaint, straight curls, like horns;
And all about her clings an old, sweet smell.
5   Prim is her gown and quakerlike her shawl.
Well might her bonnets have been born on her.
Can you conceive a Fairy Godmother
The subject of a strong religious call?

211

10   In snow or shine, from bed to bed she runs,
All twinkling smiles and texts and pious tales,
Her mittened hands, that ever give or pray,
Bearing a sheaf of tracts, a bag of buns:
A wee old maid that sweeps the Bridegroom's way,
Strong in a cheerful trust that never fails.

XXI
ROMANCE

'Talk of pluck!' pursued the Sailor,
    Set at euchre on his elbow,
    'I was on the wharf at Charleston,
    Just ashore from off the runner.

5   'It was gray and dirty weather,
    And I heard a drum go rolling,
    Rub-a-dubbing in the distance
    Awful dour-like and defiant.

'In and out among the cotton,
10   Mud, and chains, and stores, and anchors,
    Tramped a squad of battered scarecrows—
    Poor old Dixie's bottom dollar!

'Some had shoes, but all had rifles,
    Them that wasn't bald was beardless,
15   And the drum was rolling *Dixie*,
    And they stepped to it like men, sir!

'Rags and tatters, belts and bayonets,
    On they swung, the drum a-rolling,
    Mum and sour. It looked like fighting,
20   And they meant it too, by thunder!'

XXII
PASTORAL

It's the Spring.
Earth has conceived, and her bosom,
Teeming with summer, is glad.

Vistas of change and adventure,
5   Thro' the green land
The gray roads go beckoning and winding,
Peopled with wains, and melodious

With harness-bells jangling:
Jangling and twangling rough rhythms
10   To the slow march of the stately, great horses
Whistled and shouted along.

White fleets of cloud,
Argosies heavy with fruitfulness,
Sail the blue peacefully. Green flame the hedgerows.
15   Blackbirds are bugling, and white in wet winds
Sway the tall poplars.
Pageants of colour and fragrance,
Pass the sweet meadows, and viewless
Walks the mild spirit of May,
20   Visibly blessing the world.

O, the brilliance of blossoming orchards!
O, the savour and thrill of the woods,
When their leafage is stirred
By the flight of the Angel of Rain!
25   Loud lows the steer; in the fallows
Rooks are alert; and the brooks
Gurgle and tinkle and trill. Thro' the gloamings,
Under the rare, shy stars,
Boy and girl wander,
30   Dreaming in darkness and dew.

It's the Spring.
A sprightliness feeble and squalid
Wakes in the ward, and I sicken,
Impotent, winter at heart.

XXIII
MUSIC

Down the quiet eve,
Thro' my window with the sunset
Pipes to me a distant organ
Foolish ditties;

5   And, as when you change
Pictures in a magic lantern,
Books, beds, bottles, floor, and ceiling
Fade and vanish,

And I'm well once more. . . .
10   August flares adust and torrid,
But my heart is full of April
Sap and sweetness.

213

In the quiet eve
I am loitering, longing, dreaming ...
15   Dreaming, and a distant organ
Pipes me ditties.

I can see the shop,
I can smell the sprinkled pavement,
Where she serves—her chestnut chignon
20   Thrills my senses!

O, the sight and scent,
Wistful eve and perfumed pavement!
In the distance pipes an organ ...
The sensation

25   Comes to me anew,
And my spirit for a moment
Thro' the music breathes the blessèd
Airs of London.

XXIV
SUICIDE

Staring corpselike at the ceiling,
    See his harsh, unrazored features,
    Ghastly brown against the pillow,
    And his throat—so strangely bandaged!

5   Lack of work and lack of victuals,
    A debauch of smuggled whisky,
    And his children in the workhouse
    Made the world so black a riddle

That he plunged for a solution;
10   And, although his knife was edgeless,
    He was sinking fast towards one,
    When they came, and found, and saved him.

Stupid now with shame and sorrow,
    In the night I hear him sobbing.
15   But sometimes he talks a little.
    He has told me all his troubles.

In his broad face, tanned and bloodless,
    White and wild his eyeballs glisten;
    And his smile, occult and tragic,
20   Yet so slavish, makes you shudder!

XXV
APPARITION

Thin-legged, thin-chested, slight unspeakably,
Neat-footed and weak-fingered: in his face—
Lean, large-boned, curved of beak, and touched with race,
Bold-lipped, rich-tinted, mutable as the sea,
5   The brown eyes radiant with vivacity—
There shines a brilliant and romantic grace,
A spirit intense and rare, with trace on trace
Of passion and impudence and energy.
Valiant in velvet, light in ragged luck,
10   Most vain, most generous, sternly critical,
Buffoon and poet, lover and sensualist:
A deal of Ariel, just a streak of Puck,
Much Antony, of Hamlet most of all,
And something of the Shorter-Catechist.

XXVI
ANTEROTICS

Laughs the happy April morn
    Thro' my grimy, little window,
    And a shaft of sunshine pushes
    Thro' the shadows in the square.

5   Dogs are tracing thro' the grass,
    Crows are cawing round the chimneys,
    In and out among the washing
    Goes the West at hide-and-seek.

Loud and cheerful clangs the bell.
10   Here the nurses troop to breakfast.
    Handsome, ugly, all are women . . .
    O, the Spring—the Spring—the Spring!

XXVII
NOCTURN

At the barren heart of midnight,
    When the shadow shuts and opens
    As the loud flames pulse and flutter,
    I can hear a cistern leaking.

5   Dripping, dropping, in a rhythm,
    Rough, unequal, half-melodious,
    Like the measures aped from nature
    In the infancy of music;

Like the buzzing of an insect,
10   Still, irrational, persistent . . .
        I must listen, listen, listen
        In a passion of attention;

Till it taps upon my heartstrings,
        And my very life goes dripping,
15   Dropping, dripping, drip-drip-dropping,
        In the drip-drop of the cistern.

XXVIII

DISCHARGED

Carry me out
Into the wind and the sunshine,
Into the beautiful world.

O, the wonder, the spell of the streets!
5   The stature and strength of the horses,
        The rustle and echo of footfalls,
        The flat roar and rattle of wheels!
        A swift tram floats huge on us . . .
        It's a dream?
10   The smell of the mud in my nostrils
        Blows brave—like a breath of the sea!

As of old,
Ambulant, undulant drapery,
Vaguely and strangely provocative,
15   Flutters and beckons. O, yonder—
        Is it?—the gleam of a stocking!
        Sudden, a spire
        Wedged in the mist! O, the houses,
        The long lines of lofty, gray houses,
20   Cross-hatched with shadow and light!
        These are the streets. . . .
        Each is an avenue leading
        Whither I will!

Free . . . !
25   Dizzy, hysterical, faint,
        I sit, and the carriage rolls on with me
        Into the wonderful world.

THE OLD INFIRMARY, EDINBURGH, 1873–75

Notes

WILLIAM BARNES

In the Dorset dialect 'd' is habitually used for 'th' ('drough' instead of 'through'), 'v' for 'f' ('vield' instead of 'field'), 'z' for 's' ('zee' instead of 'see'), and 'en' for 'ing' ('whistlen' instead of 'whistling'). There are many diminished forms ('o' and 'an' for 'of' and 'and') and in some cases 'wo' is used instead of 'o' ('wold' for 'old'). The diæresis is used to indicate that both vowels are pronounced ('païns'), and 'mid' is the Dorset form of 'may' and 'might'.

From *Poems of Rural Life in the Dorset Dialect* (1844)

p. 1. Evenen in the Village. Note the careful choice of detail, particularly auditory detail, that goes to make up this magical picture of rural dusk. The two stanzas are subtly differentiated as Barnes portrays the transition from labour to recreation made necessary by the limitation of artificial light.

p. 1. Woodley.
3. *clotes* yellow water-lilies.
6. *blooth* a mass of blossom.
8. *grægles* wild hyacinth.
18. *knaps* hillocks.
19. *hatch* half door.
21–4. Barnes often employs sharp visual antitheses of this nature, to great effect.

p. 2. Eclogue: The Common A-Took In. This poem was first published in 1834 at a time of great social unrest; it was the year of the Tolpuddle martyrs. Barnes's social criticism is most explicit on the subject of enclosure, which he regarded as an unmitigated social evil. Not only did it destroy the landscape and cause financial hardship by depriving the poor of their grazing rights, but the villagers lost their sense of community, and consequently their culture. Enclosure came late to Dorset: Barnes is protesting against a social upheaval already deplored by John Clare in his native Northamptonshire. See Clare's eloquent poem 'Remembrance'. It is noteworthy that Barnes, more sophisticated than Clare, uses the classical form of the eclogue, or pastoral dialogue.
40. *emmet* ant.
53. *vuzz* furze, gorse.

p. 5. Grammer's Shoes.
4. *girt* great.
10. *gramfer* grandfather. *clocks* stocking ornaments.

21–2. The best example in the poem of a device borrowed from Eastern poetry which Barnes called 'adorning': 'in which every word of a line is answered by another of the same measure and rhyme in the other line of the distich'.
32. *reely* to dance a reel.
35. *clavy* mantelshelf.

From *Hwomely Rhymes: A Second Collection of Poems in the Dorset Dialect* (1859)

p. 6. A Father Out, An' Mother Hwome.
8. *leäze* an unmown field.
12. *car* to carry.
13. *heft* weight.
35. *a-croopen* bending.
38. *lewth* shelter.
40. *tack* shelf.

p. 7. Day's Work A-Done.
7. *tweils* toils.

p. 8. Hallowed Pleaces. The continuity of memory is preserved through the Christmas fellowship of the community, and asserts its supremacy over time and decay—expressed by the hard winter around the warm house.
47. *holm* holly.
61. *drong* path.

p. 10. The Water Crowvoot. The manner in which the purity of the crowfoot bloom extends outwards into the tranquil scene and transports the poet and the boy is worthy of the best seventeenth-century emblem poems.
1–4. The yellow water-lily (*clote*) roots in mud, and favours the slower-moving River Stour. The water crowfoot is a non-rooting water plant with a small white blossom.
20. *laïtren* loitering.

p. 11. Lydlinch Bells. As in 'Hallowed Pleaces', the poet moves from the rigours of winter to the consolations of community life.
15. *orts.* bundles of hay put out into the fields for the cows.

p. 000. The Wife A-Lost. Barnes married Julia Mills, the daughter of a Dorchester excise officer, in 1827, and was grief-stricken at her death in 1852. He wrote a number of plangent poems celebrating their life together and mourning her death, in a manner that anticipates Hardy's poems to his first wife, but without the younger poet's lacerating sense of guilt.

From *Poems of Rural Life in the Dorset Dialect. Third Collection* (1862)

p. 13. Naighbour Playmeates.
7. *vlee* fly.
14. *panken* panting.
26. *tutties* nosegays.
38. *staïd* steady.

p. 14. **Woak Hill.** The manner in which the last line of each stanza is matched in rhyme and quantity has been adapted from Eastern prosody.
19. *ho* to feel a weight of care.
23. *house-ridden* moving house.
30. *light* the imagined presence of the dead wife.

BOOKS FOR FURTHER READING
Bernard Jones (ed.), *The Poems of William Barnes* (1962).
Geoffrey Grigson (ed.), *Selected Poems of William Barnes* (1950).
Lucy Baxter, *The Life of William Barnes* (1887).
G. Dugdale, *William Barnes of Dorset* (1953).
William Turner Levy, *William Barnes: the man and the poems* (1960).
R. A. Forsyth, 'The Conserving Myth of William Barnes', in *Romantic Mythologies*, ed. Ian Fletcher (1967).

R. S. HAWKER

p. 16. **Featherstone's Doom.** Featherstone was a ship wrecker, whose spirit is supposed to dwell on the Blackrock, a striking rock on the shore of Widemouth Bay, near Bude.

p. 17. **The Silent Tower of Bottreau.** Hawker's note is as follows: 'The rugged heights that line the seashore in the neighbourhood of Tintadgel Castle and Church are crested with towers. Among these, that of Bottreau, or as it is now written, Boscastle, is without bells. The silence of this wild and lonely churchyard on festive or solemn occasions is not a little striking. On inquiry I was told that the bells were shipped for this church, but that when the vessel was within sight of the tower the blasphemy of her captain was punished in the manner related in the poem. The bells, they told me, still lie in the bay, and announce by strange sounds the approach of a storm.'

p. 24. **The Fatal Ship.** This poem commemorates the loss of an ironclad ship, H.M.S. *Captain*, lost off Finisterre on 6th September 1870. It was the ship's first voyage, and her designer, Captain Coles—the 'kingly mind' of verse 4—was one of those who perished. In some respects this poem anticipates Hardy's poem on the loss of the *Titanic*.

BOOKS FOR FURTHER READING
S. Baring-Gould, *The Vicar of Morwenstow* (3rd edition, 1876).
John Heath-Stubbs, *The Darkling Plain* (1950).

ELIZABETH BARRETT BROWNING

p. 25. **The Cry of the Children.** The epigraph is from Euripides' *Medea*:
'Alas, alas, why do you look at me, children?' This is spoken by Medea before she kills the children. The poem first appeared in *Blackwood's Magazine* in August 1843, and antedates Thomas Hood's better known 'The Song of the Shirt'. Elizabeth Barrett was moved to write the poem by the Parliamentary Reports of a Commission inquiring into the employment of children; one of her friends, the writer R. H. Horne, was a member of the Commission.

p. 29. **Sonnets from the Portuguese.** This set of forty-four sonnets was written to Robert Browning before the marriage. Browning had a profound dislike of showing emotions plainly in poetry, and Elizabeth did not show him the sonnets until some years after the marriage. They conceived the idea of calling them 'Sonnets from the Portuguese' to conceal their true origin.
l.1. *Theocritus* Greek pastoral poet, who lived *c.* 270 B.C.

p. 31. **A Musical Instrument.** The poem is based on the myth of Pan and Syrinx, from Ovid's *Metamorphoses*, I. Pan became enamoured of Syrinx and attempted to ravish her, whereupon she was changed into a reed by the gods, and Pan made himself a pipe with the reed. The poem is a powerful expression of the sweetness and power of poetry and the suffering, destruction and labour which it entails for the poet.

BOOKS FOR FURTHER READING
Dorothy Hewlett, *Elizabeth Barrett Browning* (1952).
Gardner B. Taplin, *The Life of Elizabeth Barrett Browning* (1957).

CHARLES TENNYSON-TURNER

p. 34. **The Steam Threshing-Machine.**
10. *him* Virgil (70–19 B.C.), whose *Georgics* served as a model for writing on country occupations. The force of the allusion lies in the disruption of these traditional methods by new farm machinery. For the impact of just such a machine on another part of the country, see Hardy's *Tess of the D'Urbervilles*, chapter 47.

p. 35. **The Seaside.**
2. *frith* estuary.
8. *jellies* jelly-fish.

p. 36. **Old Ruralities.**
2. *heath-bell* any bell-shaped flower growing on heaths, particularly the bluebell.
3. *slip-shoulder'd flail* a small flail carried over the shoulder, here used only by the poor who could not afford a new steam threshing-machine.
7. *house-leek* a wild plant that grows on walls and roofs.
8. *herbal* a manual of herbs and plants useful for medicinal purposes.

p. 38. **To A 'Tenting' Boy.** To 'tent' is to look after something, usually to prevent someone or something from doing harm to it.

BOOKS FOR FURTHER READING
James Spedding (ed.), *Collected Sonnets of Charles Tennyson-Turner* (1880).
John Betjeman and Sir Charles Tennyson (eds), *A Hundred Sonnets* (1960). Both of these editions have useful introductions.

ARTHUR HUGH CLOUGH

For this selection we have used the 1869 edition by Clough's wife. The dates refer to the period of composition, as far as this can be ascertained.

p. 40. Duty. Written in 1840, when Clough was still an undergraduate. It is an early example of his satirical exposure of Victorian shibboleths, and appears to be addressed to a woman. Clough had enjoyed the Roman satirists, especially Juvenal, at Oxford, and the title of his first published volume, *Ambarvalia*, refers to a Roman festival of purification.
41. *exinanition* condition of exhaustion and emptiness.

p. 41. 'Is it true, ye gods'. This was the kind of irreverent, sceptical poem that Arnold disliked; he called Clough 'a mere d—d depth hunter in poetry'. Here Clough rejects 'poeticisms' for a precise yet colloquial style. The open ending is typical of his best poetry.
7. *Apollo and the Nine* the god of poetry, and the nine muses.
8. '*the vision and the faculty divine*' Wordsworth's description of the poetic gift (*The Excursion*, I. 79).

p. 42. Qui laborat, orat. Title: 'He who works, prays'. This is a majestic agnostic's hymn with the generalizing weight and clarity of the best Augustan verse. The scrupulous qualifications, far from dissipating the meaning, reinforce and sharpen its sustained ambiguity to a triumphant conclusion.

p. 43. Qua cursum ventus. Title: 'Where the wind [chooses] the course' (from Virgil, *Aeneid*, III. 269). It has been suggested that the background to this poem is the break-up of Clough's friendship with his Oxford tutor, W. G. Ward, when the latter became a Roman Catholic. Clough's preference for the simile over the metaphor is well illustrated here. The poem dates from 1845.

p. 44. Epi-Strauss-Ium. The title is an adaptation of 'Epithalamium', a marriage song praising a bride, and Clough is here writing in praise of Strauss. Strauss was the author of *Das Leben Jesu* (1835), a work which conveniently summed up the thinking of a number of German scholars, who declared that the gospels were historically inaccurate and not wholly the work of their supposed authors. *Das Leben Jesu* was translated into English by George Eliot in 1846, and Clough's poem dates from 1847. The poem is a sustained conceit, with the sun as Christ, and hence religious truth, and the Evangelists as stained glass windows to the east of the church. The clear light of late afternoon is here preferable to the mystical gloom of morning. 'Epi-Strauss-Ium' and 'Easter Day' are two of several poems which Clough wrote out of a crisis of faith, though neither was published during his lifetime. As statements of doubt and hope they should be compared to Matthew Arnold's 'Dover Beach' and 'Stanzas from the Grande Chartreuse'.
11–12. This trick of turning the argument on a rhyming word set on a line apart is used to great effect by Gerard Manley Hopkins in 'The Leaden Echo and the Golden Echo'.

p. 44. Natura Naturans. The title is a term of mediaeval philosophy, which divided nature into *natura naturans*, the creative force lying behind all things, and *natura naturata*, the material form which was the effect of this cause. The terms were later used by Spinoza, where Clough found them. The force of the poem lies in its daring insistence that man is part of nature and must seek his fulfilment in nature. Not surprisingly, this frank, rather puckish treatment of sexual attraction in a second-class railway carriage did not amuse a contemporary reviewer of *Ambarvalia* (who called it 'the very worst type of Cloughage') or Clough's wife, who omitted it from the 1862 edition of his poems. Its ambiguous tone and shifting stance, its burlesque and serious foolery, are reminiscent of Andrew Marvell.

38. *Hymen* the goddess of marriage.

p. 46. Easter Day, Naples, 1849. Clough's passionate statement of religious despair and stoical resolution has the structure of a formal ode, with elaborations round a central theme. The effect of the poem is cumulative, and relies on the reiterated negatives and the ironic reversal of phrases of consolation from the New Testament and the Burial Service.

12. *Joseph* Joseph of Arimathea, who took care of the burial of Christ.

24. *the women* St Mary Magdalen and the other women, who came to the tomb early on the first Easter Day.

28. *Peter or the Ten* St Peter, or the other ten faithful disciples.

29. *blind Saul* St Paul, at the moment of his conversion (Acts 9)

30. *after Gospel and late Creed* one of the discoveries of nineteenth-century biblical scholarship was that the gospels were not written at the time of Christ; the creeds were the result of church councils in the ensuing centuries.

35. *Emmaüs inn* where Christ revealed himself to two of the disciples (Luke 24: 13–32). *Capernaum's Lake* the sea of Tiberias, where Christ also appeared (John 21: 1–13).

39. *'some'* after the resurrection 'some doubted' (Matt. 28: 17).

56. *Ashes to ashes* from the burial service, *Book of Common Prayer.*

57. *unjust . . . just* Acts 24: 15.

98–9. See Matt. 6: 19–21.

106. A reference to the ascension (Luke 24: 51).

110. See Mark 1: 16–17.

138. Mary Magdalen, meeting Jesus in the garden on Easter Day, took him for the gardener (John 20: 15).

p. 50. Easter Day II. This philosophical counter-statement, in which Clough sought hope through assertion of mythological truth over historical evidence, has been found too abstract to carry much conviction.

p. 51. Say not the Struggle. This was written as a result of watching the defence of the Roman republic in the summer of 1849 (see 'Amours de Voyage'). Clough's democratic sympathies had earned him the nick-name 'Citizen Clough' at Oxford.

p. 51. Amours de Voyage. Clough visited Rome in the spring of 1849, where he witnessed Garibaldi's defence of the new Republic and its eventual capitulation to the French at the end of June (see G. M. Trevelyan, *The Defence of the Roman Republic*). Clough's letters make an interesting comparison with this poem, drafted on the spot. In *Amours de Voyage* Clough was able to use and sustain the full complexity of his poetic personality. Three principal factors enabled him to achieve this integration: firstly his use, in Claude, of a sympathetic yet detached poetic *persona*; secondly, the immediacy produced by the epistolary form; and thirdly, the versatility of the hexameter line. Clough had already employed this unusual metre with remarkable effect in 'The Bothie of Tober-na-Vuolich';

here it enabled him to capture the ebb and flow of the vacillating mind in a manner that baffled many Victorians but which has been found more congenial in recent years.

Considerations of space have prevented us from including all of this poem, which runs to five cantos; we have chosen to print all Canto I and most of Canto II (apart from the short introductory and concluding passages). The remainder of the poem parodies the traditional happy ending of a love affair: Mary Trevellyn leaves Rome for northern Italy and Switzerland, and Claude pursues her; through a series of mishaps he never finds her, and returns disconsolate to a Rome which has been occupied by the French.

Canto I

2. *en rapport* in harmony, in connection.
4. *the Lateran* a church on the southern wall of Rome, overlooking the Campagna and the Alban Hills, *S. Giovanni in Laterano*.
19. *assujettissement* obligation.
28. *Monte Testaceo* an artificial hill of ancient broken pottery.
33. *Bernini* Baroque sculptor (1598–1680).
38. *Emperor* Augustus (27 B.C.–A.D. 14).
44. *Piazza di Spagna* a quarter frequented by English visitors. There is a fine representation of Georgina's empty chatter in this letter.
62. *thy Dome* the dome of St Peter's.
65. *Stoic-Epicurean* Claude sees these fine ancient philosophies as reflected in the buildings of Renaissance Rome, although overlaid with the 'gewgaws' of the Counter-Reformation.
71. *Spaniard* Ignatius Loyola (1491–1556), founder of the Jesuits who spearheaded the Counter-Reformation. He was, in fact, neither rigid nor ignorant; Claude returns to his violent attack at line 91.
78. *Leo the Tenth* Pope, 1513–21, at the time of Luther's rebellion.
81. *Thomas Aquinas* the principal mediaeval theologian (c. 1225–74).
82. *Wittenberg* where Luther taught.
83–8. Claude, who is a most 'literary' correspondent, refers to the story of Noah's Ark (Gen. 6–8).
93. *Alaric, Attila, Genseric* Barbarian invaders of Rome.
98. *Gesu* the *Gesu* is the Jesuit church in Rome, where Loyola is buried.
102–3. Claude here celebrates various Renaissance triumphs in architecture (Michelangelo using the dome of the Pantheon as inspiration for St Peter's), painting (Raphael) and astronomy (Galileo).
111. *bajocco* a small coin.
132–3. *Iago* from *Othello*, II. i.
135. *the garden* here Claude parodies Gen 2: 19–20.
141. *Dome of Agrippa* the Pantheon, or temple of all the gods, which survives in Rome because it was later used as a Christian church.
150–6. Claude's version of Horace, *Odes* III, 4: 58–64.
172. *Malthusian doctrine* T. R. Malthus (1766–1835) advocated smaller families as a solution to the problem of population exceeding food supply.
175. *marvellous Twain* giant statues of Castor and Pollux, the 'horse tamers', in the *Piazza del Quirinale* (also called *Monte Cavallo*). Pope Pius VI added an obelisk crowned with a cross.
190. *Chapel of Sixtus* the Sistine Chapel.
197. *affecteth the blue* has intellectual pretensions.
198. *Childe Harold* Byron's *Childe Harold's Pilgrimage*, a poem which the fastidious Claude dislikes.

210. *Laissez faire, laissez aller* let things go as they please.

214. *juxtaposition* a favourite word of Claude's to express the arbitrary nature of physical attraction.

225. *moly* the plant given by Hermes to Ulysses which enabled him to visit Circe's palace unharmed and rescue his men whom the sorceress had turned into beasts. See *Odyssey* X.

226. Claude alludes to the story of Theseus and the Minotaur (from Ovid, *Metamorphoses* VIII), in which Theseus was given a ball of thread by Ariadne to guide him out of the labyrinth.

230. *the clue* the ball of thread.

230–41. The image of the explorer in danger dramatizes Claude's fear of emotional involvement. At several points in the poem sea imagery is used to point to the natural, instinctive life that Claude is attracted to and yet fears.

252 .*Mazzini* Giuseppe Mazzini (1805–72), head of the newly declared Roman Republic. Many apocryphal stories were spead of his irreligion.

Canto II

6–8. A parody of Rev. 21: 2, suggesting the impossibility of a change of heart on the part of the French government.

9. *the Gaul* French troops.

11. In spite of the 1848 revolutions, Austrian rule had been restored in northern Italy, and a Sicilian uprising against King Ferdinand II of Naples had failed.

16. *The Times* at this time it was strongly anti-nationalist.

18. *the Apollo* the famous statue of the Apollo Belvedere in the Vatican Museum.

19. *Civita Vecchia* a sea-port near Rome.

20. *Dulce* from Horace, *Odes* III: 11, 12: '*Dulce et decorum est pro patria mori*'.

39. *He* Oudinot, the French commander.

39–42. *Palo* ... places on the road from the coast to Rome.

47–8. *tell it not* ... a parody of II Sam. 1: 20. St James's and Christ Church were centres of fashionable and aristocratic life in London and Oxford.

49–50. From the *Marseillaise*: 'If our young heroes fall, the earth will bring forth new ones ready to fight against you all'.

86. *Murray* Murray's *Handbook to Rome*, the most widely used guide-book of the time.

90. Claude calls for white coffee and the waiter informs him that 'there's no milk'.

93. *nero* black coffee.

101–2. The *Via del Corso* and the *Via Condotti* are two streets near the *Piazza di Spagna*.

103. *the Pincian Hill* a safe vantage-point to view the battle on the other side of the city.

108. *Cavalleggieri* light horse.

129. *Quinquagenarian* fifty-year-old. Claude's exuberant language underlines his ironic detachment.

135. This refers to the battle of 30th April, which the French lost.

136–7. From Psalm 48: 4–5.

181. The Neapolitan army also threatened Rome.

190. *Quidnuncs* gossips. *Monaldini's* a bookseller in the *Piazza di Spagna*, with reading rooms where tourists could read English and continental newspapers and exchange news.

202. *Trastevere* an old quarter of Rome across the Tiber.
208. *Garibaldi* Giuseppe Garibaldi (1807–82), the Italian general and later the famous liberator. He lived in exile in South America from 1834 to 1848, returning just in time to take part in the defence of the Roman Republic.
230. *osteria* tavern.
254ff. The hexameter line allows Claude to make his scrupulous qualifications in this passage.
261. *factitious* artificial.

From '*Dipsychus*'. These two songs have been extracted from the debate between Dipsychus and the 'Spirit of the World'. With 'The Latest Decalogue' and 'In the Great Metropolis', they represent the best of Clough's satires on mid-Victorian complacency. They do not do justice to the range and variety of 'Dipsychus' itself, however, which is a difficult work to anthologize.

p. 68. **'As I sat at the café'.**
2. *pelf* wealth.
7. *en grand seigneur* like a great lord.

p. 70. **'The Latest Decalogue'.** The sustained, controlled irony and bitterness of this piece incline critics to place it in the London years when Clough taught at University Hall.
Decalogue the ten commandments. As in 'Easter Day', Clough startles the complacent reader by his modification of biblical injunctions.

p. 70. **'In the Great Metropolis'.**
8. *On 'Change* at the Stock Exchange.

BOOKS FOR FURTHER READING
A. L. P. Norrington (ed.), *The Poems of Arthur Hugh Clough* (1968).
John Purkis (ed.), *A Selection from Arthur Hugh Clough* (1967).
Michael Thorpe (ed.), *A Choice of Clough's Verse* (1969).
(The edition by Norrington is sufficiently complete for most purposes; the selection by Purkis has the advantage over that by Thorpe, in that it has detailed annotation.)
F. L. Mulhauser (ed.), *The Correspondence of Arthur Hugh Clough* (1957).
Isobel Armstrong, *Arthur Hugh Clough* (1962).
(This British Council pamphlet is still the best short introduction to Clough's poetry.)
Katherine Chorley, *Arthur Hugh Clough: The Uncommitted Mind* (1962).
(Though its psychological approach is not in favour, this is a sympathetic and stimulating biography.)
Walter E. Houghton, *The Poetry of Clough: an Essay in Revaluation* (1963).
Michael Timko, *Innocent Victorian: the satiric poetry of Arthur Hugh Clough* (1966).
John Goode, '*Amours de Voyage:* The Aqueous Poem'; and Barbara Hardy, 'Clough's Self-Consciousness': in *The Major Victorian Poets: Reconsiderations*, ed. Isobel Armstrong (1969).
R. K. Biswas, *Arthur Hugh Clough: towards a Reconsideration* (1972).
(A comprehensive critical biography which places Clough in the intellectual context of his age.)
Michael Thorpe (ed.), *Clough: the Critical Heritage* (1972).

COVENTRY PATMORE

From *The Angel in the House*: this, Patmore's best-known poem, was published in two parts, in 1854 and 1856. Each section, entitled a 'Canto' after Dante, contains 'Preludes' and a narrative sequence, which describes the courtship and marriage of Felix Vaughan (the 'I' of the poem) and Honoria Churchill (daughter of the Dean of Salisbury). The poem is notable for its combination of trivial domestic detail with a sublime and sacramental view of love in marriage.

p. 72. **'The Cathedral Close'** is the narrative section of Book I, Canto I; the lady in section 3 is the Dean's wife.

p. 74. **'Love at Large'** is the second Prelude of Book I, Canto II.

p. 74. **'The County Ball'** is the narrative section of Book II, Canto III, when Felix has been accepted; but before the wedding Fanny Fry, his earlier love, appears from time to time as a foil to Honoria.

From *The Unknown Eros* (1877).

p. 76. **The Toys.** *The Unknown Eros* continues many of the themes of *The Angel in the House*, though Patmore was now a widower, and the celebration of wedded bliss is replaced by an expression of grief at the loss of his wife. The combination found here of a very human moment and the deeper significance of man in relation to God is typical of Patmore, and common to both poems. In 1893 Patmore wrote to Arthur Symons: 'The meats and wines of the two are, in very great part, almost identical in character; but, in one case, they are served on the deal table of the octosyllabic quatrain, and in the other, they are spread on the fine, irregular rock of the free tetrameter.'

p. 77. **Magna est Veritas.** In this, and other poems, divine truth and love are seen in relation to the community.

p. 77. **1867.** Patmore's attitude to Disraeli (the 'Jew' of line 2) and his Second Reform Bill, though shrilly and violently stated here, was not uncommon.

p. 79. **Night and Sleep.** First published in *Fraser's Magazine*, 1854. Patmore thought that 'the six-syllable "iambic" is the most solemn of all our English measures'. Tennyson disagreed. See Frederick Page, *Patmore, A Study in Poetry*, pp. 162–3, 167, for a discussion of the metre of this poem.

BOOKS FOR FURTHER READING
Frederick Page, *Patmore, A Study in Poetry* (1933).
J. C. Reid, *The Mind and Art of Coventry Patmore* (1957).

GEORGE MEREDITH

p. 82. **The Old Chartist.** The Chartist movement was a popular campaign for parliamentary reform, which began in 1837 and reached its climax in 1848, in sympathy with revolutionary disturbances in Europe. Partly because of strong action by the government, and partly because of differences among the leaders, the movement petered out after 1848. Many Chartists were arrested, charged with conspiracy, and sentenced to various periods of transportation to Australia. Meredith's poem emphasizes the human participants—the lord and the convict, the bourgeois linen-draper, the convict's old wife with the tea-can under her shawl—and contrasts them with the freedom of the natural world which the returned convict appreciates with a lively patriotic enthusiasm. Like Rossetti (with whom he lived for a time after the breakdown of his marriage), Meredith was influenced by the work of Browning: this may be seen in the abruptness, the odd rhymes, the rapid and allusive use of metaphor, and the unusual phrasings.

1. *dam* mother.

90. *to screw me for my work* to screw me up to endure the trial.

p. 86. Modern Love. This is a sequence of fifty-one short poems, written like a sonnet sequence but with sixteen lines to each 'sonnet'. It tells the story of an unhappy marriage: the wife ('Madam' in the poem) falls in love with another man, and the husband attempts to console himself by having an affair with another woman ('My Lady'). At the end the wife commits suicide.

I. 'he' is the husband; in the later sonnets of this selection he speaks, and becomes 'I'.

XII. The husband muses on the destruction which his wife's unfaithfulness has brought about: not only the happy future, but also the spoilt past.

XIII. The husband suggests that it is a law of nature that everything changes, including love.

15. *for ever* here used as a noun, the subject of 'Whirls'.

XXX. The husband addresses this sonnet to the other woman; it reflects his disillusion with his attempt at an affair.

XXXVI. Like Patmore, Meredith here makes poetry out of a trivial social occasion; the husband marvels at the women's composure, and their ability to compliment one another.

XLIII. Having tried to make love to his wife, the husband walks unhappily by the seashore, reflecting that neither is entirely to blame but that the attempt has shown how dead their love is.

XLIX. 'He' is again the husband.

16. Lethe: the river of forgetfulness in Hell, here a shorthand for death.

L. The poet speaks.

p. 89. Lucifer in Starlight.

10. *the old revolt from Awe* Satan's rebellion against God.

14. *The Army* Satan sees the stars as the soldiers of the army of right. T. S. Eliot uses this last line humorously in 'Cousin Nancy', to refer to the dashing Miss Ellicott's old-fashioned uncles, Matthew and Waldo.

p. 89. Love in the Valley. This version dates from 1878: an earlier, shorter version from 1851. The poem is notable for its metrical skill; the basic unit is a line of four strong beats, with a varied number of unstressed syllables. In Meredith's hands it becomes remarkably effective as an expression of exuberant and happy love, with a subtle combination of natural beauty and sexual attraction.

BOOKS FOR FURTHER READING
G. M. Trevelyan (ed.), *The Poetical Works of George Meredith* (1912).
G. M. Trevelyan, *The Poetry and Philosophy of George Meredith* (1906).
Lionel Stevenson, *The Ordeal of George Meredith* (1953).
Ioan Williams (ed.), *Meredith: the Critical Heritage* (1971).
John Lucas, 'Meredith as Poet', in *Meredith Now*, ed. Ian Fletcher (1971).

DANTE GABRIEL ROSSETTI

p. 95. **The Blessed Damozel.** An early version was written in 1847, when Rossetti was nineteen, and published in *The Germ* in 1850. The celebrated painting of this subject dates from much later (1875–9). Rossetti said that the poem originated in his love for Edgar Allan Poe's 'The Raven', which shows the lover on earth grieving; Rossetti reverses the process, showing the lover in heaven longing for the loved one who remains on earth. The influence of Dante, which is found almost everywhere in Rossetti's work, is very strong here.
105. *five handmaidens* like many of the details of this poem, these five handmaidens are purely decorative. They are chosen for the music of their names, and seem to have no other connection with each other—in fact, there does not appear to be a St Rosalys.

p. 99. **Jenny.** Another poem which, in its earliest version, dates from 1847. The description of Jenny's room, and the combination of her qualities as a beautiful girl and a prostitute, recall a Pre-Raphaelite painting like Holman Hunt's 'The Awakening Conscience'. Rossetti's only picture of a contemporary subject, 'Found', also deals with a fallen woman; but it has little resemblance to Jenny, and it was never finished. Rossetti's painting, like his poetry, is more inclined towards the mysterious, the mystical and the dream world of symbolism; though his poetry, as in 'Jenny', is capable of a skilful and accurate delineation of contemporary life. The use of the dramatic monologue suggests the influence of Browning, of whom Rossetti was an early admirer.
Vengeance of Jenny's case! from Shakespeare, *The Merry Wives of Windsor*, IV. i. Mrs Quickly is herself a corrupt go-between, simulating indignation.
100. *the lilies of the field* Matt. 6. 28.
117. *purfled* adorned.
166. *Lethe* the river of forgetfulness. The speaker wonders whether it is wise to try to waken Jenny from her present existence.
230. *aureole* the gold disk, or halo, surrounding saints in pictures.
365. *the Paphian Venus* the goddess of love, called Paphian because she was reputed to have been born at Paphos, in Cyprus, rising from the foam.
369. *Priapus* the god of sexual love, often portrayed with an erect penis.
379. *Danaä* Jupiter seduced Danaë by appearing as a shower of gold.

p. 108. **The Paris Railway-Station.** From *A Trip to Paris and Belgium*, of which it forms part III. Rossetti did the trip in 1849, and sent these verse impressions back in letters to his brother, William Michael. They are good illustrations of Rossetti's power of delineating common life. The style

with its numerous parentheses, and the subject, are again reminiscent of Browning.
5. *the Morgue* mortuary.

p. 109. **Alas, so Long!** Influenced by Keats, Rossetti was acutely aware of change and decay.

p. 110. **The Woodspurge.** *Euphorbia amygdaloides* is the botanical name for this plant. It is illustrated at plate 75 of W. Keble Martin's *Concise British Flora in Colour*. The poem is a beautiful example of the concentration on detail in nature which is a distinctive feature of Victorian poetry and painting.

p. 110. **An Old Song Ended.** A poem which links Rossetti's favourite theme of separation with the kind of mediaevalism which is found more vigorously in the work of William Morris.

p. 111. **The House of Life.** This is a collection of sonnets written between 1848 and 1881. Some were published individually and in groups between 1863 and 1870, and the sequence appeared in its final version in 1881. The sonnets probably refer, in different places, to all three of the women whom Rossetti knew intimately, Elizabeth Siddal, Jane Morris and Fanny Cornforth, but the poems are best read without autobiographical preoccupations. They are sensitive impressions of love in all its moods and forms (its suggestions of physical love led to Robert Buchanan's vulgar attack on 'The Fleshly School of Poetry'), and of love seen against a background of change and mortality.

BOOKS FOR FURTHER READING
Oswald Doughty, *A Victorian Romantic* (1949).
C. M. Bowra, *The Romantic Imagination* (1949).
Graham Hough, *The Last Romantics* (1949).
B. Ifor Evans, *English Poetry in the Later Nineteenth Century* (2nd edition, 1966).
Robert M. Cooper, *Lost on Both Sides* (1970).
Ronnalie Roper Howard, *The Dark Glass* (1972).

CHRISTINA ROSSETTI

p. 114. **Goblin Market.** Influences on the poem include the *Arabian Nights* and other stories from Christina Rossetti's childhood reading. The poem retains something of the magic and freshness of a child's story, but beneath there is the very serious theme of the temptation of sensual delights. Lizzie refuses to have any dealings with the goblin men except on the most businesslike terms; Laura cuts off her hair, enjoys the fruit, and experiences the bitterness of unsatisfied longing. Lizzie's defeat of the goblins is followed by a restorative process which is obscure; the moral at the end is clearly inadequate as an explanation of the poem's meaning. Throughout the poem there is a very interesting contrast between the Victorian moral which is the overt message of the action and the enthusiasm and energy with which the tempting fruit are described.
22. *bullaces* wild plums.
75. *wombat* an Australian animal, like a small bear.
76. *ratel* a South African animal, also called the honey badger.
258. *succous* juicy.

p. 127. **Remember.** A good example of the Victorian interest in death and mourning.

p. 127. **A Birthday.** It is not known if this poem refers to any specific event, and it is probably an expression of a happy moment by a poet who was more than usually subject to moods of elation and depression.

p. 127. **Maude Clare.** An unusual example, for Christina Rossetti, of a poem with its own dramatic situation; but with the triumph of conventional love and the promise of domestic felicity at the end.

p. 131. **Up-Hill.** Here the traditional symbols of the journey and the inn are used to make a powerful and economical statement of life as a struggle ending in rest, an idea found elsewhere in Christina Rossetti's religious verse.

BOOKS FOR FURTHER READING
C. M. Bowra, *The Romantic Imagination* (1949).
B. Ifor Evans, *English Poetry in the Later Nineteenth Century* (2nd edition, 1966).
Lona Mosk Packer, *Christina Rossetti* (1963).
(This should be used with some caution because of its theory that the painter William Bell Scott was the object of Christina Rossetti's secret love, but in every other respect it is the best critical biography available.)

ALEXANDER SMITH

p. 132. **Glasgow.**
53. *When* all editions known to us print 'with'; we have amended to improve the sense.

BOOKS FOR FURTHER READING
J. H. Buckley, *The Victorian Temper* (1951).
(This contains the best discussion of the 'Spasmodics'.)

JAMES THOMSON

p. 136. **The City of Dreadful Night.**
Epigraphs: (a) 'Through me is the way into the sorrowful city' (Dante, *Inferno* III. 1).
(b) 'Then I cannot discover any use, any profit in so much exertion, in so much movement of all things in heaven and on earth, turning without a pause to return always to their starting point.' (Leopardi, *Canti* XXIII, 93–8.)
(c) 'Alone in the eternal world, towards which all created things move, in you, death, our naked lives find rest; not joyful, but safe from the old sorrow . . . for fate denies happiness to the living and the dead.' (Leopardi, *Operette Morali*, 'Coro di Morti' from 'Dialogo di Federico Ruysch e delle sue Mummie', 1–6, 31–2.)

Proem. This seven-line stanza is the staple one of the poem, and is used in the odd-numbered meditative sections. These alternate with sections of a more episodic and narrative character in a more variable metre. Edmund Blunden has written that 'this recurrent, slow-moving, backward-coiling stanza, with its overhanging rhymes towards the close only suggesting a freedom of movement in order that the close may be more ironically definite, is the pulse of the City.' (Introduction to his selection of Thomson's poems, 1932.)

1–2. From Shakespeare, *Titus Andronicus* III. i.

Section I. Though Thomson's city is more phantasmagoric than Alexander Smith's Glasgow, it shares many of its salient features: it is at night that the city stands fully revealed in its unnaturalness. Illuminated yet empty, it is seen as a self-sufficient landscape in itself, more exotic and strange than the wildest jungle. T. S. Eliot also wrote of a deserted city 'held in a lunar synthesis' (in 'Rhapsody on a Windy Night'), and Thomson anticipates *The Waste Land* both in his preoccupation with images of sterility, and in his absorption of Dante.

24. *Resurging* surging back.

78. From Dante, *Inferno* III. 9: 'leave behind all hope, ye who enter'.

84. Thomson's footnote runs: 'Though the Garden of thy Life be wholly waste, the sweet flowers withered, the fruit-trees barren, over its wall hang ever the rich dark clusters of the Vine of Death, within easy reach of thy hand, which may pluck of them when it will.'

Section II

10. *God's-acre* cemetery.

48. Thomson's footnote runs: 'Life divided by that persistent three $= \dfrac{LXX}{333} = \cdot 210$'. The 'perpetual recurrence' is the ·210 recurring, which is the result of dividing Life (LXX for 70 years) by 333, standing for dead Faith, dead Love, dead Hope.

Section IV. Gustave Doré's illustrations to Dante's *Inferno*, Blake's visions and Browning's 'Childe Roland' have all been cited as possible sources for this horrific landscape. Thomson habitually referred to life as a desert.

Section V

25. *dree his weird* endure his fate.

Section VI

37. *Pandora's Box* Pandora was a beautiful and mischievous woman created by Zeus to avenge himself on mankind for Prometheus's theft of fire. She opened a box that contained all the ills of mankind, and so let them loose upon the world.

56. *Limbo* a region on the fringe of Hell. The just people who lived before the coming of Christ, and unbaptized infants, were supposed to dwell there.

'The City of Dreadful Night' was composed in two distinct stages: in 1870 the first seven sections, and nos. 10, 11, 18 and 20 were written; the rest were added in 1873. Thus Thomson attempted to broaden his own sense of despair into a more coherent and comprehensive statement of philosophical pessimism.

Section X

37. *The Lady of the Images* the figure of an angelic dead girl appears in

several of Thomson's poems, and much has been made, without substantial evidence, of an obsession with an early love, Matilda Weller, who died young.

Section XII
13. The formula and response in the following stanzas parody the litany, just as the central statement of Thomson's atheistic belief in 'Necessity Supreme' is delivered in the form of a sermon (Section XIV). Thomson's language draws heavily on evangelical hymnology and the Bible.
34–5. From Isa. 1: 18: 'Though your sins be as scarlet, they shall be white as snow; though they be red like crimson, they shall be as wool.'
45. *a great work Paradise Lost*, referred to in this and the previous verse. To 'justify the ways of God to men' (1: 26) was Milton's own statement of his intention.

Section XVIII Blake's drawing of Nebuchadnezzar has been suggested as the source for this debased man-beast. The language of this section has several Blakean echoes, without Blake's vision of childhood innocence.

Section XX
9. *couchant sphinx* the sphinx is here the 'Spirit of the Universe', indifferent to man's aspirations throughout history.

Section XXI
16. *the pure sad artist* Albrecht Dürer (1471–1528). His famous engraving *Melancolia* is referred to here.
74. *teen and threne* sorrow and lamentation.

BOOKS FOR FURTHER READING
Anne Ridler (ed.), *Poems and Some Letters of James Thomson* (1963).
Bernard Dobell, *The Laureate of Pessimism* (1910).
H. S. Salt, *The Life of James Thomson* (1914).
I. B. Walker, *James Thomson (B.V.), a Critical Study* (1950).
John Heath-Stubbs, *The Darkling Plain* (1950).
R. A. Foakes, *The Romantic Assertion* (1958).
W. D. Schaeffer, *James Thomson (B.V.): Beyond 'The City'* (1965).

WILLIAM MORRIS

p. 166. **The Defence of Guenevere.** This is the title poem of Morris's first collection of poems, published in 1858. The story is told in Book I of Malory's *The Most Piteous Tale of the Morte Arthur sans Guerdon*. Guenevere, Arthur's queen, is arraigned on a charge of adultery, having been discovered with Sir Lancelot in her chamber. Gawain nobly attempts to defend her, suggesting that although Lancelot was there, nothing wrong may have taken place. Guenevere's defence is therefore a defiant admission of her love for Lancelot.
153. *your mother sleeps* Gawain's mother, Queen Morgawse, was unfaithful to her husband, king Lot of Orkney, with Sir Lamerok. According to Malory she was slain by her son Sir Gaherys; Morris makes the slayer Sir Agravaine, another son. This happened at Camelot ('far down in the south', 154).
168. *Mellyagraunce* Malory tells the story in *Launcelot and Guinevere* of

how Mellyagraunce attempted to ravish Guenevere: he surprised her with a number of unarmed knights and forced them to go to his castle ('*la Fausse Garde*' as opposed to Lancelot's castle, *Joyous Garde*). Lancelot came to Guenevere's rescue, and cut his hand when breaking open the bars of her chamber window. The next morning Mellyagraunce saw blood upon the bed, and accused Guenevere of unfaithfulness with one of her knights. Lancelot agreed to defend Guenevere's good name, and in spite of some trickery appeared in the lists and overcame Mellyagraunce. Mellyagraunce begged for mercy, whereupon Lancelot agreed to fight him with his left side uncovered, and with one hand tied behind his back. In spite of this handicap, he slew Mellyagraunce. The story is a good one for Guenevere to remember, for it illustrates the nobility of Lancelot and herself, as opposed to the shameful conduct of Mellyagraunce. In the same way, her reference to the story of Morgawse is a clever reminder that she is not the only queen who has committed adultery.

267. *a bawling* Sir Agravaine and Sir Modred, with twelve other knights, surprised Lancelot and Guenevere together in her chamber. When they attempted to break the door down, Lancelot let one in, killed him, dressed in his armour and then slew the others, all except for Modred who was wounded. Modred told King Arthur the story, and thus initiated the trial of Guenevere.

295. As Guenevere was about to be condemned to the fire, Lancelot arrived, slew all the knights who opposed him, and took the queen off to his castle.

Morris's allusive employment of these stories gives the poem remarkable force and immediacy; also notable is his employment of the *terza rima* form, and the power of his physical description, both of Guenevere herself and of the fight between Lancelot and Mellyagraunce.

From *The Earthly Paradise*. This poem tells how 'the wanderers' in the Middle Ages escaped the plague by sailing across the sea in search of happiness. They find a city, inhabited by descendants of the Greeks and full of beauty: they are welcomed by the inhabitants, and an interchange of stories follows. The Greeks tell stories from classical legend, and the wanderers stories from Norse and mediaeval sources. There are two stories in each month, and delightful interludes which describe the passing of the months.

p. 175. **An Apology.** Here Morris is strongly influenced by the romantic movement, seeing himself as a dreamer offering beauty to a heedless world.

25. *the ivory gate* in Homer (*Odyssey* XIX, 562) and Virgil (*Aeneid* VI, 893–8) the ivory gate is the outlet by which false dreams come from the underworld to the earth.

p. 176. The opening lines of the 'Prologue: The Wanderers' are among the finest of Morris's visions of the Middle Ages.

p. 176. **The Outlanders.** This Christmas song comes from 'The Land East of the Sun and West of the Moon', the story told by the wanderers in September. Morris was very fond of refrains in the manner of ballads or carols, and often uses them to great effect.

pp. 178–80. **August, October, February.** These are three of the descriptions of the months which act as interludes to the tales. The poem begins with March, which is why February comes last. Reading these beautiful descriptions one is made aware of Morris's deep love for nature in all its changing forms. His character Ellen, in *News from Nowhere*, cries: 'How I love the earth, and the seasons, and weather, and all things that deal with it, and all that grows out of it.'

p. 180. **L'Envoi.** The 'sending out' of the poem, a conclusion common in mediaeval poetry. Morris uses the form to bid a moving farewell to the poem, and to pay tribute to his master Chaucer.

BOOKS FOR FURTHER READING
J. W. Mackail, *The Life of William Morris* (1899).
E. P. Thompson, *William Morris: Romantic to Revolutionary* (2nd edition, 1961).

ALGERNON CHARLES SWINBURNE

p. 183. From *Atalanta in Calydon:* **Chorus.** This drama, in the form of a Greek tragedy (published 1865), tells the story of Atalanta hunting the Calydonian boar, and the subsequent death of Meleager. This first chorus, distinguished by its marvellous surge of controlled rhythmical energy, is addressed to Artemis, the goddess of hunting.
2. *The mother of months* May. (Cp. Chaucer, *Troilus and Criseyde* II. 51: 'In May, that moder is of monthes glade'.)
5–8. These lines refer to the legend of Philomela, who married Tereus, king of Thrace. Tereus became enamoured of her sister Procne, whom he ravished; to prevent her from telling Philomela he cut out her tongue and imprisoned her in a castle. Procne then wove the story into a tapestry which she conveyed secretly to her sister; and in revenge Philomela killed her son Itylus, and served him up to his father at a feast. This happened at Daulis (in Phocis, another part of Greece from Thrace) which accounts for the 'Thracian ships and the foreign faces'. Tereus tried to kill Philomela and Procne, but they were changed into birds, Philomela into a nightingale and Procne into a swallow. In this poem Swinburne sees the nightingale as half consoled by spring for all the sadness that has passed. Swinburne wrote another poem on the subject, 'Itylus'.
10. *Maiden* Artemis, usually represented with bow and quiver.
38. *oat ... lyre* the oaten pipe, the traditional shepherd's instrument, is heard above the more sophisticated poet's lyre.
39. *satyr* country demigods, represented like men, but with the feet and legs of goats, horns on their heads, and bodies covered with hair. The first fruits of all country things were offered to them.
41. *Pan* the god of shepherds, huntsmen and all country things. According to one legend he gained the favour of Artemis by transforming himself into a beautiful white goat. His followers were the Maenads.
Bacchus the god of wine and of drinkers, who, according to one legend taught man the cultivation of the earth. His followers were the Bassarids or Bacchantes (here one is called a 'Bacchanal').
48. *The god pursuing, the maiden hid* Pan pursued a beautiful maiden, Syrinx, who was changed into a reed. See above, note to Elizabeth Barrett Browning's 'A Musical Instrument'.

p. 185. **The Triumph of Time.** The background to this poem is uncertain:

the most likely explanation is that it refers to Swinburne's love for his athletic and adventurous cousin, Mary Gordon, and his shock at being told that she was to marry someone else. She married Colonel Leith in 1865. The poem was published in *Poems and Ballads* (1866).

321. *a singer in France* Rudel, a Provençal troubadour, fell in love with a princess of Tripoli. He sailed across the Mediterranean ('the tideless dolorous midland sea') to see her but died, as it was thought, on the way. Touched by his devotion, the princess came to see his body, whereupon Rudel revived, though only for a moment. Swinburne may have found the story in Browning, who published 'Rudel to the Lady of Tripoli' in *Dramatic Lyrics* (1842).

p. 194. **Hymn to Proserpine.** The most likely event to which this refers is the proclamation of Theodosius I in A.D. 391, which closed all temples and forbade all forms of pagan worship. In this poem Swinburne cleverly uses the *persona* of an old pagan to enlist sympathy for the sensuous delights of the ancient religions.

Epigraph: 'Thou hast conquered, Galilean'; words traditionally supposed to have been spoken on his death-bed by the Emperor Julian, who died (perhaps killed by a Christian) in A.D. 363 after attempting to revive the pagan religions.

4. *Proserpina* queen of the underworld, and goddess of forgetfulness and death.

7. *Apollo* god of poetry; here the difficulty of following Apollo, and the way in which the laurel crown, or 'bays', brings no delight, is contrasted with the repose of death.

15. *New Gods* the speaker sees Christ and the saints as new gods.

26. *Loves* the Amoretti, winged children who accompanied Venus, goddess of love.

36. *Lethean* belonging to Lethe, the river of forgetfulness.

73. *the throned Cytherean* Venus, who according to Hesiod, the ancient writer, was born at Cythera and not at Cyprus (see note to Rossetti's 'Jenny').

80. *mother of Rome* Venus was thought of as the mother of Rome because her son, Aeneas, was the founder of the city.

91. The speaker returns to Proserpina; her flower is the poppy (97), the flower of sleep.

108. The line is a translation of one of the 'sayings' of Epictetus, a Stoic philosopher (A.D. 60–140). Swinburne probably found it in the writings of Marcus Aurelius; see *The Communings with himself of Marcus Aurelius Antoninus* IV. 41.

p. 198. **The Lake of Gaube.** This lake is in the Pyrenees, near Cauterets; it is high above sea level, and the water is very cold. Swinburne stayed at Cauterets in 1862, and swam in the lake in defiance of all warnings from the local people. The poem was first published in *The Bookman* in 1899, and may not have been written much before. It is an unusually fine poem for this period of Swinburne's life, perhaps because it returns to the expression of physical excitement which is so frequently found in his best poetry. The swimmer dives into the dark and cold water, feeling to the full the joy of living and escaping from the base world of fear and self-perservation.

53–4: 'If life could be like this, and death could be like this without the restriction of time, then heaven would be like the lake of Gaube.'

BOOKS FOR FURTHER READING
Cecil Y. Lang, *The Swinburne Letters* (1959–62).
T. S. Eliot, 'Swinburne as Poet' (1920), reprinted in *Selected Essays* (3rd edition, 1951).
C. K. Hyder, *Swinburne's Literary Career and Fame* (1933).
Mario Praz, *The Romantic Agony* (revised edition, 1961).
Thomas E. Connolly, *Swinburne's Theory of Poetry* (1964).
C. K. Hyder (ed.), *Swinburne: the Critical Heritage* (1970).
Jerome J. McGann, *Swinburne: an Experiment in Criticism* (1972).

W. E. HENLEY

p. 201. **In Hospital.** Printed here from *A Book of Verses* (1888). An earlier version, entitled 'Hospital Outlines: Sketches and Portraits' and consisting of eighteen sonnets, was published by Leslie Stephen in *The Cornhill Magazine* in July 1875. The sequence in its final form is composed of regular sonnets, unrhymed poems in metre, and the occasional poem in free verse.
Epigraph: 'It is not possible to tell at what point a man, alone and ill in his bed, becomes self-absorbed.'

p. 202. *II. Waiting.*
10. *bluestone* copper sulphate, used as an emetic.

p. 202. *IV. Before.*
14. *You carry Caesar and his fortunes* spoken by Julius Caesar to a boatman during his war with Pompey, and quoted in Plutarch's *Life* of Caesar.

p. 204. *VII. Vigil.*
33. *bull's eye* a torch, here shaded by the nurse's apron.

p. 205. *VIII. Staff-Nurse: Old Style*
2. Rembrandt and Sir Walter Scott were both famous for their portrayal of ordinary people, especially old women of character.
10. *Syme* James Syme (1799–1870) was the former chief surgeon of the Edinburgh Infirmary.

14. *'The Chief'* Lister.

p. 206. *X. Staff-Nurse: New Style.*
7. *chignon* hair-piece worn at the back.
10. Balzac was a novelist whose realism was much disapproved of at this time; the allusion to George Sand probably refers to her well-publicized amours with Alfred de Musset, Chopin and others. Henley had a great interest in French literature.

p. 206. *XI. Clinical.* As in 'Before', Henley describes his own ordeal in detached terms ('Behold me waiting . . .').
27. *serry* press together in ranks.
33. *the hiss of the spray* a reference to Lister's carbolic spray, used to destroy germs in the atmosphere.
47. *red* one of the few, and therefore memorable, flashes of colour in the whole sequence.

p. 208. *XIII. Casualty.*
20. *writhen* contorted.

p. 209. *XIV. Ave Caesar!* The title, 'Hail, Caesar!' opens the speech of the gladiators before death.

p. 209. *XV. 'The Chief'.*
12. *Herakles* Hercules. In Euripides' *Alcestis* Herakles wrestles with Death and brings back Alcestis from Hell.

p. 209. *XVI. House-Surgeon.*
11. *Schism* sect or creed.
14. *Philistinism* a term for middle-class complacent materialism, popularized by Matthew Arnold in *Culture and Anarchy*.

p. 211. *XVIII. Children: Private Ward.*
5–8. Roden Shields and Willie Morrison shared the other bed in a small ward that Henley was moved to about half way through his stay. He called it a 'transformed back-kitchen'.

p. 211. *XIX. Scrubber.*
13. *Trailing her coat* being provocative.

p. 212. *XXI. Romance.*
1. *the Sailor* Captain Boyle, who also shared Henley's hospital room; his sister Anna became Henley's wife.
2. *euchre* an American card game.
3. *Charleston* a Confederate sea-port during the American Civil War. The Captain is narrating a tale of blockade running.
12. *Dixie's bottom dollar* poor Negro soldiers of the Confederate army.

p. 213. *XXIII. Music.*
18. *sprinkled pavement* in hot weather city streets were sprinkled with water to keep the dust down.

p. 215. *XXV. Apparition.* This is a portrait of Robert Louis Stevenson (1850–94), who was introduced to Henley in hospital by Leslie Stephen, and who became a close friend.
14. *Shorter-Catechist* member of the Church of Scotland subscribing to the Shorter Catechism, or summary of belief.

p. 215. *XXVI. Anterotics.* The title is presumably a combination of 'antics' and 'erotic'. A letter of Henley's, dated 17th May 1874, shows how close the poem is to the original experience: 'I am close to the window and through it I can see the grass-plot in the quad, the sweet sun shining down on the daisies and dandelions, chasing the shadows slowly from point to point along the windows and flashing on the skylight, like the admirable tyrant he is. I can see the quick, bright sparrows fighting over the crumbs I throw them, the corpulent crows wandering about, breast-high in the grass, after belated worms, the hospital terrier ... larking with his friends ... I can also see the whole body of nurses and probationers go to dinner and tea ...'.

BOOKS FOR FURTHER READING
Henley's complete *Works* (7 vols) were published in 1908: the complete poems have been reprinted several times.
J. H. Buckley, *William Ernest Henley: a study in the counter-decadence of the 'Nineties* (1945).
John Connell, *W. E. Henley* (1949).

Index of First Lines

A square, squat room (a cellar on promotion)   202
Across the gap made by our English hinds   178
Ah! dear one, we were young so long   109
Ah, let me look, let me watch, let me wait, unhurried, unprompted!   66
Ah, what a shame, indeed, to abuse these most worthy people!   55
All night fell hammers, shock on shock   80
Although lamps burn along the silent streets   141
Anear the centre of that northern crest   163
An' oh! the jaÿ our rest did yield   7
As I sat at the café, I said to myself   68
As ships, becalmed at eve, that lay   43
As with varnish red and glistening   208
'At eve should be the time,' they said   21
At last, dearest Louisa, I take up my pen to address you   52
At the barren heart of midnight   215
At Woodcombe farm, wi ground an' tree   8

Because he seemed to walk with an intent   140
Before our lives divide for ever   185
Behold me waiting—waiting for the knife   202
Behold those wingèd images   22
Belovèd, thou hast brought me many flowers   30
Beside me,—in the car,—she sat   44
Blue-eyed and bright of face but waning fast   206
But I am in for it now,—*laissez faire*, of a truth, *laissez aller*   57
But, knowing now that they would have her speak   166
By this he knew she wept with waking eyes   86

Carry me out   216
Come to me in the silence of the night   129
Contemptuous of his home beyond   130

Dear Eustatio, I write that you may write me an answer   51
Dearest Louisa,—Inquire, if you please, about Mr. Claude——   58
Do ye hear the children weeping, O my brothers   25
Does the road wind up-hill all the way?   131
Down the deep sea, full fourscore fathoms down   24
Down the quiet eve   213
Dulce it is, and *decorum*, no doubt, for the country to fall,—to   59
Duty, that's to say, complying   40

Each for himself is still the rule   70
Early thou goest forth, to put to rout   38
Exceeding tall, but built so well his height   209

Flush with the pond the lurid furnace burn'd   34
Forget six counties overhung with smoke   176
From the winter's gray despair   209
Full often as I rove by path or stile   33

Good morn t'ye John. How b'ye? How b'ye?   2

He found her by the ocean's moaning verge   88
He has not woo'd, but he has lost his heart   39
He served his master well from youth to age   38
He stood alone within the spacious square   142
Her little face is like a walnut shell   211
Here are we for the last time face to face   180
Here in this dim, dull, double-bedded room   211
Here, in this little Bay   77
His brow spreads large and placid, and his eye   209
Hist? . . .   206
How do I love thee? Let me count the ways   30
How he arrives there none can clearly know   144
'How should I your true love know   110
How strange at night to wake   79
How the moon triumphs through the endless nights!   158

I am in love, meantime, you think; no doubt you would think so   66
I do seem to zee Grammer as she did use   5
I have been here before   109
I have lived long enough, having seen one thing, that love hath an end   194
I never gave a lock of hair away   30
'I play for Seasons; not Eternities!'   86
I sat forlornly by the river-side   145
I sat me weary on a pillar's base   162
I thought once how Theocritus had sung   29
I wandered in a suburb of the north   159
In France, (to baffle thieves and murderers)   108
In summer-time it was a paradise   35
In the year of the great crime   77
Is it true, ye gods, who treat us   41
It is full strange to him who hears and feels   148
It is most curious to see what a power a few calm words   65
It's the Spring   212

Large glooms were gathered in the mighty fane   154
Laughs the happy April morn   215
Lazy laughing languid Jenny   99
Like as a flamelet blanketed in smoke   204
Lived on one's back   204
Lo, thus, as prostrate, 'In the dust I write   137
Look in my face; my name is Might-have-been   113
Luther, they say, was unwise; like a half-taught German, he could not   53

Mark where the pressing wind shoots javelin-like   88
Matthew and Mark and Luke and holy John   44
Morning and evening   114
My heart is like a singing bird   127

My Lady unto Madam makes her bow   87
My little Son, who look'd from thoughtful eyes   76

No, great Dome of Agrippa, thou art not Christian! canst not   55
No, the Christian faith, as at any rate I understand it   53
Noon—and the north-west sweeps the empty road   179
Not I myself know all my love for thee   111
Not solely that the Future she destroys   86
Now supposing the French or Neapolitan soldier   60
Now the light o' the west is a-turn'd to gloom   1

O jaÿ betide the dear wold mill   13
O love, turn from the unchanging sea, and gaze   179
O only Source of all our light and life   42
O rich red wheat! thou wilt not long defer   36
O small-feäc'd flow'r that now dost bloom   10
O, the fun, the fun and frolic   210
Of all things human which are strange and wild   153
Of Heaven or Hell I have no power to sing   175
On a starred night Prince Lucifer uprose   89
On goes the age with footsteps fleet and strong   37
On to the beach the quiet waters crept   39
Once more I came to Sarum Close   72
Once more the changed year's turning wheel returns   112
One little noise of life remain'd—I heard   35
Only think, dearest Louisa, what fearful scenes we have witnessed!   65
Our isolated units could be brought   151
Our shadowy congregation rested still   157
Out of the church she followed them   127
Outlanders, whence come ye last?   176

Poor malkin, why hast thou been left behind?   37
Poor rocking-horse! Eustace and Edith too   34

Remember me when I am gone away   127
Rome disappoints me still; but I shrink and adapt myself to it   52

Say not, the struggle nought availeth   51
She died in June, while yet the woodbine sprays   33
She's tall and gaunt, and in her hard, sad face   211
Since I noo mwore do zee your feäce   12
Sing, Poet, 'tis a merry world   132
So, I have seen a man killed! An experience that, among others!   63
So in the sinful streets, abstracted and alone   50
Some say that phantoms haunt those shadowy streets   147
Some three, or five, or seven, and thirty years   205
Staring corpselike at the ceiling   214
Sweet Woodley! oh! how fresh an' gaÿ   1

'Talk of pluck!' pursued the Sailor   212
The blessed damozel leaned out   95
The City is of Night; perchance of Death   138
The Feast is o'er—the music and the stir   37
The gaunt brown walls   202

The greater masters of the commonplace 205
The mansion stood apart in its own ground 149
The mighty river flowing dark and deep 161
The morning mists still haunt the stony street 201
The poor have hands, and feet, and eyes 18
The snow-white clouds did float on high 6
The sun is lord and god, sublime, serene 198
The taper wastes within yon window-pane 35
The wind flapped loose, the wind was still 110
There are two different kinds, I believe, of human attraction 66
'There is no God,' the wicked saith 67
These are the facts. The Uncle, the elder brother, the squire 57
Thin-legged, thin-chested, slight unspeakably 215
Thou shalt have one God only; who 70
Through the great sinful streets of Naples as I past 46
Thus piteously Love closed what he begat 88
Tintadgel bells ring o'er the tide, 17
'Twer when the busy birds did vlee 9
Twist thou and twine! in light and gloom 16
Two and thirty is the ploughman 207
Two separate divided silences 112

Under yonder beech-tree single on the green-sward 89

Victory! Victory!—Yes! ah, yes, thou republican Zion 63

Well, Heaven be thank'd my first-love fail'd 74
What are we first? First, animals; and next 87
What do the people say, and what does the government do?—you 59
What men are they who haunt these fatal glooms 151
What was he doing, the great god Pan 31
Whate'er I be, old England is my dam! 82
Whene'er I come where ladies are 74
When skies wer peäle wi' twinklen stars 11
When sycamore leaves wer a-spreaden 14
When the hounds of spring are on winter's traces 183
Wherefore and how I am certain, I hardly can tell; but it is so 67
Wherever men are gathered, all the air 156
Which of three Misses Trevellyn it is that Vernon shall marry 54
While I still lingered on that river-walk 147
Why were you born when the snow was falling? 129
Will they fight? They say so. And will the French? I can hardly 60
With joy all relics of the past I hail 36

Ye, too, marvellous Twain, that erect on the Monte Cavallo 56
Yes, we are fighting at last, it appears. This morning, as usual 61
Yet it is pleasant, I own it, to be in their company; pleasant 56
You are carried in a basket 203